HOUR OF DESTINY

THE GERMANS OPENED UP, with their long overhanging cannon. 75mm shells ripped the air apart, howling flatly toward the tank destroyers. The first tank destroyer . . . panicked . . . and went slipping helplessly into the drainage ditch. In virtually the same moment, the second tank destroyer was struck a great blow. It shuddered to a sudden stop, its commander and gunner killed outright. . . .

Abruptly, Murphy's men realized that they were without their armored protection and 200 German infantry dressed in "spook suits" and yelling their heads off like men demented, were running straight for their positions. Murphy sprang into action. He ordered his men to fall back to a prepared position some half a mile to the rear . . . Later he would write that the reason he sent his men back was because he "couldn't see why all had to get killed when one man could do the job that had to be done."

Now he was all alone . . . Murphy waited, armed only with a battered carbine and field telephone, a baby-faced 20-year-old who would go down in the history of the United States Army as its "greatest fighting soldier." Audie Leon Murphy's hour of destiny had come.

AMERICA'S FORGOTTEN ARMY

ARMY

THE STORY OF THE U.S. SEVENTH

CHARLES WHITING

St. Martin's Paperbacks

Published by arrangement with Sarpedon Publishers

AMERICA'S FORGOTTEN ARMY: THE STORY OF THE U.S. SEVENTH

Copyright © 1999 by Charles Whiting.

ISBN: 0-312-97655-0

Printed in the United States of America

Sarpedon hardcover edition published 1999
St. Martin's Paperbacks edition / February 2001

St. Martin's Paperbacks are published by St. Martin's Press, 175 Fifth Avenue, New York, N.Y. 10010.

10 9 8 7 6 5 4 3 2 1

CONTENTS

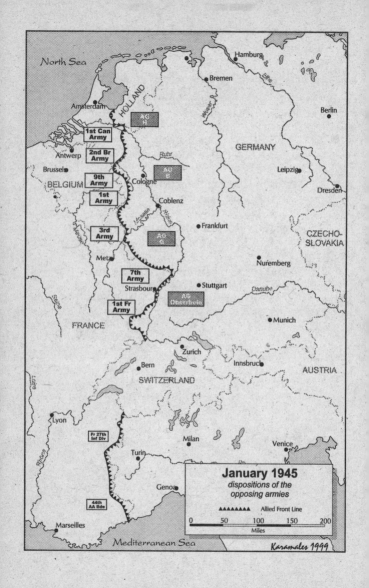

January 1945
dispositions of the opposing armies

▲▲▲▲▲▲▲▲▲▲ Allied Front Line

0   50   100   150   200
Miles

Karamales 1999

INTRODUCTION

"Silent cannons, soon cease your silence. Soon unlimber'd
to begin the red business."

—WALT WHITMAN, *Drum Tap*

ALL this long day of 9th July 1943, the storm had raged,
whipping the Mediterranean into a wild white fury. The
great fleet of transports and escorts wallowed up and down
in the tossing green waves, their bows taking tons of angry
white water every time they struck the sea.

By mid-afternoon the eighty thousand men of the US invasion were deadly sick and not a little afraid. Clinging to
the ladders, stanchions and poop decks of heaving, plunging
transports, their faces were a sickly sweaty green as they
retched and vomited miserably. The invasion fleet, it
seemed, was in serious trouble.

Tough veteran Admiral Henry Hewitt, who was in command on his flag ship, the *Monrovia*, definitely thought so.
Late on that same afternoon, as a full gale raged, buffeting
the big vessel like blows from some gigantic fist, he went
looking for General Patton, who would lead the invasion
force on the morrow.

"George," he said when he found him, facing up to the
tall, graying three-star general, "this shows every sign of becoming more intense. I think I'll signal Ike and Cunningham
to delay the landings."

Apparently unaffected by the ship's heaving and tossing,
Patton said, "Wait a minute, Henry. Have you spoken to
Steere?"

Lt. Commander Steere was an aerologist, who the previous year had restored Patton's faith in the science of meteorology—and the United States Navy—during another huge storm that broke just as Patton had sailed in to invade North Africa. Now Patton regarded the hard-pressed naval scientist as something of a good luck charm. "Yes," Hewitt replied.

"Did he say how long this goddam storm will last?" Patton queried.

"Well," Hewitt said, "he thinks it will calm down by D-Day!"

Steere's prediction gave Patton new hope. He sent for the lieutenant-commander. "Well, Houdini," Patton demanded, calling the naval officer by the nickname he had given him back in November, 1942, "what do you say?"

"This is the *mistral*, sir," Steere answered, refering to the brisk north wind, "violent but abrupt. I would say it will moderate by 2200 and the weather will be fine by H-Hour, General."

Patton gave him a hard look. "It had better!" he rasped.

Steere was confident. "I'm positive, sir," he answered.

At ten o'clock that night, the full gale still raged but then "Houdini's" prediction came right, only thirty minutes behind schedule. Half an hour later, the wind began to ease. Slowly but surely, the green heaving sea calmed down and the miserable seasick soldiers who littered the vomit-stained decks of the transports started to realize that they were not going to die after all—not just yet at least.

At midnight, when the *Monravia*'s radarscope picked up the pear-shaped outline of the island of Sicily, their objective off the coast of Italy, the wind had died away almost altogether.

It was Patton's hour of glory.

Hastily Patton's staff—plodding General Lucas, one-eyed General Gay, dashing Colonel Codman—assembled on the bridge deck and Patton, now Commanding General of the first real American army in Europe in World War II, made a little speech to the officers who would follow him over the next two years, "Gentlemen," he said in that curiously high-pitched voice of his, "It's now one minute past midnight, July 9th–10th, 1943, and I have the honor and privilege to activate the Seventh United States Army. This is the first army in history to be activated after midnight—and baptized in blood before daylight!"

Admiral Hewitt signalled to his flag lieutenant. In marched a smart, precise honor guard. With them they bore the US Navy's gift to Patton. A brand new flag for a new army; blue, yellow and red silk bearing the letter "A" for army. Thus as Patton began to cry a little, the U.S. Seventh Army was activated on the high seas, with the invasion of Sicily only two and a half hours away.

Observing the scene at that historic moment, Commander Brittain, USN, "could see the fire of pride" in Patton's glistening eyes. It seemed to the naval officer that "it was to him (Patton) not a ship's deck he stood upon but a peak of glory. . . ."

Now the first American army to fight on European soil in World War II got off to a good start. The plan had envisaged the American "new boys" playing the role of a mere flank guard to Bernard Montgomery's veterans of the British Eighth Army. "Get yer knees brown, Yank!" the bronzed veterans of two years of desert warfare had sneered when they had first seen the pale-faced soldiers of the Seventh. Patton changed all that. He wasn't going to let that "little fart" Monty relegate his new army to a side–show. Under Patton's dynamic, aggressive leadership, the Seventh surged through Sicily "like shit through a goose," to use another of Patton's favorite expressions. That July, Patton's Seventh Army was in the headlines all the time. "PATTON DRIVES FOR PALERMO" . . . "PATTON'S SEVENTH TAKES TROINA" . . . the banner headlines back home screamed. "PATTON TAKES MESSINA" . . . "PATTON FORCES SICILY'S SURRENDER" . . . .

Then came tragedy. After that notorious slapping incident, Patton fell from grace and with him his beloved Seventh Army. While he brooded in his gloomy palazzo HQ in Sicily, unit after unit of his Seventh was taken from him and fed into the Fifth Army of his hated rival, General Clark, in Italy. By the winter of 1943–44 the Seventh was less than five thousand HQ troops: a mere token force. Already it seemed that the US Seventh Army had become "America's Forgotten Army."

It was a year before this forgotten army went into action again. Merely three divisions strong now, it landed off the coast of southern France in August 1944. It was a landing that the British strongly opposed as a side-show, a weakening of Allied strength, with no real strategic purpose behind it. Indeed, British Prime Minister Churchill had once threatened to resign if it were not called off. American commanders, such as General Clark in Italy, too, felt it diverted from what he believed should be the Allies' main effort. Naturally in his own theater of operations.

The landing was relatively unopposed. At a cost of three thousand casualties, in a month-long campaign, the Seventh Army punched right through southern France to join up with Patton's Third in Lorraine by September. Critics of the Seventh thought it had all been too easy; they called it with a sneer, "the champagne campaign."

While the Seventh had been going through France virtually unnoticed by the general public back home, Omar Bradley's armies in the north had been hitting the headlines as they raced for the border of the Reich. The new commander of the Seventh, General Alexander "Sandy" Patch was indeed a brave, competent combat soldier, but he was no Patton. He had little charisma and could not provide that exciting "copy" for the newshounds, which profane, dramatic "Ole Blood and Guts" could. The Seventh continued to remain forgotten.

It was no different in January 1945 when the Seventh was attacked in what Hitler code-named "Operation Northwind," an eight-division-strong German assault in French Alsace–Lorraine. There, Patch's Seventh fought a desperate, touch-and-go "second Battle of the Bulge." But that month-long battle was totally overshadowed by the dramatic events further north in the Belgian Ardennes. Even today, when virtually every aspect of World War II in Europe has been extensively written about, made the subject of movies, TV films, and the theme of a hundred novels, the Seventh's fight to save Alsace during "Operation Northwind" is totally unknown.

It was the same two months later when the Allies crossed the Rhine. Every student of military history—and most of the general public too—is aware of that dramatic seizure of the railroad bridge at Remagen during the first week of March 1945, "the most important bridge in the world." Patton's surprise crossing at Oppenheim is familiar too. "Brad, don't tell anyone, but I'm across!" he yelled over the telephone to his boss, Bradley, carried away by his own triumph in beating that "little fart" Montgomery over the river by a day. But who has ever heard of the Seventh's crossing three weeks after that celebrated attack at Remagen?

Indeed the only incident worthy of remembering of the Seventh's assault on the Rhine was that one white NCO and nine black soldiers of the French Division attached to the Seventh made their own lone crossing in a rubber dinghy. Of all the hundreds of thousands of Allied troops who finally crossed, those ten were the only ones to have a memorial erected to that feat. It is still there. Naturally they "assaulted" the Rhine in their own unique fashion on April 1, 1945—April Fool's Day!

Even the final surrender of one million German soldiers to the victorious Sixth Army Group, to which the Seventh belonged, was marred by the fact that their French comrades-in-arms continued to fight the enemy because they were jealous they had not been represented at the surrender negotiations. In the end, The French, a constant pain-in-the-neck to the American Seventh, gave up their private war for lack of Germans to fight. Anyway what did it matter? The massive surrender of German troops to the Seventh was completely upstaged by that "little fart" Montgomery high up in North Germany. One day before the Seventh's surrender went into operation, he had "bagged" the whole of the German Army, Navy, Air Force and what was left of the battered Nazi state, including its last Führer. To the very end, the US Seventh Army seemed involved in sideshows, forgotten by the media. By VE Day, 1945, the Seventh had achieved its victory in Europe at a cost of 15,271 dead, 58,342 wounded, plus twice that number of non-battle casualties between August 1944 and June 1945. Now it seemed about to pass into history.

In the years to come, veterans of the campaign in the E.T.O. would be able to say proudly, when they were asked what they had done in the "big war" in Europe: "Why, I served with Patton's Third!" or "Hodges' First" perhaps, or even "'Big Simp' Simpson's Ninth; you know, the general who looked like an Indian chief with his shaven skull?" The replies were a kind of proud shorthand and their listeners would know what they were talking about immediately. They had fought at D-Day, raced for the Reich's frontiers, held at Bastogne, slogged it out in the Hurtgen, jumped the Rhine and had almost reached Berlin. But what did Patch's Seventh Army stand for? Where had it served? What had it done? "The US Seventh Army—never heard of it!" As the years passed after World War II, the deeds of the Seventh Army became mere footnotes to the brave, bold accounts of other US armies. They had fought in sideshows, minor campaigns in exotic places like Sicily, the Riviera, Austria, which had not had much effect on the course of the war. After working on it for forty years, the US Department of Defense did not produce its long promised official history of the Seventh Army "From the Riviera to the Rhine" until 1993. That must be significant in itself. Truly a forgotten army . . . .

On Friday, December 15, 1944, the Seventh's Army's 45th "Thunderbird" Division was the first of its outfits to cross the German frontier. They entered Germany at the little Saar hamlet called Bobenthal. But they would soon be chased out of the place and it would be another three months before they saw it again.

But on that Friday afternoon, with the sky already darkening and the guns rumbling in the distance, the GIs flopped down in the mud and rested. There were cold rations out of a can, but there was a mail call, which made the weary infantrymen's day; for some of them had been fighting and away from home for two years now. A platoon commander came up and told the men squatting in the cold mud that it was "an historic moment"; they were the first of the Seventh's soldiers to enter Hitler's Reich. The GIs were not particularly impressed. But they might have been if that young "second looey" had informed them that the same Seventh Army, to which they belonged, would still be in Germany nearly fifty years later!

Never in their wildest dreams could those infantrymen of so long ago have imagined that their sons, and their sons too, would serve in the Seventh as well; that their own "second looeys" and "chicken captains"—if they survived—would one day be colonels, perhaps even generals, commanding that same Seventh Army. But it would come true—all of it.

First came the victory of 1945 and the job of tackling the appalling ruins of the Third Reich, which Hitler had boasted would last "One Thousand Years," but which fell apart in exactly twelve years, four months and nine days. Those were the days of "Frowleins" and non-fraternization, the runaway VD epidemic among the troops, black market, "re-education," the Nuremberg Trials in that same city where the year before the 45th Division had slogged it out for six days with fanatical Nazis. For a while there was no water, gas or electricity. Communications had broken down completely. The Seventh had a million prisoners to deal with, millions of displaced persons and wandering refugees from a dozen European countries. Somehow the Seventh Army coped and helped to get Germany started again.

When the Cold War commenced, the 7th Army tackled it from its huge infrastructure sprawling right across Germany from the border with East Germany and Czechoslovakia over the Rhine into France. To the casual visitor to the Army in those days, it must have seemed that the Seventh's soldiers led a good life. They served in refurbished "Kasernen," or barracks, built by Hitler and now named after the American heroes of the "Old War"—Robinson, Rose, and Patch.

Their families lived segregated from the Germans in the ghettoes of "Base Housing," complete with PX, snack bars, movie theaters, bowling alleys, and Rod and Gun clubs— US provincial life transported wholesale three thousand miles across the Atlantic into Germany. No wonder the Germans called these places scornfully "Little America." For the single soldier, there was cheap sex aplenty. The callow young draftees now had the choice of "B" girls from the tawdry GI bars who seemed mostly to be spying for the Russians, or the roadside whores who worked from trailers or even in the bushes of roads leading out of town, charging five dollars a dance. No wonder the GIs called them with grim humor "Veronika Dankeschöns" (i.e., "Veronica Thank-yous," a name which could be reduced to the forbidding initials "VD"). And if the "frowleins" didn't suffice, there was always a three-day pass to the (then) "Gay Paree" and "Pig Allee" (Place Pigalle).

But behind the superficially good life that the US Seventh Army led in the late fifties and sixties, there hovered all the while the threat just over that silent sinister frontier, which always seemed so strangely deserted, but wasn't. All of them knew, even the dumbest private of the Seventh Army, that at any moment the "balloon" might go up and that "Red Force," as the enemy was always known in the annual fall maneuvers, might instantly be replaced by the real thing, the Red Army.

Occasionally someone from the "World," as the draftees longingly called the USA, would publicize the role these thousands of young American soldiers were playing in far-off Germany. Somewhere about 1959, a slack-hipped, loose-lipped Private First Class, Elvis Presley, made his appearance in the Seventh in the unlikely role of a scout for the 3d Armored Division. The world press went wild. The reporters, eager for a story, never learned of course that PFC Presley was driven to his barracks in the morning by a chauffeur in a white BMW and that he lived in a private house at a rental of eight hundred dollars a month, four times the going rate. But for a while, at least, the "folks back home" became aware that they had a huge army in Germany.

Two years later the "Wall" went up. Suddenly America realized that it had—and vitally needed—an army in Germany. Vice President Johnson flew to Berlin and threw the western part of the city into a tizzy by demanding the shoe shops should be opened on Saturday afternoon. (In Germany all stores are closed on Saturday afternoons save for the first Saturday in the month). Johnson felt, for some strange reason, that it was his first priority in this grave crisis to buy a pair of shoes for his outsize feet. President Kennedy followed and told the cheering populace in a great speech that: "I am a doughnut" (*Ich bin ein Berliner*). The crowd cheered even more. At that moment of grave crisis there were those who demanded that armored divisions should break through to West Berlin as a show of strength. But wiser heads at Seventh Army's HQ prevailed and prevented the Cold War from turning into a very hot one indeed.

But once the situation had cooled down, the Seventh Army again lapsed into its usual obscurity; once more the forgotten army. Again the dreary routine of guarding the border, practicing the defense of the "Fulda Gap," going off on those back-breaking annual maneuvers at muddy Grafenwöhr, trying to keep control of an army plagued by boredom, drugs and outbreaks of racial tension, commenced. Then at the other side of the world another hot war broke out in Vietnam, while back home youth revolted against the army. "Flower power" turned into riot power.

The Seventh Army provided much of the manpower. Those young second looeys of the battles in France and Germany now were the generals commanding the divisions fighting in Vietnam. As for the younger officers when they returned to Germany, decorated now, sporting their Purple Hearts and Combat Infantryman Badges, more often than not they were morose and not a little bitter. All their effort and sacrifice had meant nothing to the folks back home.

Then "Nam" was over and those embittered young men

vanished to be replaced by the "new professionals," for the draft was finished. Still the job in Germany remained the same: patrolling the border, defending the Fulda Gap, maneuvers at Grafenwöhr. It was the same dreary boring routine in a forgotten army preparing for a war that might come, but never did.

Fifty-five years after the Seventh "Thunderbirds" first crossed the frontier into Hitler's Reich, the "Forgotten Army" was still fulfilling its traditional role. Then suddenly things began to happen in Central Europe. The Wall crumpled, the Cold War died. As one intelligence officer told the Press in that exciting year of 1989, "the threat just went away."

For nearly five decades, the forgotten army had fulfilled a vital role. It had helped to keep the Russians east of the Elbe and at the same time, as NATO's major component, it had kept the Alliance together. American strength on the ground and American willpower had convinced the waiverers in Europe to keep on doing their bit. But what was to be the future role of this forgotten army now?

By October 1990, Germany was no longer divided by the victorious powers of World War II. The hard fact was that NATO's fate and that of the Seventh Army now rested with Germany. With the country reunited, Germany, it appeared, would soon rid itself of those one-time conquerors and occupiers who had become its allies. To most observers, it seemed that the future role of NATO and the Seventh Army would be decided not by the Russians or the Americans, but by the Germans themselves. The days of the Seventh Army were numbered, or so it appeared.

With startling suddenness, after nearly a half of a century of armed peace, the Seventh Army was alerted for action once again. A grave crisis had erupted in the Persian Gulf. By the end of 1990, half of the Seventh Army and all of its armor had gone to the Middle East. There, commanded and directed by generals such as Norman Schwartzkopf and Colin Powell, who as young officers had spent years of their lives in that forgotten army in Germany, the men of the Seventh helped to achieve a brilliant victory in a war of 100 hours: vindication of all that hard slog, decade after decade, in faraway Germany.

Now the fate of the Seventh Army still hangs in the balance. It seems to the author that the time has come to relate the battle history of that force which did so much to win World War II and the victory in the Gulf so many decades later: the US Seventh—"AMERICA'S FORGOTTEN ARMY . . . ."

Charles Whiting
York, England and Bleialf, Germany

ACKNOWLEDGMENTS

For their kind help in the preparation of this book, I would like to thank General G. Blanchard, General F. Sparks, General T. Mataxis, Colonel G. Clarke, Major D. Pence, Professor H. Morris, Rev. D. Docken, Mr. B. Clarke, Mr. G. Inzer, Mr. T. Lea, Mr. E. Taylor, Mr. B. Sieman, Mr. K. Corrigan, Mr. L. Froberg, and Mr. Hy Schorr.

My special thanks go to Mr. Tom Dickinson of the New York Public Library. Without his unflagging help, this book would not have been possible.

C.W.

1

SICILY: BAPTISM IN BLOOD
July–August 1943

"It is true, I suppose, that the Americans consider that we have led them up the garden path in the Mediterranean—but what a beautiful path it has proved to be! They have picked peaches, here, nectarines there. How grateful they should be!"

—WINSTON CHURCHILL, 1943

THE great deception had started innocently enough, far away from the scene of the bloody battle to come. Indeed nothing could have been more remote from combat than the sedate, silent rooms of the Junior Carlton Club in the heart of London's clubland in that winter of 1943 when the first tentative plans were laid.

Over coffee that gray winter's afternoon, with the club's ancient waiters creaking back and forth and the fat gray barrage balloons floating in the sky outside like tethered elephants, the smart young officer from Naval Intelligence, Commander the Hon. Ewen Montagu, listened attentively as the white-haired pathologist, who was perhaps the world's greatest authority in his field, answered his carefully phrased questions.

"Death would probably result from a lowering of the person's temperature, especially if the man in question were to float by means of a life-belt," Sir Bernard Spilsbury lectured him in that pedantic manner of his. "First he would fall unconscious . . . death would occur several hours later . . ." On and on the old man droned.

Montagu posed the key question, "Would there be any outward signs of how the man had met his death, sir?"

Sir Bernard considered for a moment, a cup of thin, weak wartime coffee poised at his thin lips. He wasn't given to answering questions of that nature lightly. How many times in the past had the life of a man or woman accused of murder depended upon the answer he had given to the court in the Old Bailey just across the road? "No," he said finally, "in my opinion there would be no outward characteristics of the manner of death."

The young Royal Naval Officer's heart skipped a beat. It was the answer he had been hoping for ever since that hush-hush intelligence organization, the XX Committee, i.e., the double-cross committee, had first dreamed up "Operation Mincemeat." All he needed now was the right body.

"But you can't get bodies just for the asking!" Sir William Bentley-Purchase, the Coroner for the London Borough of St. Pancras, objected pompously one week later. "I mean even with bodies all over the place"—he meant the many air-raid victims which that area of Central London had suffered over the last months—"each one has to be accounted for."

But the middle-aged knight, who affected spats and a wing collar, did not realize just how powerful the "Double Cross Committee" was and how much depended on finding the right body in the icy Victorian vaults of St. Pancras' Morgue. Discreet pressure was applied right from the very top—and that meant the Prime Minister, Winston Churchill himself. Sir William gave in. His bodies were available to this clever young officer, the product of both Cambridge and Harvard Universities.

Thus it was that Sir Bernard, Sir William and Montagu met behind the locked doors of St. Pancras' Morgue. A century after the last body snatcher had been arrested and imprisoned in that same London borough, the three men set about finding the corpse that Montagu needed so urgently for the great deception. In the harsh white light cast by the naked bulbs they viewed a number of corpses laid out on slabs in the yellow-tiled Victorian house of death.

One by one they were all rejected, save one. It was the

corpse of an unknown thirty-year-old man, who had died in a London hospital of pneumonia. According to the eminent pathologist, any unsuspecting enemy doctor examining the body would conclude that, due to the fluid in the dead man's lungs, he had died of drowning.

Montagu nodded his approval. That was exactly what the "Double Cross Committee" would want the enemy to think. Glad that the macabre business was over, he explained that the unknown man would be "called for" but he would have to be dressed before he was tucked back in his vault, to await "collection."

But an unexpected difficulty cropped up. The dead man's feet were frozen solid and couldn't be parted. Sir William was equal to the occasion. He ordered one of his attendants to go upstairs and bring down the hot plate on which they boiled the water for their afternoon tea. Minutes later the Coroner was plugging it in and stretching the solitary red ring close to the corpse's iron-hard yellow feet.

Montagu turned away sickened as the first drop of thawed water started to drip to the floor, but Sir William didn't bat an eyelid. "We'll thaw the feet out," he announced in a matter-of-fact manner, "and as soon as the boots are on, we'll pop him back in the refrigerator and refreeze him . . ."

On April 19, 1943, "Operation Mincemeat" was finally ready. The dead man had now been transformed into "Major Martin" of the Royal Marines. His wallet was filled with fake letters and theatre stubs and contained a photo of a mythical girlfriend inscribed "With love from Pam." (At the time of writing Mrs. Gerard Leigh, as she is now, is still alive). More importantly the Major bore with him a brief-case, carrying a private letter from the British Deputy-Chief of Staff in London to General Alexander, commanding the armies in Africa. "This private letter," as Montagu wrote later, "enabled him [the Deputy Chief of Staff] to mention small transparent details . . . which would make the enemy believe that we were going to land troops in both Greece and Sardinia."

Now with the specific approval of President Roosevelt

himself, "Major Martin" was packed in dry ice and put into a container labeled "Optical Instruments." This was loaded into the British submarine HMS *Seraph* at Holy Loch (from whence American nuclear subs start their patrols today) and in due course the craft sailed.

Two days later it made landfall off the Spanish coast near Punta de Umbria. Here the sub's skipper, Captain Jewell, ordered the craft to surface and, clearing the deck of all save officers, told the latter what their mission was.

It must have been an eerie scene as "Major Martin" was unpacked from the dry ice and the officers made sure that his precious briefcase was secured to his dead wrist by means of a little chain. Somehow they managed to fit him into his "Mae West" before Captain Jewell clasped his hands together, lowered his eyes and muttered the committal ceremony for the body lying there on the wet deck. That must have been one of the strangest "burials" in the history of the Christian Church! Gently the body was thrust over the side. Jewell's voice rose a couple of octaves. Once again he was a Royal Navy officer. He rapped out a command. The engines commenced throbbing once more. The sub swung round. The ripples grew into waves again. Slowly but surely, as the sub began to return the way it had come, "Major Martin" and his briefcase were driven towards the Spanish coast— and the waiting Germans.

"Father Christmas," they called him behind his back in Berlin. Indeed he did have a shock of snowy white hair like that celebrated children's figure; he cultivated a benign, gentle appearance and was given to the very un-German habit of donning an apron and cooking grand dinners for his spies and operatives. But Admiral Canaris—"Father Christmas"—the head of the Abwehr, or German secret service, was no simple, gentle old man despite his appearance. William Shirer has written of him, "He was so shadowy a figure that no two writers agree as to what kind of a man he was, or what he believed in, if anything much."

Now this shrewd, long-time spymaster was given the task

of evaluating the papers found on "Major Martin" by a Spanish fisherman off the port of Huelva on the morning of April 30th and promptly handed to the Germans—for a consideration, of course. In the end, he forwarded Hitler the copy of the letter to General Alexander, with an accompanying note which read: "There is no doubt about the genuineness of the captured documents. We are checking, however, whether they have been played into our hands deliberately and whether the enemy is aware of their loss or that we have gained possession of them. It is possible that the enemy has no knowledge of this fact."

Thereafter, things moved fast. The top secret British code-cracking operation Ultra picked up Berlin's signal ordering the 1st Panzer Division to move in the direction of the Balkans from southern France. Another signal from Field Marshal Keitel, Hitler's Chief-of-Staff, was decoded, commanding the strengthening of German garrisons in that same area; while the celebrated "Desert Fox" himself, Field Marshal Rommel, was sent hot foot to Greece. All was rapid movement and change.

As an afterthought, Montagu had decided to put a notice for "Capt. (A/Major) W. Martin" in the London Times "List of Missing" columns. This was picked up by the Germans, too, and for Canaris it clinched the case. "Major Martin" was genuine. The Western Allies were going to attack from North Africa into the Balkans!

By mid-May, when it was quite certain that the Germans had swallowed the bait, Churchill, who had first sanctioned the deception months before, was in Washington. Here, not long after his arrival in the American capital, he received a cryptic and prophetic message from home. It read simply: "MINCEMEAT SWALLOWED WHOLE."

Now "Operation Husky" could go ahead in safety.

To Winston Churchill, the Balkans and, in particular, Italy were the German and Italian enemy's "soft underbelly." For him and the British Imperial General Staff it seemed self-evident that once the enemy was driven out of North Africa, the island at the tip of the "boot" of Italy should be the Anglo-Americans' next objective. For Churchill, Sicily and then Italy were the easiest means of gaining an entry into Hitler's vaunted "Festung Europa." The Italians were war-weary and reluctant soldiers and Germany's weakest ally on the Continent. Knock them hard in Italy, he reasoned, and Mussolini, the Italian dictator, would be toppled. Besides, the invasion of Europe through Normandy was still a year away. What was one going to do with the victorious Anglo-American troops in North Africa? As Churchill told the House of Commons: "We have to fight them somewhere, unless we are just to sit back and watch the Russians."

In reality, Churchill would have liked nothing more than that: to sit back and watch the Germans and the Russians fight each other to exhaustion. But he could not tell the House that. In 1943, the Prime Minister's instinct told him that the right place to meet the Russians when they started advancing westwards was not in a conquered Germany, but in Central Europe. The farther away Stalin's Red Army was kept from the West, the more it pleased that supreme realpolitiker, Churchill.

Craggy-faced General George Marshall and the American Chiefs-of-Staff thought differently. In those days Marshall knew little of politics, save office ones. He was strictly a soldier. He believed that Nazi Germany should be finished by one single thrust to its evil heart, across the English Channel and on to Berlin. Nothing should be allowed to divert men and material from that main effort. Anything else would be a sideshow and Marshall, that stern unyielding figure in Washington, whom even the President of the United States called "General" and Supreme Commander Eisenhower addressed as "sir," was against sideshows.

As late as May 1943, Marshall told the US Combined Chiefs-of-Staff: "The Mediterranean is a vacuum into which America's military might could be drawn off until there is nothing left with which to deal the decisive blow on the Continent."

But Marshall had not reckoned with Churchill's influence

on Roosevelt, and in the end Marshall was overruled. The US Army was committed in that sea for the time being, at least, to the invasion of Sicily. As US General Wedemeyer, the only senior US commander to have studied in the German Kriegsakademie before World War II, wrote in a bitter letter: "We lost our shirts and are now committed to the subterranean umbilious operation." He was referring, of course, to that phrase so often used by Churchill when promoting operations against Germany's Mediterranean flank—"the soft underbelly of Europe."

In the end that "soft underbelly" would take two long bitter years to conquer and would have become for the men who did the fighting there, "the tough old gut!"

By the summer of 1943, with the Axis defeated in North Africa, "Operation Husky" as the plan for the invasion of Sicily was code-named, had been approved both in Washington and London. It consisted of five stages, but all depended on the second stage, which envisaged "airborne and glider landings on the night of July 9/10, to disrupt enemy movement and communications, and to help to secure the important airfields in the Gela sector. Beginning in the predawn hours (approximately 0245 hours), assault forces of Seventh and Eighth Armies would land along 150 miles of the southeastern coast of Sicily to seize the airfields and the ports of Syracuse and Lacata." In essence, it was an operation devised to win more laurels for the "Victor of El Alamein," General Bernard Law Montgomery, who would command the British Eighth Army; and if it was carried out the way the planners in Algiers envisaged, it would relegate the new US Seventh Army, under the command of General George Patton, to the role of little less than a flank guard to the British.

Naturally General Patton did not quite agree with that . . .

It was Friday, July 9, 1943. For most of the voyage from North Africa, the weather of the greatest invasion fleet ever assembled had been calm. Now during the dog watch, the wind had begun to freshen abruptly. It grew in intensity by the second.

A terribly hot wind, straight from the heart of the Sahara, had struck the huge convoy. Within minutes the troopers were plowing up and down on the heavy gray-green seas as if on a giant roller-coaster. Valiantly the skippers of the big troop transports, packed with miserable, seasick American, British and Canadian soldiers, strained to keep to the all-important timetables. They punched their way through the howling storm, shipping tons of water.

Relentlessly, hour by hour, the storm, which threatened the whole bold operation, grew in fury. As the 2,500-ship invasion fleet came ever closer to the enemy shore, the gale continued to grow in strength. Force Two became Force Three and that was followed by Four and Five on the Beaufort Scale. Desperately the convoys tried to keep together as the wind reached Force Seven.

On board the *Monrovia*, his command ship, a grim Patton summoned his Meteorological Officer to his cabin and was reassured that the storm would not last.

Back in Malta, waiting for the invasion to start, General Eisenhower also worried about the weather. Later he would state, he felt as if "my stomach were in a clenched fist." He knew that if the wind kept blowing at 40 knots, it would ruin the Seventh Army's landings. Already some of his more anxious staff officers were suggesting he should postpone the Invasion before it was too late.

Chain-smoking those 60 cigarettes he consumed a day, Eisenhower conferred with "old ABC," as British Admiral Cunningham was known on account of his initials. The Briton was a veteran of four years of war in the Mediterranean. He knew the island sea like he did his own wrinkled face. Cunningham assured Eisenhower that the velocity of the wind in that sea often changed after sunset. By midnight just before the airborne assault on Sicily was due to start, conditions might have improved.

A little reassured, Eisenhower took "Old ABC" out for a walk. Above them the gliders and transports of the airborne attack were flying over Malta at a mere four hundred feet, their dim navigation lights just visible. To Eisenhower they looked "like flights of giant bats."

Just about then a wire came in from General Marshall in Washington. "Is the attack on or off?" he demanded to know in that brisk, no-nonsense manner of his.

Eisenhower, who had just rubbed his seven "lucky" coins for the success of the airborne attack, wished he knew. All the same he decided that the operation must continue, storm or no storm. He signalled Marshall accordingly. As that long nerve-racking evening unfolded and the wind velocity continued to increase, Eisenhower felt that "there was nothing we could do but pray."

In the planes which Eisenhower and "Old ABC" had seen, a lot of other, younger men prayed that night. This was the first major Allied airborne assault of the war and already things were going badly wrong. It had been planned that the C-47s carrying the 82d Airborne Division would approach Sicily at 200 feet above the sea before climbing to 600 feet for the drop itself.

Now, as the transports started to climb, some of their windshields were splattered with salt spray because they had flown so low—many of their pilots discovered that not only were they miles off course, but that also they could not identify one single landmark! Confusion followed. Many pilots flew back out to sea to regroup. Others chanced their luck and ran into intense anti-aircraft fire. Within minutes eight transports had been shot down.

In that one hour between midnight and one o'clock in the morning of July 10, the paratroopers of the 82d Airborne Division's 505th Regiment ended up dispersed over a thousand square miles of an island as big as the state of Vermont. At the very moment that America's newest army—the Seventh—was being created on board the *Monrovia*, it seemed that disaster had already struck.

Patton's comment that his Seventh Army would be baptized in blood was very true that grim morning. Everywhere the paras of Colonel Gavin's 505th Regiment were hunted down ruthlessly by the German and Italian garrison of Sicily. Trooper Mike Scambelluri was captured and stripped of his weapons and valuables by a group of Italians, who tied his hands behind his back. When he spoke to them in Italian, they called him a traitor. An Italian captain drew his pistol and shot the helpless captive seven times. But Scambelluri refused to die. His own grenade was thrown at him and riddled his body with shrapnel. Somehow the grievously wounded trooper managed to survive and several hours later Scambelluri was able to identify one of his torturers from a group of newly captured Italian POWs. Thereupon three angry fellow paras marched the screaming Italian out and shot him behind the nearest hill. Trooper Scambelluri died of his terrible wounds a day later. Sergeant Frank Harkness remembered afterwards he was the last to jump from his transport, which was belting along at 200 mph instead of the usual 100 mph for jumping. "The plane seemed to be going unusually fast. My chute snapped open with a terrific jerk and my carbine disappeared . . . so the only weapon I had was a long trench knife."

Soon Harkness was to use it. For almost immediately he bumped into two civilians—and one of them was carrying a stiletto clearly visible in the moonlight. The two men ran at each other and a vicious knife fight developed. But the American slipped and the Italian lunged. His razor-sharp knife slashed open the Sergeant's leg to the very bone. He rolled backwards into a ditch and lost consciousness— something which undoubtedly saved his life.

His lieutenant was not so fortunate. Together with another trooper he was captured immediately upon landing and thrown to the floor of a hut where they were bound hand and foot. Subsequently the two of them were shot in cold blood by an elegant Italian officer, moments before British infantry stormed the place.

That night their commander, Colonel James M. "Slim Jim" Gavin, who had worked himself up from private to colonel after 20 years of service, now found himself commanding exactly five soldiers instead of the several thousand he had anticipated. Undeterred, the Colonel set off, slipping through the shadows cast by an olive grove, heading for the sound of the guns. Suddenly he heard a man whistling. As he recorded later, "After twenty years of military service, I was about to meet the 'Enemy' face to face!"

The "Enemy" turned out to be a terrified Italian soldier. The latter had obviously heard the frightening rumors spread by the Germans that the American paras were all long-term convicts who had been granted their freedom if they became paratroopers.

One of Gavin's band, a Captain Vandervoort, had taken an intelligence course and had learned that the best way to immobilize a prisoner was to slice through his belt and fly so that he would have to hold up his pants and couldn't run away. Now he stepped forward to do so, his knife glistening in the moonlight looking to Gavin like "a foot long." Vandervoort managed to cut the Italian's belt, but when he reached for the prisoner's fly, the terrified man gave a shrill scream which Gavin felt could be "heard all the way to Rome." The Italian thought the "American criminals" were going to castrate him.

He threw himself at Vandervoort and they fell to the ground in a "kicking, yelling, fighting mass." In the end the prisoner managed to escape, fleeing into the darkness, leaving Gavin "madder than hell."

"Slim Jim's" first taste of "combat" had been highly unsuccessful. Soon he would be experiencing the real thing though, storming the high ground at Biazza Ridge with 200 paras and losing a staggering 165 men in the process!

Now the loudspeakers were crackling into life: "Attention Serial One. To your boat stations now . . . move . . . let's go." It was H-Hour, 0245, July 10th. Everywhere in that vast fleet of 600 big ships and 2,100 small landing craft, the mainly seasick soldiers were struggling into their packs and moving forward, their hearts beating faster. This was it. They were going to land soon.

Stiffly the serials, with numbers marked on their helmets in white chalk, shuffled forward, each man's fingers hooked in the web belt of the man in front of him, platoon linked to platoon until a whole company would coil in and out of the deck like a human snake. Laden like pack animals with rifles, automatics, picks, shovels, packs—almost 100 pounds of equipment in some cases—they clambered down the swaying rope nets and ladders into the bobbing landing barges, which seemed so far below.

Colonel Darby's Rangers had preceded the main Seventh Army assault. At exactly 2:34 a.m. they had assaulted the enemy defenses at Gela, to be followed ten minutes later by the 16th and 26th Regimental Combat Teams of the US 1st Infantry Division.

Now as the 1st Division's assault waves approached in 200 craft, the sea turned rough again. Once more the soldiers started to vomit into their helmets. One GI clambered to the side of the swaying craft, fumbling with his pants. An ensign ordered him to crouch down again.

"I have to move my bowels, sir," the GI moaned.

Someone laughed nervously.

"Jesus!" another GI exploded, "What's so funny about that?!" He got up and said, "Here Joe, hold on to me!"

Dutifully the GI did as he was ordered, and so he advanced into Europe with his pants around his ankles.

Indeed that first American assault on Europe was altogether a little ludicrous and confused. In one landing craft commanded by Major Grant of the 1st Division, not one single man moved when the ramp clattered down.

"Jump off!" Grant yelled. "You want to get killed here? Get on the beach!"

Angered beyond measure, Major Grant invaded Europe himself, while his men watched to see if anything happened to the red-faced commander. When nothing happened, they followed the irate Major.

The situation was little different on the beach at Scoglitti, where Patton's second assault division, General Middleton's completely inexperienced 45th Division, landed. There the landing was total confusion. Units got split up. Others landed on the wrong beach. Within the hour some 50 percent of the landing craft used were lost. But there was little sign of the enemy, save for some sporadic machine-gun fire.

Now as the infantry of the "Thunderbird Division," as the National Guard outfit was named after its divisional patch, started to trudge inland, the beach engineers got completely out of hand. Neglecting their mission, which was to clear up the invasion beach, they started to loot the 45th Division's stores, even rifling the men's personal kits. So the "Thunderbirds" marched into battle without their logistical support. Not that it seemed to matter. The opposition was laughable, it appeared.

First Lt. Thomas Akers and his driver Private Weaver were first into Scoglitti. As they entered the little coastal town, they spotted Italian soldiers everywhere.

"Oops!" exclaimed the 1st Lieutenant. "Turn round, Weaver!"

They belted back down to the rest of the advancing division. With 25-foot sloggers Akers returned to the central square of the Italian town where he drew a Swastika in the dust. "Then I stamped on it with my foot. The people came running out of the houses waving white handkerchiefs and some soldiers came too. They threw down their guns and surrendered. We brought back about 50 of them and they all seemed glad to be with us."

Subsequently the "45th Division News," which boasted it was the "first US newspaper to be printed in Nazi Europe," to which Akers related his adventure, headlined it as "Dance in Dirt Captures Prisoners." To the average American soldier coming off the beaches that blazing hot July morning, this first invasion of Hitler's Festung Europa seemed a bit of a joke.

It appeared little different on the front of Patton's third and final assault division, the 3rd Infantry, which landed near Licata. Advancing with the forward elements, newspaperman Jack Belden, crouched behind a stone wall, listened to the roar of motors coming ever closer. "We waited in ambush beneath the wall, taut and silent. Like a crackling fire, rifles and machine guns split the air. Outlined in the shooting light of tracer bullets we saw wheel spokes and the red flashes of bullets shooting through them.

"A louder explosion shook the wall where we huddled. Lieutenant Thomas Rodgers was firing his anti-tank gun. A flash of flame tore the darkness and spotlighted the careering truck and the white frightened face of the driver. . . . The night was upside-down with shouts, bullets and moving figures. We could not know what was happening. A private clapped his hand on somebody's shoulder and said, 'What unit you from buddy?'

"A voice answered 'Mein Gott!'

"A shot rang out. Someone howled, then gurgled . . ."

Supporting the 3rd Division that morning was Combat Command A of what had once been Patton's own division, the 2d Armored, nicknamed the "Hell on Wheels." Its landing had also been something of a fiasco. As radios were forbidden for communication between the Command's scattered landing craft, an officer, 1st Lt. Cameron Warren, had to strip naked and relay his chief's messages to his troops by swimming from craft to craft. Then the naval ensign in charge of the little fleet confessed he couldn't recognize a single landmark ashore and the senior officer, Captain Perkins, was forced to draw a profile of how the shore might look from the sea.

Finally the tankers managed it and rolled into Licata, the 3rd's first objective that morning, losing two tanks, not to the enemy, but to the mud.

Here they encountered some resistance and started blasting away with their tank cannon, orders being relayed over the radio by a Sergeant Gwinn, as Colonel Quillian, a battalion commander, listened in and questioned Gwinn's superior Captain Perkins on how the fire fight was going.

Owing to the terrain Perkins could hear Gwinn, but he couldn't hear Colonel Quillian. Thus it was an irate Gwinn, after listening to "Hazel 6, this is John 6, what is your position and situation?" took matters into his own hands. Thinking that there was a German, speaking fluent English, tapping their radio network, he snorted, "Listen, you lousy son-of-a-bitch, if you are a goddam Nazi just keep listening. Maybe you'll learn something."

After a brief battle, Colonel Quillian joined Gwinn's company and asked to meet the sergeant who called him a son-of-a-bitch. Captain Perkins obliged. He introduced the two men, "Sergeant Gwinn, this is John 6." Everyone laughed at the look on the big noncom's face.

So it had been easy after all. The US Seventh Army had fought its first battle in Europe—if it really could be called a battle—and had won without even really trying. It had been part "SNAFU" and part a good story, the kind you'd be able to tell your kids, to explain the way that the Army always got things "screwed up" in that old war fought so long before.

But on that first day, the 82d Airborne, the 1st, 3d and 45th Infantry Divisions, plus the men of the 2nd Armored and Darby's 3rd Rangers had fought the Italians, and the Italians had little will to fight and die for Mussolini. They were mostly Sicilians, and what had Rome ever done for Sicily? Soon, however, the Americans would meet the first team, the Germans, and then things would be different.

As Eric Severeid, one of the best of American war correspondents, would depict them: "They understood the war's meaning no more than others—which is to say hardly at all. Their country, their families were not in mortal danger . . . and yet they plodded on . . . They did not hate Germans . . . They did not hate the concept of Fascism because they did not know what it was. But they struggled on, climbing the hills, wading through rivers until they dropped . . . and died in ignorant glory . . ."

It was Sunday, D-Day plus One. Just after six, Brigadier General Roosevelt, deputy commander of the 1st Infantry Division, who would be dead within a year, went to visit one of the division's forward command posts. It was another beautiful morning, already very warm, and the heat haze rippled in blue wavelets over the burnt hills of Sicily. But the General

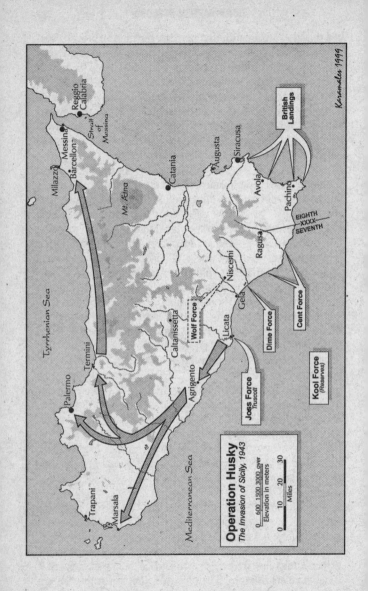

Operation Husky
The Invasion of Sicily, 1943

0 600 1500 3000 over
Elevation in meters

0   10   20   30
Miles

Korsmeyer 1999

British
Landings

EIGHTH
XXXX
SEVENTH

Cent Force

Dime Force

Wolf Force

Joss Force
Truscott

Kool Force
(Reserves)

Reggio
Calabria

Strait
of
Messina

Messina

Milazzo

Barcellona

Catania

Mt. Etna

Augusta

Siracusa

Avola

Pachino

Ragusa

Niscemi

Caltanissetta

Gela

Licata

Agrigento

Termini

Palermo

Trapani

Marsala

Tyrrhenian Sea

Mediterranean Sea

had things other than the scenery on his mind that morning. Yesterday the Italians had attacked the 1st with light tanks. They had been beaten off easily. Now there were persistent rumors flooding the bridgehead that the Germans themselves were heading for the beaches. There were only two tanks ashore in the 1st's sector, and most of the Division's 57mm anti-tank guns had been lost the previous day when the landing ship carrying them exploded and went down.

Roosevelt had barely reached the command post of Colonel Bowen's 26th Infantry Regiment when the balloon went up. Italian dive-bombers fell out of the sky, sirens howling, hurtling downward at Gela. Ten minutes later an excited telephone call from his 3rd Battalion informed Bowen that German medium tanks were attacking the Battalion. Already they had broken through in several places. Help was needed urgently.

Roosevelt acted promptly. He called the divisional commander, General Terry Allen. "Terry, look," he said urgently, "the situation isn't very comfortable out here. The 3rd Battalion has been attacked by tanks and has been penetrated. If we could get that company of medium tanks it sure would help."

The tough little General answered that he'd do everything he could. But an hour passed and there were no tanks. The Germans were pressing hard and the situation was deteriorating rapidly. Roosevelt called Allen again.

"Situation not so good," he said. "Out of communication with our 3rd Battalion, Terry. Any news of what's to be expected? Now, what about those medium tanks? God damnit, I'll come back and pull 'em out myself!" Again Allen promised him tanks from the 2nd Armored Division, unaware that two-thirds of the "Hell on Wheels" were still at sea. On the front held by the "Big Red One," as the First Division called itself after its divisional patch, things were starting to fall apart.

It was about just then that the commander of the Seventh Army, General Patton, made his celebrated landing on enemy soil. Immaculately dressed in a tailor-made uniform, tie knotted, a pistol in an open holster and with a big cigar stuck between his thin lips, he waded to the shore backwards. He was shooting the scene with his own camera. Then he repeated the memorable event—going the right way this time—for the benefit of the US Signal Corps photographers.

But, in spite of the histrionics, Patton soon made his presence felt. Almost immediately he realized just how dangerous the situation was on the US beaches. As he told "Old ABC" Cunningham later: "Admiral, I was no longer in command of an Army, but merely a reconnaissance unit"—and that reconnaissance unit was in serious danger.

He took off for Gela, now under attack, and could see on the horizon the packed German tanks. Indeed seven of the squat sinister Mark IIIs seemed to be bearing down on him personally.

Patton spotted a young naval ensign who carried a radio. Shouting above the roar of the guns, he cried, "Hey, you with the radio!"

The sailor called, "Can I help you, sir?"

Patton, who had little respect for the US Navy, bellowed back, "Sure as hell. If you can connect with your goddam navy, tell them for God's sake to drop some shell-fire on the road." He pointed to the dusty white road ahead.

The young officer, who suddenly found himself being enrolled as the commanding officer's personal radioman, started to call the battlewagons.

Meanwhile the 1st Division's front was crumbling rapidly. Colonel Bowen signalled he was "dispersing" his command post. In truth, he was forcing anyone capable of holding a rifle into the firing line. Cooks, clerks, drivers—all were rushed up to bolster his endangered 1st Battalion, while behind him the 1st Division's artillery commander lined up every gun he had on the dunes. They were to fire until their ammunition was exhausted. In the minds of the division's officers there was not going to be another Kasserine Pass debacle for the "Big Red One" here in Sicily. They would fight to the end, rather than run and surrender as they had done at Kasserine in North Africa.

Just about then, the Division's 18th Infantry Regiment was struck by 40 German tanks. A little later it was the turn of the 16th Regiment. Shell-fire fell on the regimental command post and most of the staff were hit. Two battalion commanders became casualties. By noon, the 16th's 3rd Battalion was being commanded by a 28-year-old captain, Boyce Denno, who was barely three years out of West Point.

Someone signalled the 16th's harassed regimental commander, Colonel Taylor. "We are being overrun by tanks!" Taylor signalled back: "Everyone just stays where he is. Under no circumstances will anyone be pulled back. Take cover from tanks. Don't let anything else get through. The Cannon Company is on its way. Everyone is to hold present position!"

But the Cannon Company did not arrive and the German tanks, now thrusting their way through the 16th positions, started to head for the beaches.

General Bradley, the commander of II Corps, to which the 1st Division belonged, was running the battle from a jeep, seated on a rubber cushion on account of his piles. He called General Terry Allen and asked: "Are you in trouble, Terry?"

Bravely the tough little General, whom Bradley would fire before the campaign in Sicily was over, replied, "We haven't begun to fight yet. Our artillery hasn't been overrun."

But even as he answered, the leading German tanks were within 500 yards of those guns and the artillery was beginning to run out of ammunition. By now, too, all naval personnel on the beach had been ordered to drop everything, grab a rifle and flesh out the 1st's line. Things were getting very desperate.

In the very last instant, when it seemed the 1st Division would be overrun, Patton's call to the Navy paid off. The heavy guns of the US cruiser *Boise* thundered into action. The shells screeched over the heads of the hard-pressed American infantry and slammed down right upon the panzers. The German attack rumbled to an abrupt halt, just as Shermans from the "Hell on Wheels" were diverted to restore the situation on the Gela front.

The crisis was over and that night Patton could write in his diary, "This is the first day in this campaign that I think I earned my pay."

But Patton's troubles were not altogether over this Sunday. For on this day occurred what the 82d Airborne Divisional History called "One of the war's greatest tragedies." It had been planned to drop 2,300 paratroopers of Colonel Reuben Tucker's 504th Regimental Combat Team as reinforcements for the Gela beachhead. In theory, the force carried by 144 C-47 transports should have been a milk run; the planes would fly over their own fleet and land behind their own lines. In the event it turned out to be a nightmare.

As the force approached the Allied fleet anchored off the beach, a nervous machine-gunner on an American ship spotted one of the low-flying, bomber-like planes and opened fire. The fleet had been under constant Luftwaffe attack all day—even hospital ships had been hit and sunk—and the gunner was understandably jittery. That lone gunner's burst seemed to act as a signal. Suddenly flak and fire opened up on all sides, even from the beachhead itself.

Chaos ensued. Everywhere the pilots took violent evasive action as the paras rushed to the doors to jump before they were shot down out of the sky by their own people. Desperately the pilots fired recognition flares. The gunners below were too carried away to notice. Flak exploded on all sides. The sky was criss-crossed with tracer.

Plane after plane started to go down. One bore the assistant divisional commander of the 82d, Brigadier-General Charles Keenans. He died instantly like so many of his men that terrible day. In the end, "friendly fire" took a terrible toll on the paras and their transports. Only 400 men finally reached the Gela bridgehead, while 23 aircraft were lost and never seen again and another 37 were severely damaged. Colonel Tucker, whose plane twice flew the length of Sicily, survived, but his C-47 suffered a staggering 2,000 hits.

"Why did I have to go on deck?" a distraught Machinist's Mate, Herbert Blair, told the press after the tragedy. "Hit after hit we scored until ship after ship bursts into flames or falls spiralling into the sea. But something is wrong. From the wounded ships parachutes come fluttering, some to fall in flames into the sea . . . others to billow out in slow descent. Then some trigger-happy gunner aboard another ship decides to pick off the supposedly helpless Jerries. Soon every gunner is firing away at the troopers dangling limply beneath the umbrellas of their chutes.

"Cease firing . . . Stand by to pick up survivors.

"Only then does the dreadful realization descend like a sledgehammer upon us. We have wantonly slaughtered our own buddies . . . I feel sick in body and soul."

That night one troop carrier pilot was reported to have said cynically, "Evidently the safest place for us over Sicily tonight would have been over enemy territory."

Now, however, things started to brighten for the Seventh Army. The Italian Army opposing them was falling apart, with thousands of demoralized Sicilian soldiers deserting to their homes or surrendering to the Americans daily, many with their hands outstretched for what they could get from these rich young men from the land of their dreams.

"They all acted like a bunch of spoiled brats," said one disgusted officer later. "From somewhere they got the idea that the American troops would come marching in, loaded down with food and money. Some were expecting new donkey carts, cigarettes, new homes. It took a while before they understood."

Patton didn't mind. Let them all think that they could join their relatives across the ocean—they all seemed to have an "Uncle in Brooklyn"—as long as they got out of his way and surrendered. From now on he determined that his new army would eat up territory and objectives. Why should he continue simply to play "flank guard" to Montgomery— "the little fart," as he invariably referred to the commander of the British Eighth Army to his staff? He wanted conquests, and the headlines in the papers back home that went with those conquests.

To speed up his advance, Patton formed a provisional corps under the command of one of his staff, General Keyes. It consisted of General Truscott's Third Division, what was left of the 82d Airborne, and his old division, "Hell on Wheels." This corps would now race for Palermo, to the northwest. The fact that the only real strategic target in Sicily was Messina, through which the German Army would finally escape to fight again in Italy did not bother Patton. As he radioed Truscott, "I want you to be in Palermo in five days!"

It was a tall order. Truscott's men and those of the 82nd and the attached Third Ranger Battalion would have marched the whole way over hilly terrain under the burning hot sun of mid-summer Sicily. Although, according to the Official US History of the War, the advance was "little more than a road march," it was a strange business "unlike anything else I encountered during the war," as Colonel Gavin of the 82nd recalled. "Suddenly a machine gun or anti-tank weapon would open up and then the white flags would appear. A shot had been fired for 'honor' but it was just as likely to cause casualties as a shot fired in anger."

Truscott set a cracking pace for his division. Back in North Africa he had trained his 3rd Division to do what his weary GIs called the "Truscott Trot": a 30-mile hike, the first five miles of which were done at a run for one hour, thereafter followed four miles in the hour, with the rest of the march being done at three and a half miles an hour. It had been very tough training and the men had bitched and cussed their divisional commander. But now it paid off.

All the same it still was tough, especially as water in that part of Sicily was in very short supply. First the sweat-lathered men of the 3rd, slogging their way northward, threw away their gas masks—they always went first. Overcoats followed, sometimes their packs as well. But to the very last they kept their rifles and perhaps the most important piece of military equipment of all—their canteen. Some men marched with up to four of them attached to their belts, dreaming of cool beers and freezingly cold ice-cream, risking their lives in some cases to obtain cold water from a spring which was under enemy fire or had been booby-trapped.

Taking part in that race for Palermo was a skinny, freckle-faced 3rd Division infantryman from Texas who didn't look a day over 16.

As he recalled after the war, "Dust lay over the highway like a smoke screen; not a cloud appeared in the sky. Often we could not stop even to eat. We gulped our rations as we walked. My brain swam; my internal organs rumbled. Finally I could take it no longer. I fell out of the ranks, lay down at the roadside and heaved until I thought I would lose my stomach."

A major rolled up in a jeep. He called, "What's wrong? Are you sick, soldier?"

The young Texan raised himself and said, "No sir, I'm just spilling my guts for the hell of it."

"Maybe you'd better report to the medics."

"Yessir," the Texan replied.

But he did not. He rose to his feet "and staggered up the road, cursing the war in detail."

That young Texan would become America's most decorated soldier ever, but that war he cursed that hot July day would be with him forever, until the day he died nearly 30 years later. He would survive while everyone else in his company that day would be killed or wounded in the years to come. But that war would haunt him always. His name was Audie Murphy . . .

While Keyes' Provisional Corps slogged away to capture Palermo, Bradley's II Corps doggedly fought against ever-increasing enemy resistance; first, elite troops from the best of Italy's armored divisions, then the Germans themselves, whose combat experience had been gained in the tough battles of Russia.

One lieutenant of the 45th Division recalled afterwards,

"German atrocities were rampant and so were ours in retaliation. My driver was captured, tied to a tree and shot by the Goerings [the Hermann Goering Panzer Division]. Then we encountered another German trick. They would rise without weapons, waving their hands in the air and shouting 'Kamerad.' Then when we went to round them up, they would fall flat and other Germans, concealed behind them, would open up on us. We lost many men due to this. Casualties were severe and the procedure of taking prisoners was abandoned by both sides."

It was not surprising, therefore, that Patton's Seventh Army soon involved itself in the first recorded atrocity of the campaign, especially after the pep talk Patton had given the green division just before it had left for Sicily. There in North Africa, he had told the 45th: "To be very careful when the Germans or Italians raise their arms as if they want to surrender . . . watch our for treachery . . . kill the SOBs . . ."

And that was exactly what the "Thunderbirds" did. British war correspondent Alexander Clifford saw men of the 45th mow down a truckload of German prisoners as they climbed down at Comiso airfield. But this war crime was never followed up.

On July 14th though, one was. On that day a company of the 45th's 180th Regimental Combat Team was ambushed. A bitter three-hour fight followed. Thereafter 36 Italians were rounded up, some allegedly in mufti. The mood of the 180th was bitter and angry. One of the regiment's battalions had taken a severe mauling the previous day—now this. The officer in charge took justice into his own hands. He had the prisoners lined up along the edge of a nearby ravine and executed by a group of infantrymen.

On that same day a Sergeant West was ordered to take 37 Italian prisoners to the rear. It was getting dark and the NCO became increasingly nervous; in the end he machine-gunned them by the roadside, killing the lot.

It says much for Bradley, the II Corps commander, that he did not attempt to hush the two incidents up, although he, as commanding officer, was technically responsible for the deeds of his men. He reported them to Patton.

Cynically Patton noted in his diary that Bradley had stated that Captain Compton had shot the prisoners down "in cold blood and also in ranks, a greater error." Airily Patton dismissed the matter, "Tell the officer," he ordered Bradley, "to certify the men were snipers or had attempted to escape." Later when General Bradley ordered an official investigation, Patton wrote scornfully to his wife, "Some fair-haired boys say I kill too many prisoners. Yet the same people cheer at the far greater killing of the Japs. Well, the more I kill, the fewer men I lost, but they don't think of that. Sometimes I think that I will quit and join a monastery."

Today, of course, in our supposedly more enlightened times, it is easy to condemn Patton's apparent cold-bloodedness in such matters. But if we do so, we forget that Patton was born in a time when Americans were still slaughtering Native Americans without the slightest compunction. He was a product of an older and more simplistic America, untouched by the social changes and political doubts of our own time. Things for him were black and white—there were no grays.

The year before, after inspecting a bunch of new recruits and mentally comparing them with the tough, keen "doughboys" he had commanded in World War I, Patton had thrown up his hands in that melodramatic fashion of his and exclaimed in apparent disgust, "We've pampered and confused our youth . . . Now we've got to try to make them attack and kill. God help the United States!" It is in this light that we must see Patton's attitude to the massacres committed by the 45th Division's soldiers, and his own involvement in the celebrated slapping incidents soon to come.

But for the time being Patton had much more pertinent matters on his mind than what had happened to the unfortunate Germans of the Hermann Goering Panzer Division. Bradley's II Corps was in serious difficulties at Troina, and the Germans were making the nearly exhausted "Big Red One" pay for gaining every foot of ground.

Patton ordered that the 39th Infantry Regiment, belonging to the 9th Infantry Division, should be thrown into the fray. It was commanded by Colonel "Paddy" Flint, a cavalryman like Patton, and one of the latter's closest friends.

Flint was a colorful eccentric who ordered his regiment to paint the letters "AAA" on their helmets. This stood for "Anything, Anytime, Anywhere—Bar Nothing." At Troina, Flint made himself easily identifiable by walking about the front line bare-chested save for a black silk scarf, rifle in hand, often rolling a cigarette as he moved about. Warned several times, he snorted contemptuously, "There's nothing to be afraid of. The damn Krauts couldn't hit anything in the last war. They can't hit anything in this war. They can't even hit an old buck like me." In the end they would, but that would be in another battle.

Both Patton and Bradley went up to Flint's command post to wish him luck, advising him that there would be little opposition facing him now. At first they seemed to be right, and Flint's 39th Infantry Regiment made good progress across the high ground a mile west of Troina. But that same night the 39th ran out of luck. A savage counterattack "thumped the hell out of A and C companies," as an officer described the fight afterwards.

Now General Allen commanding the "Big Red One" which had made the first attacks on Troina and which was now about to be relieved by the whole of the 9th Infantry Division, changed his mind about the 39th Infantry. He decided that it was a matter of pride for the 1st Division to take the place itself. So he ordered that Flint could attack again, but he would be supported by the 1st's 26th Infantry Regiment.

Colonel Bowen of the 26th Infantry did not share his commanding general's conviction that this time they would take Troina. He warned Allen that there were "very strong defenses." "I think there is a hell of a lot of stuff there . . . We'll be moving right into the teeth of the enemy."

Allen did not share his subordinate's fears. But Bowen

proved right. Although the two attacking regiments were supported by nine battalions of artillery, the Germans stopped them in their tracks.

All that hot day Patton waited for news of the attack. But none came, for the situation at Troina was terribly confused. That mid-day some companies up on the heights were being commanded by sergeants, as the Germans now went over to the counterattack. The 26th Infantry Regiment alone held fast against 13 German assaults, but the cost was high.

So when finally Patton called Bradley at sunset to find out what was going on at Troina, Bradley was forced to tell him miserably, "Terry was hit by a powerful counterattack and thrown back to his line of departure."

"Goddamnit!" Patton cursed over the telephone, "It's just like Terry." Bradley tried to defend his subordinate, saying "No General, Allen can't be blamed for the setback. Troina was going to be tougher than we thought. The Kraut is touchy as hell there."

Nevertheless the defeat at Troina meant the end of General Terry's career with the Seventh Army in Sicily. Both he and his assistant, divisional commander General Roosevelt, were removed from command because, according to the rumor circulating among the 1st Division, they had "spoiled the Big Red One."

Allen was replaced by Major General Clarence Huebner, a no-nonsense disciplinarian who had been in the Army since 1910, rising from enlisted man to general in that time. During World War I he had served in the "Big Red One" himself, but he had little time for that division's high opinion of itself. As one US officer complained bitterly, "The 1st thinks the US Army consists of the Big Red One—and ten million replacements!" As his first act in his new command he singled out the 26th Infantry Regiment, which Bradley thought was the most ill-disciplined in the 1st Division, and started them off at target practice on a makeshift range which had been a battlefield 24 hours before!

It was now that Patton, worried about the 1st and the 45th Division, which was also stalled and seriously under-strength, made his fatal error. On the following day he went up to visit the 1st. His aim was to put some spirit into the infantry and their commander. As he had explained to Bradley more than once, "I am the best damn butt-kicker in the whole United States Army."

But he had little success with the men of the "Big Red One." The men he met thought the Division had been overused both in North Africa and here in Sicily. They had been the first US troops to fight in World War I as had also been the case in World War II. It seemed that the 1st did all the fighting. Where was the rest of the Seventh Army?

Patton was also told by the divisional surgeon that more and more of the men were breaking down, weeping and throwing away their weapons, refusing to fight, pleading that they couldn't stand the noise and danger any more.

Naturally "combat fatigue" as the media were now calling it (in Patton's day as a fighting man back in the "Old War" they had called it "shell-shock"), was anathema to Patton. It was an affliction he could and would not understand. In his book, a man who wouldn't stand and fight was "yellow." After all, where would an army be if its soldiers were the ones who made the decisions when or whether they would fight?

Accordingly, next day when Patton spotted a sign on the roadside, reading "15th Evacuation Hospital," he told the driver, Sergeant George Mims, "Take me to that Evac." He'd visit the wounded and then he'd see about the malingerers, as he thought the "combat fatigue" cases undoubtedly were. After chatting with a few of the wounded stretched out on the cots under canvas, he came across a soldier in his mid-20s squatting on a box and obviously not wounded.

This was Private Charles Kuhl of the 26th Infantry of the "Big Red One," the same outfit general Huebner was currently trying to discipline. According to Patton, Kuhl eyed him in what Patton thought was a "truculent manner," as he asked him what was the matter with him.

"I guess I can't take it," the soldier replied.

What happened next was described in a letter home which Kuhl wrote to his father: "General Patton slapped my face yesterday and kicked me in the pants and cussed me. This probably won't get through [the censorship]. Just forget about it in your letter."

Patton, boiling with rage, then turned to the Hospital Commander, Colonel Warden, and yelled, "Don't admit the sonovabitch! I don't want yellow-bellied cowards around here, stinking up this place of honor."

Turning back to Kuhl, Patton shouted, red in the face, "You're going back to the front—at once!"

And there the matter appeared to end. Kuhl was ushered away and Patton and the hospital staff got on with the business of war, though later Patton did issue a memo, telling his commanders not to send men to hospital who said they were suffering from "combat fatigue." "You will take measures," he wrote, "to see that such cases are not sent to hospital but are dealt with in their units. Those who are not willing to fight will be tried by court-martial for cowardice in the face of the enemy."

Seven days later Patton did it again. Visiting the 93rd Evacuation Hospital he came across an artilleryman, Private Paul Bennett, assigned to the 13th Field Artillery, who lay shivering on his cot. When Patton asked what was the matter with him, Bennett replied, "It's my nerves."

"What did you say?" Patton bellowed.

"It's my nerves, I can't stand the shelling any more," Bennett sobbed.

Patton shook as much as Bennett, but his shaking was due to anger. "Your nerves! Hell, you are just a goddamned coward, you yellow son of a bitch. Shut up that goddamned crying! I won't have these brave men here who have been shot seeing a yellow bastard sitting here crying." He then ordered the man to be sent back to the front, telling Bennett, "You're a disgrace to the Army and you're going back to the front to fight although that's too good for you. You ought to be lined up against a wall and shot. In fact, I ought to shoot you myself right now, God damn you!"

With that, Patton pulled out a pistol and waved it threateningly in front of the terrified artilleryman's face.

The tumult brought the hospital commander, Colonel Donald Currier, up at the double. Patton turned on him and cried, "I want you to get that man out of here right away. I won't have these brave boys seeing such a bastard babied." And unable to contain his rage any longer, Patton then slapped Bennett across the face. Patton started to leave, but as Bennett continued to weep, he strode back to his cot and struck him with such force that his helmet liner rolled to the floor.

Muttering, "I won't have these cowardly bastards hanging around our hospitals. We'll probably have to shoot them some time anyway, or we'll raise a breed of morons," Patton stalked out.

As Eisenhower once told Patton, "You're your own worst enemy," which he was. Not only had the scene been observed by several nurses and doctors of the hospital, the chief of whom would be bound to report it, but now returning to Bradley's HQ, he started to boast to the latter about what he had just done.

Bradley did not like Patton. He did not like his self-dramatization, his style of living (Patton was privately wealthy and before the war had kept a string of horses when Bradley had thought himself lucky to possess a small car), or Patton's attitude that he was beyond the law.

His conduct of operations in Sicily so far had "sickened and soured me on Patton," he commented later, and stated, "We learned how not to behave from Patton's Seventh Army." Now Bradley was faced with what to do with Colonel Currier's report on the incident. In the end, he decided to lock it in his safe and not forward it.

But the slapping incident would not go away. A copy of the report was already being forwarded by Bradley's own corps surgeon, Colonel R. Arnest, through medical channels. Soon it would reach Eisenhower's own surgeon, Brigadier General Frederick Blesse, and then the fat would be in the fire.

* * *

With Palermo captured and Montgomery stalled at the Etna Line on his right flank, Patton now sent his Seventh Army rushing forward to capture the key town of Messina. In his own mind, he seemed to have thought that he was racing the "little fart," Montgomery, for the place.

That other prima donna of the Allied armies, Montgomery, seemed, however, to be totally unaware of the race. After an entry in his diary for July 28th, 1943, Patton is never again mentioned. In the British sector he had an account of Patton slapping his soldiers suppressed and told General Alexander that the slapping was "a family affair," which the Americans themselves would have to deal with.

Many years later, Montgomery's long-suffering chief-of-staff, Freddie de Guingand, who had little reason to be loyal to his old boss (after the war Montgomery treated him very badly), maintained there was neither a "race for Messina" nor rivalry between the two generals, as far as Montgomery was concerned. "It was all balls that about who was going to get to Messina first. We were delighted when we heard that Patton had got to Messina first—and about that fictitious scene in the film *Patton*—absolute cock! . . . Monty marching at the head of the Highlanders—all balls!"

Be that as it may, Patton pulled out all the stops in order to be in Messina first. He told Bradley, who commanded his II Corps, "in a grandiose fashion," "I want you to get into Messina just as fast as you can. I don't want to waste time on these maneuvers even if you've got to spend men to do it. I want to beat Monty into Messina!"

A shocked Bradley said he understood. Using the 3d Division he made an amphibious landing behind the German San Fratello Line. After some bitter fighting, the landing succeeded and the Germans started to retreat towards Messina. But the terrain, and the enemy's liberal and cunning use of mines, made the advance of the 3rd very slow. Colonel Ben Harrell remembered long afterwards: "How damn tired we got just going day after day."

Patton wasn't tired, however. He was simply damned im-

patient. Montgomery was advancing again and there were
reports that the British were planning commando landings
just south of Messina. He bore down on Bradley, insisting
that he make a second amphibious landing, 25 miles further
east of the San Fratello Line, at a place called Brolo.

Bradley didn't like the idea. Nor did Truscott of the 3rd
and General Keyes, formerly of the Provisional Corps. Both
Generals spoke with Bradley, who agreed to the postpone-
ment. Thereupon, Keyes called Patton and informed him of
the decision.

Patton's reaction was explosive. General Truscott
recorded after the war: "An hour later, General Patton came
storming into my command post giving everybody hell from
the Military Police at the entrance right on through until he
came to me. He was screaming angry as only he could.
"Goddamnit, Lucian, what's the matter with you? Are you
afraid to fight?"

Truscott bristled right back. "General, you know that's
ridiculous and insulting. You have ordered the operation and
it is now loading. If you don't think I can carry out orders,
you can give the division to anyone you please. But I will
tell you one thing, you will not find anyone who can carry
out orders they did not approve as well as I can do."

Patton's anger vanished at once. He put his arm round Truscott's shoulders and said affably, "Damnit Lucian, I know
that. Come on, let's have a drink—of your liquor."

They did.

The operation was postponed.

Two years later when Patton opened his mouth once too
often and Eisenhower fired him at last from his beloved
Third Army, it would be General Truscott who took over the
command: a suitably ironic reversal of the roles they played
that hot August evening in Sicily.

So the landing went ahead. It ran straight into serious
trouble. The beach was mined, the Germans attacked both
with tanks and fighter-bombers and by mid-afternoon the
commander of the landing force was signaling General

Truscott desperately, "Enemy counterattacking fiercely. Do something!"

In the end the Germans pulled out and were able to continue their general withdrawal to Messina, from which they were already beginning their 100 percent successful evacuation to the Italian mainland.

Undeterred, Patton planned yet another landing, this time by the 157th Regiment Combat Team of General Middleton's 45th Division. Again Truscott protested to General Keyes for the simple reason that his 3rd Division had already advanced beyond the proposed landing site. But after the dressing down the two subordinate generals had received over the Brolo landings, this time neither general dared protest to Patton.

So the 45th's landing went ahead. It was totally unopposed, of course, and Truscott's staff were waiting on the beaches when the first wave of Middleton's "Thunderbirds" came charging ashore, prepared to do bloody battle. No one cheered.

It was almost over now. On the evening of August 16th, 38 days after the Allies had landed, the first elements of the weary 3rd Division started to enter Messina. In the early hours of the following morning the local civic dignitaries offered to surrender the city to General Truscott. But Truscott had been ordered to leave that honor to Patton. So he waited for the Seventh Army Commander to make his triumphant appearance.

Meanwhile the British 4th Armored Brigade, under the command of a Brigadier Currie, was also heading for Messina, supported by Colonel Churchill's No. 2 Commando. Colonel Churchill, distant cousin of the British Prime Minister, was carrying a large Scottish broadsword and had a set of bagpipes in his jeep, which he intended to play when he entered Messina. (Besides his sword, one of the big tough Commando's favorite weapons was a bow and arrow.)

But "Mad Jack" Churchill was out of luck He wouldn't play his pipes as the first to enter Messina. For Patton was on his way, while Truscott and Bradley fumed at the delay. Indeed, the latter wrote later that he was "so angry at Patton's megalomania that I was half tempted to enter the city myself and greet him on a street corner when he arrived." But that, he admitted, "would have been playing Georgie's game."

At ten o'clock the great man himself arrived, signalling his approach with his usual howling sirens. He glared down at the waiting brass, with Bradley conspicuously absent, and snarled, "What in hell are you all standing around for?"

They moved and Patton personally led them into the city to the accompaniment of harassing fire from the mainland, for now the whole German Army had safely crossed the Straits of Messina, leaving their erstwhile Italian allies to their fate.

Messina was not much of a prize that particular day. Allied bombing had reduced it to a pile of rubble. But the "people came streaming out of their caves," one eyewitness recalled, "marching through the streets, yelling and cheering . . ." while "in the back streets we could see old people and kids and pregnant women loaded down with sacks of flour and boxes of canned goods. Too long starved, they had broken into an Italian warehouse, almost rioting, grabbing as much as they could carry. The slow-moving convoy was a picture of the worst of war."

General Lucas of Patton's staff was more concerned with the "doughboys moving down the road towards the city. They were tired and incredibly dirty. Many could hardly walk but were pushing on. These American boys of ours have remarkable stamina and are terrible in battle. I'm glad I'm on their side."

It was about now that "Mad Jack" Churchill and Brigadier Currie of the Eighth Army appeared. Currie saluted Patton and extended his hand. "I congratulate you, sir," he said in his fruity cavalryman's voice. "It was a jolly good race!"

* * *

That "jolly good race" had cost the Western Allies some 30,000 men dead, wounded and missing. Of these, 8,781 casualties were incurred by the US Seventh Army. At the time it was thought that these losses were worth it, because the generals claimed they had killed a large number of Germans. The contrary was the truth. The Germans had succeeded in evacuating the bulk of their army and its equipment over the Straits of Messina, leaving behind only a few thousand dead. Those German divisions, supposedly written off in Sicily, would still be fighting the Allies two years later. The only real achievement of Sicily, and it was a very important one, was that it led to the downfall of Mussolini, the Italian dictator on July 25th, and would soon result in Italy renouncing its alliance with Germany.

But whatever the long-term result of the Invasion of Sicily was, the new US Seventh Army had proved itself. Back in North Africa, after the rout of Kasserine, General Alexander had asked, "Surely you must have better men than that?" The British General had told Patton, who for once had listened tamely in silence, that he found American soldiers [to be] "mentally and physically soft and very green."

In Sicily, the first army America had fielded in Europe, the Seventh, had come of age under generals such as Truscott, Middleton, and Eddy, who had transformed their divisions into first class fighting outfits. The 1st, the 3rd, the 9th, the 45th Infantry Divisions, plus the paras of the 82nd, Darby's Rangers, and their comrades of the "Hell on Wheels," had shown themselves to be tough, hard fighters.

Of course, Patton, their commander, had made several blunders during the campaign—even the US official history referred to his dash for Palermo, for example, as "almost a publicity agent's stunt."

But the flamboyant style of Patton's command had brought not only Patton, but also his Seventh Army, to the attention of the Western world. The Seventh was now a known quantity. Even such a veteran as Montgomery (contrary to the popular American myth, fostered by the post-war memoirs of American generals and the movie *Patton*) was genuinely impressed by "Seventh Army's mobility, speed and, on its eastern flank, rugged determination and professionalism"—as Montgomery's biographer, Nigh Hamilton, has written.

But now the battle of Sicily was over. Already the first British commandos were over the Straits of Messina separating Sicily from the mainland. Soon they would be followed by two armies—Montgomery's Eighth and General Mark Clark's US Fifth Army, attacking up the sides of the Italian "boot." What of the Seventh Army? Where would Patton take them now?

2

THE CHAMPAGNE ASSAULT

August–September 1944

"Whatever you do, don't crush the vines."
— GEN. LATTRE DE TASSIGNY,
First French Army, August 14, 1944

ON the same day that Patton entered Messina, thus ending the campaign in Sicily, General Blesse, Eishenhower's Surgeon-General, presented his boss with the hospital report of Patton's behavior with soldiers suffering from combat fatigue. Eisenhower was shocked, but also scared for Patton's future. He told Blesse that "If this thing ever gets out, they'll be howling for Patton's scalp and that will be the end of Georgie's service in this war!"

He ordered a letter to be taken personally to Patton, expressing his chagrin and ordering Patton to "make in the form of apology or otherwise such personal amends to the individuals concerned as may be within your power."

But Eisenhower could not sweep the slapping incident under the carpet. People in the hospital had blabbed and the many newspaper correspondents on the island now got hold of it. Several of them went to see Eisenhower. They sought a deal. In return for killing the story they wanted Patton fired. Reynolds, the most senior correspondent present, expressed the press corps' anti-Patton stance when he said that there were "at least 50,000 American soldiers on Sicily who would shoot Patton if they had the chance."

The matter started to escalate. Patton was ordered not only to apologize to the soldiers he had slapped, but also to make a public apology to all the divisions of the Seventh Army. It was an unprecedented order. Never before in the

whole history of the US Army had a senior commander
made a public apology to each individual of his command.
Surprisingly enough, knowing Patton's explosive temper, he
agreed. Patton had waited too long for his chance to achieve
glory on the field of battle, something he had dreamed about
all his life. He knew that if he refused Eishenhower's humiliating order, he would be fired and sent back to the States to
spend his declining years in shamed obscurity. So he bit the
bullet.

The reaction of most of the Seventh's combat units was
indifference. His former division, the 2nd Armored, received
him with quiet understanding. The 1st Infantry Division listened to him in stony silence. At the 3rd Division emotion
ran high and reportedly there were tears at the sight of this
gray-haired senior commander making an apology to them
because he had slapped two cowards and been found out.
When he spoke to the men of the 60th Infantry Regiment of
the 9th Division, it was Patton himself who broke down and
began to sob. In the end he could speak no more, so he left,
as one eyewitness recalled, standing up "in his command car
and saluted, crying. He was our hero. We were on his side.
We knew the problem. . . . He never came back."

But Patton couldn't be kept down for good. Not only did
he manage to retain his dignity during this long humiliating
experience, he could even be funny about it. At a large assembly of GIs in September 1943, he was introduced by the
chairman of the American Red Cross and then simply stood
there for a while, before announcing baldly, "I thought I'd
stand here and let you fellows see if I am as big a son-of-a-
bitch as you think I am!"

The assembled troops erupted into wild cheering.

But the public apologies did not succeed in getting Patton
off the hook. Already the details of the slapping incident had
reached the United States. Soon, after Drew Pearson made
them public, there would be a widespread outcry and demands made, even in the Senate and Congress, for the un-
happy General's dismissal.

So as the fall gave way to winter Patton reigned in isolated splendor in his rundown palazzo in Palermo, while bit by bit the units of his Seventh Army were taken away from him. His 3rd and 45th Divisions were sent to Italy to join the Fifth Army, commanded by General Clark—a man Patton absolutely detested. His 2nd Armored, 1st and 9th Infantry Divisions went to Britain to prepare for the cross-Channel invasion.

Bradley followed. He was to command the US First Army during the initial stages of the invasion of France, then he would be given a whole American army group. This was a bitter blow for Patton. He had "made" Bradley, and now the lantern-jawed, pedestrian, plodding infantryman was going to become an army group commander. It hurt.

Eisenhower ordered Patton to show himself publicly. He was sent to Malta, then to Algiers, finally to Cairo. Patton had now been relegated to the role of a pawn in another game of deception similar to "Operation Mincemeat." His presence in the area was to make the Germans believe that such an important general, the conqueror of Sicily, was going to lead yet another thrust somewhere in the Balkans.

The Germans were not fooled. They had their spies and agents everywhere. They knew of Patton's disgrace and that the Allies were fully committed in Italy since the Salerno invasion of September 9, aside from having sent so many troops to Britain. Patton didn't care. His mind was elsewhere. He was at the low point of his career. Once he had described himself as a "passenger floating on a river of destiny." Now it seemed that the war had passed him by. "I have absolutely nothing to do," he complained, "and hours of time in which to do it. From commanding 240,000 [men], I now have less than 5,000."

But while Eisenhower fought to retain Patton, plans were being made to employ the Seventh Army again. On December 19th, 1943, Patton's HQ received a telegram from Allied Forces Headquarters which read: "An estimate is required as a matter of urgency as to the accommodation which you

would require for your planning staffs should you be asked
to undertake the planning of an operation of similar size to
'Husky'."

Ten days later Allied Forces HQ revealed some details of
the proposed operation, which was known under the codename "Anvil" to General Gay, Patton's chief-of-staff. It involved a series of landings by both the Seventh and the
French First Army on the south coast of France. This operation would be launched in conjunction with the invasion of
that country from Britain some time in May 1944. The first
major objectives of the new landings would be Vichy, the
seat of the French government under Marshal Petain, and
Lyon, the third biggest city in France.

But Patton had only two days to remain cheered by the
news that in the coming year his Seventh would be on active
duty once more. For on New Year's Day, a "very untactful"
telegram was received (as Patton's one-eyed chief-of-staff,
General Hobart R. Gay, put it), relieving Patton of command. Without warning, "he was advised that his enemy
General Clark would take over the Seventh with effect from
that day." "It was a bitter blow," Gay wrote, "to the headquarters of the Seventh Army . . . particularly bitter in view
of the fact that it was felt the Seventh Army had just com-
pleted a brilliant campaign."

Patton's own comment was more succinct. It was "A hell
of a Happy New Year!"

Patton's relief was followed by the appointment of the two
American commanders who would direct the fortunes of the
Seventh Army for the rest of the war and set their personal
stamp upon it.

The first to arrive was General Jacob L. Devers, a 57-
year-old ex-artilleryman, who in the '20s had played polo
with Patton, Truscott and Allen, but had none of their fire
and personality. Devers, who like the Supreme Commander,
Eisenhower, had never heard a shot fired in anger at him,
was to be Eisenhower's deputy in the Middle East and to

command the Sixth Army Group, to which the Seventh and the French First Army would belong.

Despite his great responsibilities, Devers would remain unknown to the general public. Of all America's senior commanders in World War II, Devers would be the only one who would never have his biography written. Nor did he publish his memoirs, as did Eisenhower, Patton and Bradley, although he lived to the ripe old age of 92.

Devers' problem was that he wasn't flamboyant like Patton, nor did he have General Bradley's publicity machine. He lacked the flair that made him good "copy" for correspondents. They wanted stories for the "folks back home." Devers could not provide them.

Another problem was that Devers' Sixth was relegated to a sideshow—first the invasion of southern France, then the long slog in northern France and finally, after being the last American army group to cross the Rhine, the drive into southern Germany.

"Jakie" Devers, as he was nicknamed, also controlled the very touchy French, who were always eager for new glory to wipe out the shame of their defeat back in 1940. They would be very hard to handle. Time and again, Devers would clash with his French subordinate who, in reality, answered to General de Gaulle and not to him. Therefore it was deemed expedient not to publicize the Sixth Army Group so much because of the constant military-political rows which rocked his command.

A major result of all this was that the Seventh Army would never receive the acknowledgement and publicity that the other three US fighting armies in Europe did. Everyone knew what "Patton's Third" was. A lot of people knew of Hodge's First. Even the newest of those three armies, Simpson's Ninth, was known. Didn't "Big Simp," as the Ninth's Commander was nicknamed, shave his balding head so that, with his hawk-like face, he looked like an Indian chief? The Press was always photographing "Big Simp." The situation was not helped by the appointment of the new Seventh Army commander, in March 1944. General Alexander Patch, a tall man with thinning red hair which had gained for him the nickname of "Sandy" at West Point, had, unlike his chief, a fine combat record. In 1917 he had fought with the "Big Red One" in France in World War I. Thereafter he had trained raw recruits for the infantry, gaining the reputation of being a tough disciplinarian. In 1942 he was given the task of whipping the Americal (American-Caledonia) Division into shape. That done, he was ordered to take the division and relieve the Marines on Guadalcanal with this pick-up formation. It was his first battle command and within two months he wound up the campaign there successfully.

Now this lean, ramrod-straight officer, with something of the air of a scholar about him (he collected Kipling first editions, for instance) would lead the Seventh for the rest of the war. But again, just like Devers, he wasn't "good copy" for the newspaper correspondents, and he never succeeded in gaining the publicity for his divisions, which in months to come they richly deserved. After all, they would pay for their unsung victories with their blood. As for General Patch himself, he would be dead of exhaustion and pneumonia within six months of the war ending, aged only 55.

By the middle of May 1944, the plan for the assault on southern France, soon to be renamed "Dragoon," was almost perfect. It envisaged three principal assault areas along a 45-mile stretch of the Riviera coast. Four French divisions under the command of General Lattre de Tassigny would attack there, their objective the capture of Toulon and later Marseilles; while three American divisions would secure beachheads and then begin their advance, principally up the valley of the Rhone River.

The three American assault divisions were all veterans. They were the 3rd and 45th Divisions which had fought in Sicily and later in Italy; and the 36th, another veteran of the Italian fighting. Up to now the 36th, a Texan National Guard formation, had been unlucky. In January 1944, the Division had attempted the crossing of the Rapido River in Italy and had been slaughtered doing so. After the battle the divisional commander, General Walker, wrote in his diary that the disaster was "chargeable to the stupidity of the higher command." He meant Clark. One of his company commanders was more succinct. Bitterly he told a war correspondent, "I had 184 men. Forty-eight hours later I had 17. If that's not mass murder, I don't know what is!"

Now as the division prepared for the coming assault on France, a small number of the 36th's officers brought with them the secret oath they had all sworn after the Rapido fiasco. If they survived, they would call for a Congressional investigation of Clark's role in the battle. "The Butcher," as they called him, must be brought to account.

Just as in Normandy, however, there would be a prior airborne landing to ensure that enemy forces did not penetrate to the assault beaches once the alarm had been given. This task was allocated to the Seventh Army's Provisional Airborne Division, the command of which was to be given to General Robert Frederick, one of America's outstanding combat soldiers; by the end of the war, he would have been wounded no less than nine times.

In mid-July 1944 when the final details were being put to the plan, "Bob" Frederick, who up to then had commanded the 1st Special Service Force, a strange commando-airborne outfit composed of Americans and Canadians, known to the Germans as the "Black Devils," was summoned to Devers' HQ in Algiers. There Devers said bluntly, "Bob, you're going to command our airborne troops in an invasion of Southern France." Frederick's face remained expressionless, but his mind was in a whirl. He was a trained paratrooper, but he had no experience in planning a large scale combat parachute landing. "How long will we have to get ready for the mission?" he asked after a moment.

"Five weeks—D-Day is August 15."

Now Frederick did look shocked. Five weeks only to plan an airborne assault, destined to be one of the largest of the war. "Well, where are my airborne troops?" he asked finally when he recovered.

Devers looked him hard in the face and said, "So far you are the only one we have."

In the end Frederick received the 2nd British Independent Parachute Brigade, one parachute regimental combat team, two parachute battalions, one infantry glider battalion, and supporting troops. It was the kind of rough-and-ready mixed force that Frederick was used to commanding, but one component of it made even the tough ex–special forces officer take pause.

It was the group who would make up his glider force. For these little soldiers, who were his glidermen, were technically enemy aliens, at least in the eyes of the Americans. They were the men of the Japanese American 442d Infantry Regiment, which by the end of the war would have gained the honor of being the most decorated outfit in the whole US Army. Mostly Nisei, they had volunteered to fight for their country, even though back in the States many of their relatives had been forcibly dispossessed of their houses and lands and shipped into the appalling conditions of the remote Western detention camps. But these young men, whose parents had often been reviled and spat upon by their fellow citizens as they had been herded to the trains which would take them to the camps, had proved themselves in Italy. True to the 442's regimental motto "Go For Broke," they had paid the bloody butcher's bill more than once.

Now they were told that they were going to become glidermen, even though none of them had even seen a glider before. It didn't faze them. They were given two practice rides in a Waco glider, given their glider wings, and told, "OK, you're ready to go." And ready they were.

And in Naples, while German spies and agents tried desperately to find the objective of the great army being assembled in the region, "Sandy" Patch was busy too. Now he faced the greatest challenge of his military career: a full-scale landing in the south of France at a time when the public's attention was focused almost exclusively on what was happening in Normandy. Even if he did pull it off successfully, who would really care? After all, southern France was only a sideshow.

All that summer General Patch worried about that. But he had a private worry too which could be told only to the closest of friends. It was that his son, Capt. Alexander Patch, a West Pointer like his father, was in the thick of the fighting in Normandy with the US First Army which had already suffered forty thousand casualties.

Could young Alex survive?

Over five thousand American, British and Japanese-American paras and glidermen of the Seventh Army Provisional Airborne Division started to fall out of the sky over southern France at half past four on the morning of August 15th, 1944.

The weather was perfect for the jump, and although the troopers had heard rumors that the Germans knew they were coming, most of them were able to land safely before the few enemy gunners in the drop zone were aware they were there. Indeed, for most of the paras of the first wave, their major problem was that they were lost. Some managed to find Frenchmen, setting off early for their vineyards and fields, to guide them. Others set off confidently in march formation, only to be attacked by their own fighter-bombers. The pilots of the P-38s had been told that anything outside the DZ would be German and could be attacked automatically.

There was also the problem of the British "Red Devils" of Brigadier Pritchard's 2nd Independent Parachute Brigade. Many of them had been dropped outside the target area and were, like the Americans, wandering around in the pre-dawn gloom trying to find exactly where they were.

One bunch of about 80 almost stumbled into an ambush set up by their American comrades-in-arms. Only at the very last moment did one of the tense expectant paras, waiting to open fire on them as they came down the road, spot that they were wearing red berets and were, therefore, British.

Joining the Americans, the force continued their tortuous march through the rugged steep hills to Le Muy and their assembly area. On their way, they stumbled on a German convoy heading for the landing beaches. A violent fire fight erupted. Using bazookas and machine guns, the mixed force destroyed each truck and killed or captured the soldiers they contained.

General Frederick, the commander of the Provisional Airborne Division, found himself little better off than his troopers that dawn. He had landed with his bodyguard, Corporal Duff Matson, who had badly injured his left leg as he struck the earth.

Now while Frederick attempted to ascertain his position by studying the map beneath the cover of his parachute canopy, the injured bodyguard detected five or six shadowy figures edging their way through the vines toward them. "Germans!" Matson shouted a warning to the General and loosed off a burst at the enemy. Someone yelled with pain. Two of the Germans fell to the ground. The others fled.

Calmly the General looked up from his map and, after making Matson, who was in considerable pain, as comfortable as possible, the General set off alone to find his division. He had not gone far when he spotted a dim figure, wearing what he thought was a German helmet.

Frederick, the former commander of the Special Service Force, knew exactly what to do. He stalked the lone enemy soldier and then approached him from the rear. When the General knew he would be discovered any moment, he sprang forward and flung his right arm around the other man's neck. Teeth gritted, he exerted full pressure. His aim was to break the man's neck before he could shout out.

But the startled "enemy" did manage to get out one curse—and it was in English! The General was strangling one of his own men! The man was a Red Devil, who was just as lost as he was. Not overly upset that just a moment ago his commanding general had been about to kill him, the Red Devil said, "I say, old boy, you are a bit rough!"

Frederick refrained from comment.

Winston Churchill had always been firmly against "Operation Anvil." He believed that the attack diverted precious re-

sources from the Italian front and for once he was supported
in his opposition to an American plan by a senior US general, "My American eagle" (as Churchill called him fondly),
craggy-faced, big-nosed General Mark Clark.

Churchill and Clark believed that "Anvil-Dragoon"
would now make it impossible for the armies in Italy to
drive into the Balkans and stop Stalin's Red Army there. As
Clark said long after the war, "Stalin . . . was one of the
strongest boosters of the invasion of southern France. He
knew exactly what he wanted and the thing he wanted most
was to keep us out of the Balkans, which Stalin had staked
out for the Red Army."

Now, however, Churchill, who had once declared that he
would resign from office if the plan was not scrapped, was
on board the destroyer *Kimberley*, smoking a big cigar and
viewing through his binoculars the great fleet preparing to
land the first wave of assault troops. The old war horse, who
had charged with the British cavalry at Omdurman in
Africa, had escaped from a Boer prison camp in South
Africa, and had commanded a battalion of infantry on the
Western Front in the Old War, simply could not resist a
scrap. He had to be there, though "Old ABC" Cunningham
had given him an escorting officer, who had strict orders.
"Don't let the prime minister out of your sight for one
minute!" "Old ABC" knew just how much Churchill loved
to be in the center of the action.

Now as "Winnie" watched, the assault elements of the
3rd, 45th and 36th Infantry Divisions, joined together into
the US VI Corps, commanded by the former head of the 3rd,
General Truscott, headed for the beaches. Each man, laden
with equipment, weapons and extra ammunition, crouched
behind the steel plating of the landing craft, wrapped in a co-
coon of his own thoughts. Many of them were veterans of
other such landings: Africa, Sicily, Salerno, Anzio. But even
the veterans could not quite overcome their sudden nervous
tension, as they came ever closer to those hill-fringed golden
beaches, which had been the playgrounds of the very rich
before the war. Only two months before, ten thousand Allied

soldiers had been killed and wounded in a few short hours during the D-Day landings in Normandy. Was that going to be their fate, too?

In the case of the 3d Division, resistance was slight. The coastal defense battalions here mostly could not even speak German. They were made up of former Red Army men, captured by the Wehrmacht, and then impressed into the Germany Army. They had not wanted to die for Stalin; they now certainly did not want to lay down their lives for the German tyrant, Hitler. They surrendered quickly, but there were Germans who wanted to fight. "As we started inland from the water," S/Sgt Herman Nevers of the 3d recalled afterwards, "I suddenly noticed a wire just above my head." He called back to warn the others it might be attached to a mine. Too late. "In that very same instant the mine exploded and hit a fellow staff sergeant, James Connor, in the neck. The officer in charge ordered Connor to go back to the aid station. But Sergeant Connor's Irish blood was up. He refused. He had come this long way to fight and fight he would.

They pushed on. Just before a little stone bridge, a German popped up, his rifle raised. Connor was quicker. He shot him dead. That seemed to act as a signal for the Germans. With a thump and obscene howl, mortar bombs came falling out of the morning sky. Men went down everywhere. Swiftly the patrol became shaken and disorganized.

Not Connor though. He led 20 men forward again out of the barrage and straight into a sniper's bullet which penetrated his back. "For Chrissake," Nevers moaned, "Connor, stop and get medical attention for yourself!"

Connor answered thickly, "No. They can hit me, but they can't stop me. I'll go until I can't go any farther." He pushed on against ever increasing fire, being wounded yet again in the leg. He fell to the ground and was unable to stand.

Once more Nevers tried to aid him. He refused stubbornly, though he was racked with pain. Weakly he continued to urge on Nevers, his fellow noncom. "He hoped he would see me sometime. [He] told me that even if I had to get down and dig the bastards out with my bare hands to go ahead and dig them out . . ."

That day Sergeant Connor won the Seventh Army's first Congressional Medal of Honor for bravery on the European mainland. There would be many more who would do so before it was all over. But unlike the brave noncom, not many of them survived to know that their courage had been rewarded by their country's highest military honor.

One who would was that freckle-faced kid looking no more than 16 who had fallen out with exhaustion during the march on Messina the previous summer. Now he was Staff Sergeant Audie Murphy, with three amphibious landings behind him. He had learned a lot during the hard slog up the "boot" of Italy; had toughened, become remote, had learned not to make friends among scores of replacements who had come routinely to his company, decimated time and time again; for it only hurt when they were killed or wounded, as they always were. Somehow he had survived. Why, he didn't know.

Now Audie Murphy landed with the first wave of the 3rd Division's 15th Infantry Regiment on "Yellow Beach," known before the war to pleasure-seekers as "Plage de Pampelonne." As he recalled afterwards, "Under the rocket barrage, scores of landing boats churn toward the shore. I stand in one; and the old fear that always precedes action grappled with my guts."

But on the beach itself there was little danger. Beyond, as the early morning sun began to burn away the early morning mist, there was, at the fringe of scented pine wood, a steep slope of a vineyard and it seemed to the keen-eyed young noncom, there had to be Germans hiding and waiting in it. Murphy was right. As the panting men started to climb up through the vines, a German MG 42 opened up with startling suddenness. Tracer started to hiss toward the advancing Americans.

Murphy, who was somewhat to the rear of the lead platoon, cocked his head and listened for the answering fire of an American BAR. There was none. He cursed and reasoned the platoon had walked straight into a trap. Now they were pinned down and unable to get out of it. Swiftly he doubled forward, clutching his carbine. A burst cut the air near him. He dropped into a ditch, filled with terrified men. He cursed and punched and tried to get them moving once more. They wouldn't budge. That MG 42 was too lethal. Murphy gave up on them. He doubled away, somehow found a light machine gun and started shooting at the German nest from the flank. But it was no use. The angle was wrong. His slugs flew harmlessly over the heads of the Germans in their coal-scuttle helmets.

Cradling the machine gun in his arms, Murphy ran the length of the vineyard under fire, flung himself down, panting for breath, in a spot directly to the front of the Germans. Now if they wanted to fire at him, they would have to expose their upper bodies and that was exactly what Murphy was waiting for.

After the war Murphy told an interviewer that he had become a dead shot as a poverty-stricken kid in rural Texas, "because if I missed [whatever he was hunting] we didn't eat." Now as the Germans tried to kill him, exposing their bodies as they did so, Murphy went into action. Screams of pain and horror followed his first sharp burst. But then Murphy ran out of luck. The automatic stopped firing. It had run out of ammunition.

He dropped it in disgust and doubled back to the undergrowth where he had stashed his carbine. There was a rustle behind him; he swung around, murder in his eyes. But it was only Tipton, his one surviving friend of the original company he had joined back in North Africa.

Tipton was bleeding from behind the ear. For the first time in two years of combat, the tall lanky married man had been hit. Murphy urged his old buddy to go back to the beach and have his wound dressed. Tipton refused. "Come on, Murph," he said with a wry grin on his skinny face, "let's move up." And then for the last time he used the old phrase he had used so often before. "They can kill us, but they can't eat us. It's against the law."

Together they crawled down a drainage ditch. They spotted two Germans. Tipton killed one, Murphy the other. An angry burst of tracer hissed above their heads. The German machine gun was only ten yards away. The two rose to their feet. Firing from the hip, yelling obscenities, carried away by the heated, crazy logic of battle, they charged the MG post.

Two of the enemy machine gunners were killed outright and the others started surrendering hurriedly, crying in frenzied terror, "Kamerad . . . Kamerad . . . nicht schiessen!"

It was then that Tipton made his fatal mistake. He had seen some more Germans a little further off and thought they were waving something white in token of surrender. He told "Murph" that he was going to collect them.

Murphy was not so sanguine. "Goddam, Lattie," he hissed, "keep down! You can't trust them."

Tipton didn't listen. Perhaps he was dazed by his wound and the events of the last hour? Perhaps he had grown overconfident? In the past years he had seen so many others killed and he had survived. He'd survive this time, too.

But he didn't. The moment he stood up, the Germans opened fire. He reeled back, chest spurting blood. He had been shot through the heart. He choked out one word, "Murph." The next moment he was dead.

For a moment Murphy held him, and then something snapped in the young Texan. For the only time in his 33-month combat career, he went berserk. Half crazed with rage and grief, he picked up the German machine gun and, flinging two grenades to keep the heads of the surviving Germans down, he charged, firing from the hip.

Five minutes later he had taken the little ridge and shot down all the Germans dug in there, without mercy. "My whole being is concentrated on killing," he recalled after the war, "as the lacerated bodies flop and squirm, I rake them again, and I do not stop firing while there is a quiver left in them."

Then he returned to the dead Tipton, took off his pack, cradled Tipton's head on it, and, flopping down on his heels, "bawled like a baby."

The exploit in that southern French vineyard won the young noncom the Distinguished Service Cross, but also dramatically heightened the pace of Audie Murphy's life. After Tipton's death he would always seem to deliberately court danger. He would volunteer for patrol after patrol. Even when not commanded to, he would tag onto other outfits, spoiling for a fight. Finally when the 3rd put him on the divisional staff to keep him from getting killed, he would "desert" every now and again to his old B Company.

Was he trying to die? Had some dark psychological trigger been pulled within him after Tipton's death that made him court death so recklessly? We do not know. What we do know is that during the next nine months Murphy would be wounded three times, kill an estimated hundred-odd Germans and become not only the US Seventh Army's most decorated soldier, but the most decorated soldier in the whole 200-year history of the United States Army—and that by the time he was barely 20.

"Lattie" Tipton was one of the unfortunate ones during those dramatic 48 hours which it took to clear the beachheads. Of the 66,000 troops landed in the initial assault, a mere 500 and some had been killed and wounded. Now Toulon was in the hands of de Lattre's First French Army and Marseilles would soon follow, allowing just short of a million American soldiers to pass through the port on their way to the front over the next eight months. It had been a tremendous success, but it was one totally overshadowed by the events in northern France. There Bradley's divisions were already on the outskirts of Paris. Soon the whole of the Western world would be indulging itself in heady, nostalgic triumph—the liberation of Paris. Who would remember the Seventh Army's sideshow on the Riviera?

Still, the top brass felt the event worthy of some kind of

recognition and celebration. Thus it was that at nine o'clock sharp on the morning of D-Day plus One, a group of leading generals and admirals landed on the beach near La Nartelle. It included US Admiral Hewitt, commander of the naval force; Secretary of the US Navy, James Forrestal; General Patch, naturally; and the Chief-of-Staff of the French Navy, Admiral Lemonnier.

Leaving the beachhead in two jeeps, with armed escorts to front and rear, the illustrious party set off for the nearest town of any size, Saint-Raphael, now waking up to the fact that, after the tremendous bombardment of the previous day, it had been liberated.

Now as the little procession made its way through the smoking dusty streets, piled high with brick rubble and debris, hundreds of scared, cowed civilians started to peer from the doorways and shattered windows of their ruined houses.

Admiral Hewitt ordered the jeep to stop. He pointed to the French Admiral and grinned encouragingly. The civilians recognized the Admiral's naval cap which differed markedly from Hewitt's. They threw caution to the wind. Surging into the streets, cheering and shouting, crying in the ecstasy of freedom, "Vive la France!! Vive les Etats Unies!"

Then, at that first moment of liberation, there were none of those bitter accusations and counter-accusations, the recriminations, the anti-Americanism, the professed contempt of US "Coca-Cola culture," which would divide the French thereafter and continue to do so into our own time. Now, as Admiral Lemonnier, choking with emotion, the tears streaming down his face, tried to make a speech, the crowd went wild, cheering madly, shouting their slogans over and over.

In all that turmoil, a woman's voice commenced singing the "Marseillaise," the song of the French Revolution, forbidden in this part of France since November 1942 when the Allies had landed in Africa and the "Unoccupied Zone," as it had been called, had been occupied by the furious Germans.

Abruptly everyone was singing, the tears rolling down

their cheeks. Secretary of the Navy Forrestal, who would commit suicide after the war, remained expressionless and unmoved. But Hewitt and Patch, both hard-bitten veterans of the last war in France, could not help themselves. Their eyes glistened with tears, too.

In a special order of the day on the following morning, General Patch, who wanted no second Anzio or Salerno, where the advance had bogged down on the beaches for months on end, told his Seventh Army to keep moving, regardless of fatigue or shortages. "The enemy" he commanded, "is perplexed and stunned and the opportunity for decisive results is ahead of us." It was an order reinforced by General Truscott, head of VI Corps, who commanded, "If you run out of gas, park your vehicles and move on foot." Truscott, eager and ambitious, was anxious to link up with Eisenhower's armies advancing out of the Normandy bridgeheads as swiftly as possible. The pressure was on from above and he was determined to apply it to those below him. It was the old army game.

For this purpose he created a special task force under the command of Brigadier General Frederick Butler. It was set up on August 18th from mobile combat elements of the 3rd, 36th and 45th Infantry Divisions. Named aptly enough Task Force Butler, it would drive on Grenoble or Montelimar. It was to be the spearhead of the whole Seventh Army, a long exploratory finger sticking into the confused retreating troops of General Wiese's German Nineteenth Army, poking hard and fast.

But Wiese, an ash-blond, scar-faced German, was a veteran of the Russian Front. He had plenty of experience of retreating and he was not panicked by the thought that Bradley's armies racing east could cut him off from the Reich. He withdrew skillfully. He allowed his Russians, Ukrainians, Turcomen, and half a dozen other Soviet nationalities, who had been press-ganged into his army, to drift away. But he was determined to save the nucleus of the German-speaking units in his army.

Time and again he escaped, as the French and their American allies pressed hard at his heels, fighting their way up the few valley roads leading north, under the blazing August sun.

For the victorious Americans, it seemed to be roses all the way. The Krauts were on the run, the natives were—as yet—friendly, and the local girls were willing and able. In the evenings, half drunk on the unaccustomed strong red wines of Provence, the young GIs of "Butler Force" sprawled out in the tree-shaded village squares, watching the old men in their floppy black berets playing boule in the dust, ogling the dark-eyed girls in their short, floral dresses and high wooden platform heels, drinking their rouge or Ricard in the sidewalk cafes. As the historian of 3d Division would put it later, it was "the longest advance in the shortest length of time that it [the 3rd] had ever made—or would ever make in Europe."

"If this is war, we want more," General Frederick's paras said. For now they were based near newly captured Nice, sitting within shell range of the front, with, as one of them recalled afterwards, "its neon lights blazing, its modern little nightclubs filled with real Scotch whisky and beautiful women dressed in soft silk and hot pianos beating out boogie-woogie just like it was "Cafe Society" or downtown in Greenwich Village."

Occasionally the windows shivered from the shelling, "but the beautiful babes weren't paying any attention and neither was the pianist and neither was the bartender." But then one of the paras would look at his watch and say, "Well, this has to be the last drink because I have to go on patrol soon."

And sometimes it wasn't all just "babes," boogie-woogie and bubbly. Now and then, General Wiese turned and fought back with startling savageness, which reminded the gleeful young GIs that this was not just an exercise with artillery, but a real shooting war in which men could be killed. Up in the foggy, snowbound mountains around Grenoble, paratroop patrols sometimes had a habit of going out and never coming back. At Callian in the Alpes Maritimes, a garrison

of paratroopers was trapped. It was reinforced by the local
Maquis, a bunch of teenagers mainly, armed with the cast-
offs of two armies, plus whatever weapons the British had
been able to parachute into the region. But they were
doughty fighters all the same and they did their best. Twice
Callian changed hands until it finally fell to the Seventh
Army.

The 141st Infantry Regiment of the 36th Division, which
finally succeeded in taking and holding the mountain village
was now ordered with the rest of the Texans to come out of
the mountains and head for the key road and rail center of
Montelimar on the River Rhone. But just as at the Rapido,
the 36th's luck ran out. As it advanced northwest in an attempt to cut the Route Nationale 7 to the north of Montelimar and block the retreating Germans, the latter picked up
a top secret Seventh Army map of the VI Corps' disposition
in the Rhone valley. Later no one could give a satisfactory
explanation of how this could happen. Had someone at
headquarters been exceedingly careless? Was there a German spy at work? (The Germans had left a large number of
"sleeper" agents and French collaborators, including
women, behind them as they had retreated.)

At all events, General Wiese now had an ace up his
sleeve. He knew Patch's plans and he also possessed an
overlay showing the Seventh Army's relative strengths at
different positions. Swiftly General Wiese, trying to withdraw the bulk of his German division north along Route
Seven through Montelimar, ascertained that 36th's weak
spot was at the small town of Bonlieu.

Bonlieu, a typical Provencal township centered around a
dusty square shaded by equally dusty trees, to which the local peasants recoursed after the summer heat for a game of
boule, cards, a drink and gossip, was held by a composite
company of the 3rd Engineer Battalion. The parent outfit itself was spread over a front of three thousand yards, normally the frontage defended by a whole infantry regiment of
some three thousand men. It was an ideal place for a breakout and General Wiese knew it.

On the last afternoon of August 25th the Germans attacked and caught the engineers completely by surprise. According to the manual the "Hun" was always expected to attack at first light, never at night or in the evening. The engineers hadn't a chance. Covered by the fire of Mark IV tanks—naturally engineers did not have anti-tank weapons, save for their bazookas which were not particularly effective against German armor anyway—the Germans pushed through the Americans and crossed the River Roubion, forcing the surprised defenders back several hundred yards. General Wiese was elated. For the first time in the campaign here in Southern France he had forced the Amis, as he contemptuously called the Americans, back. Immediately he threw in a second assault.

This time the German attack, again fronted by tanks, cut the engineers' line in two. German troops flooded through the gap so that within the hour all contact between the 36th Division's 141st and 142nd Regiments was broken.

Hurriedly General Dahlquist, the unassuming, heavy-set commander of the 36th Division, dashed up reinforcements to the area. The battered 3rd Engineers were withdrawn from their positions and fresh infantry of the Texas Division went over to the attack. It took two days but in the end it was done. Now the Bonlieu escape gap was plugged once more. But General Wiese had managed to slip most of his 198th Infantry Division, and, more importantly, his 2nd Panzer Division, through it during the time it had been in his hands. The scar-faced German Army commander, who would fight the US Seventh Army right up to the spring of 1945, was proving a wily and tough opponent.

Now General Patch was determined to round up what was left of the German Army in Southern France below Lyon in one single blow. The Bonlieu gap had been stopped. Now the only escape route available to the Germans was centered on "Route Nationale Sept" running through Montelimar.

Montelimar's only claim to fame was that it was the center of production of nougat, that sticky tooth-breaking sweetmeat, which used to be popular with children. Even today the place still calls itself "Nougat City" and the stuff is on sale everywhere.

But it was ideally suited to defense. Centered on its ruined 18th century citadel, Montelimar blocked National Route Seven heading north in a sprawl of dingy stucco bungalows, shaded by dusty trees, spreading out to the steep foothills to the east and the broad River Rhone to the west. Choked with white dust at this time of year, the roads radiating out from Montelimar's center could be easily defended by a handful of determined infantrymen. But Truscott did not want a head-on confrontation in Montelimar if he could avoid it. He had not the troops or the desire to engage his divisions in some kind of French Stalingrad. So he prepared to maneuver, and achieve his aim of blocking that key road leading north by artillery fire before encircling it with infantry.

Now "N 925540," the coordinate for Montelimar, became the most important map coordinate in the whole of France for VI Corps' artillery. For eight long days the 105s of the divisions engaged and pounded anything that moved in or out of Montelimar.

As one artillery spotter, flying a Piper Cub, recalled afterwards, "From up there it's like a box seat at a Broadway show. The only thing is if you go too high you're liable to get hit by Jerry planes or flak and if you go too low, even small arms fire will knock you down.

"Still it's an awful, peculiar thing to sit up there and spot something and call for fire on it and just sit there and wait for 60 seconds and watch something blow up. Sometimes it's a whole convoy and you keep adjusting fire until you pick the whole thing to pieces. Or sometimes maybe, it's just a house that the Jerries use as an observation post. Whatever happens we always pass on the report to the boys of the 158th Field Artillery Battalion because they never get to see what they hit. We're their eyes."

But by now the point of the Seventh Army was over a 150 miles away from their beaches through which all their supplies were coming. Marseilles, now captured, was not yet operating as a port and all supplies had to be manhandled ashore and then brought up by trucks over winding French roads and through medieval villages, some of them only wide enough to allow one-way traffic.

Gas began to run out. The lack of rifle ammunition became acute. The shell shortage was now so bad that the gunners pounding Montelimar and its surrounds started to pass up juicy targets because they were down to their last 25 shells; and it was a standing rule among the artillery battalions of the Seventh that the last 25 rounds were saved for a possible counterattack.

Communication was also becoming increasingly difficult, especially in the mountainous areas between Grenoble and Montelimar. Patch, still back on the beaches, was losing control over his scattered command and Truscott was finding it difficult, too, to know exactly where the spearheads of his widely dispersed corps were. Of course, his divisions had radios, but in the mountains their range was limited and as the retreating Germans had systematically destroyed all land-lines, the US Signal Corps had to work flat out to lay cable between the front and the rear.

Day after day, Signal Corps trucks would be out from dawn to dusk, crawling down the dusty little French roads between the vines, reeling out cable and galvanized wire. Behind the trucks there would be soldiers, stringing the two wires together to ensure that they didn't become entangled and then hanging them on the trees bordering the roads so that the tanks wouldn't tear them up.

"It's like sleep walking," one of them explained to the correspondent of the Army magazine *Yank!* "We've been doing it all through Africa and Sicily and Italy, and we can do it blindfolded. I got so used to it that I've walked all through France stringing wires together and knocking nails in trees and all the time I was back in Philadelphia."

In the last week of August, Truscott ordered his divisions, all of them very short of gas by now, to close in on Montelimar and bring the battle for the "nougat city" to an end. By moving ammunition—by hand—from artillery battalions not in action to those that were, Truscott managed to continue blasting away at the place, as units of the 3d and 36th Divisions closed in.

Within 48 hours, the 141st Infantry Regiment of the 36th seized control of the high ground to the east of the smoke-shrouded, battered city, while "Iron Mike" O'Daniel's 3d Division reached the outskirts of Montelimar itself on the evening of August 27.

All the following day, the "Rock of the Marne" men, as the soldiers of the 3rd Division called themselves after their celebrated defense of the French river in 1918, fought the German rearguard left in Montelimar. Steadily they pushed forward through the smoking city, over which hung the sickly sweet smell of nougat like a pall, rooting out the last-ditch, suicidal snipers.

Meanwhile to the north of the city, fighter-bombers from Corsica—the Seventh's air support had still not established fighter-strips in southern France—stood waiting in "racks" until the order came: "Attack!" They'd then fall out of the sky, hurtling in at tree-top height to slaughter the massed German convoys fleeing north with their cannon and rockets. Afterwards an estimated 2,500 vehicles and over 80 artillery pieces would be found blasted to pieces on one stretch of 30 miles of Route Seven between Montelimar and the next town north, Loriol.

By midnight on the 28th, it was all over and while the 3rd rested and combed the smoking ruins for Germans and loot, the unrelenting Truscott urged his 36th and 45th Divisions forward. Supplies were about running out. At Montelimar, the three battalions of light artillery and the one medium three-quarter battalion employed had fired a staggering 37,665 shells and it was taking the artillery battalions' ammunition train a 470-mile round trip to haul ammunition from the beach at St. Maxime. Now Truscott put his weary soldiers on two-thirds rations in order to give top priority to fuel so that the headlong chase could continue.

The 45th Division was ordered to advance from Grenoble

to cut the axis connecting the city of Lyon, capital of the region, from the Swiss border, while the 36th Division was to continue its drive northward heading for Lyon itself. The German Nineteenth Army must be destroyed before it could retreat to the safety of the high Vosges mountains in northern France and from thence to the celebrated Siegfried Line itself.

By now General Wiese was putting up hardly any resistance. The main difficulties facing Truscott's sweat-lathered, hungry, dusty GIs were the distances and the lack of fuel. Even the medics of the field hospitals to the rear of the Seventh Army's columns complained about Truscott's relentless drive forward. "Seems like every time we just finished putting up our tents," one of them told the correspondent of *Yank* magazine, "we had to pull them down again and move somewhere else. We must have moved at least a dozen times in less than 30 days. The war moved so fast that we never knew where it was exactly." Somberly the medic added, "But we never had to go anywhere to find it, it always came to us!"

On September 2nd the first patrols of General Dahlquist's 36th Division entered Lyon. It had cost the Seventh Army 2,733 men, killed, wounded or taken prisoner, to reach southern France's major city. Now Patch hesitated. He did not want to lose more men in a fight for a city of some half a million citizens. He need not have worried. Although the men of the 45th's 157th Regiment fought a short, sharp skirmish with some last-ditch defenders on the main road leading into the city from the east, the rest of the ten thousand German defenders slipped out like rats in the night without a fight.

The entry of the 36th Division and their comrades-in-arms of the French 1st Division into Lyon was triumphal procession. Wynford Vaughan Thomas, the veteran BBC correspondent, recorded the scene that September day. "None of us will forget the tumultuous heartfelt welcome we've been receiving from the people of the Rhone Valley—

but in Lyons that welcome reached its climax," he reported to his listeners back in Britain. "You daren't stop your jeep in a main street without it getting almost buried with people who just wanted to see you or pat you or to just be near an Allied soldier. . . . Their bicycles and the F.F.I. [the French Resistance] coming one way and our jeeps coming the other, with four policemen blowing variations of the Marseillaise on their whistles and nobody paying the slightest attention, but getting right ahead with the celebrations and the back-slapping and the general jollifications. We looked at the barbed wire fences of the Gestapo Headquarters, then we raced to the great squares under avenues of flags that cov-ered every possible place that a flag can be put; and I got the impression of a great city rapidly wiping out all traces of the hated German occupation—tidying up the minor damage and getting ready for normal life as soon as possible."

But there was not going to be a "normal life" for the GIs of the Seventh Army for a long time to come.

On September 8th, 1944, three weeks after the invasion of Southern France, General Truscott issued an order to his corps. Truscott reasoned they had gained a great deal of ter-ritory in August, but they had not destroyed General Wiese's Nineteenth Army—and the Kraut who escaped one day would live to fight another. So his order read: "The purpose of this operation is to destroy by killing or capturing the maximum number of enemy formations. Therefore the fol-lowing should be observed:

"a. Make every effort to entrap formations regardless of size. Long range fires, especially artillery, will merely warn and cause a change of direction.

"b. All units, but especially battalions and lower units, must be kept well in hand. Commanders of all ranks must avoid wide dispersion and consequent lack of control . . .

"c. Contact once gained must be maintained. The enemy must not be allowed to escape."

The Corps Commander ended with the grim exhortation:

"Every attack must be pressed home with the utmost vigor. Be vicious. Seek to kill and destroy!"

But that was not so easy. General Wiese was using every trick of the military game to extricate his battered army. Although the Allies were sensing an easy victory, believing that Nazi Germany was finished after the slaughter of the Wehrmacht in France, he knew just how resilient the Fatherland was. Already the Nazi Party was introducing a national levee, closing all universities, technical colleges, senior schools and the like, to raise men for the new "People's Grenadier Divisions" being hastily formed in the Reich. The Luftwaffe's flying schools were being closed too, as were U-boat schools in order to release men for transfer to the infantry. That September would see German industry's production of tanks, planes and guns reach the highest level of the whole war, despite Allied round-the-clock bombing. So Frederick Wiese was still confident. He was not going to tamely surrender his army to the "Amis" while there was still a chance of victory—and he thought there was.

As August gave way to September, he pulled back at speed, abandoning town after town, which the Americans thought he would defend, without a fight. Bourg fell, then Besancon. Dijon, the capital of Burgundy, was next. On the night of September 10th-11th, elements of de Tassigny's First Armored Division met men of the 2nd French Armored Division belonging to Patton's 3rd Army at a place near the little town of Sombernoon. Now the 3rd and 7th Armies formed one continuous front. Vesoul, an ideal site for a defensive position, fell with hardly a shot being fired. Everything seemed to be going splendidly. Still, Wiese's Nineteenth Army, battered though it was, was intact and retreating.

Now the Seventh and First French Army turned eastwards, with the German border only 100 miles away. Before them lay the Moselle River and the Vosges Mountains, a formidable natural barrier. In particular, they faced the High Vosges, a northeast/southwest range which formed a major obstacle to the Plain of Alsace and the Rhine River. On September 19th, the G-2 of Truscott's VI Corps warned that "the Vosges Mountains will make an excellent position from which to defend and it is doubtful that the enemy will evacuate without being forced to do so." The G-2 was right. The days of the "champagne campaign" were about over.

On September 20th, General Truscott ordered the assault crossing of the River Moselle, which barred the way to the Vosges. In the lead would be the 36th Infantry Division, making its attack in the Eloyes area. This would be followed by the 45th's crossing at Epinal and the 3d's in the Rupt area. Once the crossings had succeeded, VI Corps would break through the Saverne Gap, one of the two major exits from the Vosges, and head for Strasbourg, the capital city of Alsace.

The 36th was not happy with its assignment. The memories of the Rapido disaster still lingered and the veterans of that bloody fiasco noted the similarity between the deadly S-bend of the Italian river and the curve of the Moselle where they were to cross. That was not their only problem, as the hastily planned assault force began to assemble. For no roads led from the assembly areas to the river; only trails leading through the rugged, thick woods of the area.

But for once the 36th was lucky—at first. Somebody announced that the mayor of the nearby village of Raon-aux-Bois would like to see General Dahlquist. The staff officers cursed. What the hell did the Frog want at a time like this? Finally the mayor, 70-year-old Monsieur Gribelin, a retired French naval officer, was ushered into the CP and when he told them what he knew, "they almost kissed him," as one GI recalled afterwards. "His was the gift of American lives."

It appeared that Gribelin knew a jeep-sized pass through the woods that led to a shallow part of the Moselle where the water was only waist deep. There the current was slow and there was plenty of cover for the Americans' vehicles. Dahlquist, perhaps suspecting a trap, asked how the mayor knew this. Gribelin explained that it was a shortcut he took every Sunday when he went to visit his daughter in Eloyes. It would take them right behind the German positions.

So they set off at midnight, plodding through the rain and fog in a long three-battalion column, with the old man marching proudly in front, his skinny chest thrust out and his eyes shining. This definitely was not going to be another Rapido when so many of their comrades had been slaughtered even before they had reached the river.

By one o'clock that morning General Dahlquist had all three battalions of his 141st Regiment spread out along a three-mile stretch of the Moselle. Unfortunately the 3rd Battalion, commanded by Major Kermit Hansen, had got lost in the pitch darkness, and was a good mile and a half downstream of the ford. But Hansen knew he hadn't the time to reach the ford. He would have to cross where he was.

Hansen personally led the first group across by wading the river. But the Germans were waiting for them, hidden on the rugged heights on the other side of the Moselle. With startling suddenness, tracer, glowing eerily, cut the dawn gloom. Signal flares hissed into the sky, burst and cast everything below in an unreal, flickering light. Men went down everywhere. Within minutes the leading group was wiped out save for four men. Major Hansen was captured, but before this he had warned the rest of the battalion to move downstream and follow the 1st Battalion across.

Meanwhile the 1st Battalion had reached Gribelin's ford. But since he had last come this way, the river had flooded. Now it was shoulder-deep. Undaunted, an engineer, Corporal Walter Lindsey, took off his boots and helmet, tied a rope to his belt, and swam through the icy water. Using this as a guide the rest of the battalion followed across, battling the stiff current, trying to keep their balance with their weapons held high above their heads.

As the lead elements clambered thankfully to the other side, coughing and spluttering, their legs frozen, the Germans spotted them. Mortars opened up and bombs started to drop into the water, hurtling up violent spouts of wild white water. Snipers joined in and splattered the surface with their

slugs. The life line was almost shot in half and another had
to be hastily rigged at a more sheltered spot so that the crossing could continue. But it was difficult. It would be afternoon before the 1st was across, to be followed by the
reorganized 3rd Battalion. While all this was going on, the
141st's 2nd Battalion made a coordinated attack on that part
of Eloyes on the west bank of the Moselle. The enemy reacted violently. But the 2nd persisted with its attack. All the
same, resistance was so stiff that the 141st was unable to
build a bridge. It would be two days before they were able to
do so. Now it was becoming quite clear that General Wiese
was sick of running. As the end of September 1944 loomed
closer it was very evident that the Germans were fighting
back. The champagne was beginning to run out . . . but fast.

At Epinal, the 45th Division was forcing the Moselle too.
But again they were paying the price. One company managed to get across, but met such a withering German fire that
it was forced to retreat back to the other side, leaving one
fifth of its number dead and dying. There the 45th's 180th
Infantry met very stubborn resistance, including mined
banks and German rocket mortars, the first they had encountered in France. They weren't very accurate, but they were
decidedly frightening, as great snake fingers were poked
into the sky, followed instants later by the banshee-like howl
of the huge canisters hurtling down.

But as usual, the Thunderbirds, a lucky division if there
ever was one, slogged it out and finally consolidated their
positions after two days of bitter fighting through the first really serious opposition they had encountered ever since
landing in France.

It was the same for the 3rd Division, only tougher. The
"Rock of the Marne" men were fighting through well-
wooded mountainous terrain, made more difficult by the
mud after the persistent rain of the last few days. Slowly
they edged their way toward the Moselle, fighting German
roadblocks every few hundred yards and the snipers who
kept infiltrating behind their lines to pick off officers and

noncoms: those brave men who kept the infantry advancing and who soon would have an average life expectancy at the front of exactly 21 days. On the same day that Truscott gave the order for the corps' attack on the Moselle, the 3d Battalion of the Third's 30th Infantry was stopped dead by snipers and crossfire. The men tried repeatedly to break through, but with fire coming in from three sides it was impossible.

One day later, the Division's 7th Infantry reported: "The fighting in the woods is pretty tough. The undergrowth makes movement difficult. The Battalion has been having quite a fire fight."

It was no different in the Division's third regiment, the 15th. That same day Staff Sergeant Audie Murphy was ordered to report back to collect some raw replacements. They were green, nervous and bewildered. Murphy had just collected them together when suddenly the air was rent apart by the howl of a mortar bomb. Thwack! The bomb exploded nearby in a ball of angry red flame. Murphy yelled with pain and blacked out. "When I come to, I am sitting beside a crater with a broken carbine in my hands. My head aches, my eyes burn and I cannot hear. The acrid greasy taste of burnt powder fills my mouth."

But Murphy had still not lost the luck of the Irish, although he was the last man of his original company to be wounded or killed. If the shell had struck home a little closer he would have been as dead as the two replacements, who lay only feet away: bloody-torn bundles of rags, killed before they had even reached the line. A few stitches, a new pair of shoes (his others had been destroyed in the explosion) and with his "lucky" carbine repaired hastily, he was back in the line again, as the autumn leaves started to fall, wondering vaguely "which of us will still be alive when the new leaves return to the trees."

General Patch threw in a large, new formation. It was XV Corps, transferred from Patton's Third Army and led by General Wade Haislip, who one day would command the Seventh Army itself. XV Corps consisted in part of the US

79th Infantry Division, a hard fighting outfit with three months of combat behind it, and the famed French 2nd Armored Division, which the previous month had taken Paris and was now intent on taking Strasbourg too. But that wasn't to be—just yet.

The new corps was low on gas and ammunition. Nor did it possess the heavy artillery needed to batter its way through the forests and mountains ahead. Still, Haislip was a fighter, and he ordered the 79th into the attack. Their first objective was to be the forest of Parroy, behind which the Germans had built up a continuous line of concrete pillboxes, trenches and anti-tank ditches.

Surprisingly enough the 79th's advance to the edge of the forest went without trouble. Army intelligence had indicated that the six-by-five-mile forest was defended by the 15th Panzer Grenadier Division, but the two regiments taking part in the attack, the 79th's 315th and the 313th, met no real opposition until they penetrated into the trees themselves.

All hell broke loose as the American artillery bombardment ceased. With a rusty creak and the crash of falling pines, several Mark IVs broke their cover and started racing down the central road straight for the astonished Americans. The German counterattack had commenced.

By nightfall all was confusion and panic in the dripping, fog-shrouded forest of Parroy. German snipers and infiltrators were everywhere. Time and time again little shock groups of grenadiers, armed with machine pistols and grenades, launched attacks on the split up squads of US infantry; a few minutes of savage, bitter action in which neither side gave nor expected quarter. Then the Germans would vanish again into the trees, leaving behind the new dead and the dying. By midnight the American attack had come to a standstill with the 79th's GIs huddled in their foxholes under constant German artillery fire, red-hot, fist-sized pieces of shrapnel scything lethally through the trees.

It was no use. General Wiese had won after all. It would take another two months before the Vosges mountains were crossed and the Seventh Army would not cross the enemy's last natural bastion, the Rhine, until March 1945. By then most of the GIs of those veteran divisions—the 3rd, 36th and 45th, who had landed so confidently back in August 1944—would be dead or broken men, the great gaps in their ranks filled with fresh-faced replacements; or "reinforcements," as they were now calling them.

Back in that August General Lattre de Tassigny had told his officers, half in truth, half in jest, "Whatever you do, don't crush the vines." Even a war must not destroy those precious vines which produced the great wines of France. And it had been that kind of a campaign: babes and booze and occasionally a little bit of battle. But now the autumn rains were falling and it had become a slow, gruelling slogging match with the weary troops plodding through hills and mud on ground that was too slick for tanks, against a determined enemy, well dug in.

Back on the plain before they had attacked into the Vosges, many of the Seventh Army's GIs had bought picture postcards to send to the folks back home. Cheaply colored sentimental things, they had featured "Big bosomed babes holding bunches of grapes between their toothpaste smiles and wearing picturesque Alsatian clothes," as one disgruntled sergeant described the cards that fall, "or else pictures of mountain scenery with happy, healthy people and an overripe moon in the background."

But that had been on the plain. In the mountains it had been different, as he explained, echoing the thoughts of many of his comrades. Here "the beautiful babes weren't beautiful anymore. The happy healthy people were hungry and thin. . . . As for the scenery, that forest full of Christmas trees was lousy with snipers; those winding streams running through the valleys . . . only made their feet wetter and the full moon shone on hills . . . making the GIs curse, thinking of the long f——ing climb and the f——ing mud and the more f——ing mud on the other side."

The time of despair had commenced.

* * *

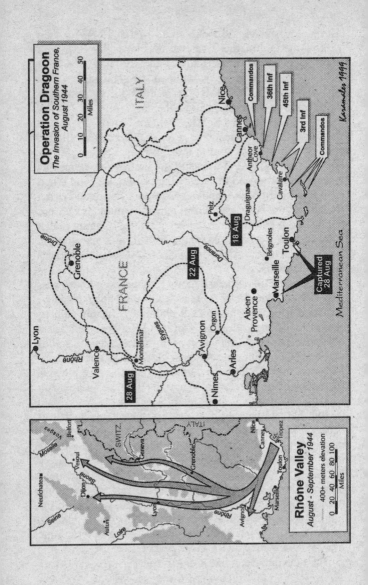

Operation Dragoon
The Invasion of Southern France, August 1944

Miles
0 10 20 30 40 50

Kaszander 1999

ITALY

FRANCE

Lyon

Grenoble

Drôme

Valence

Montélimar

28 Aug

22 Aug

Isère

Durance

Eygues

Avignon

Orgon

Arles

Nîmes

Aix-en-Provence

Marseille

Brignoles

Toulon

Bignoles

Dragুignan

Pelz

18 Aug

Cannes

Nice

Antheor Cove

Cavalaire

Mediterranean Sea

Captured 28 Aug

Commandos
36th Inf
45th Inf
3rd Inf
Commandos

Rhône Valley
August – September 1944

400+ meters elevation

Miles
0 20 40 60 80 100

SWITZ.

ITALY

Seine

Neufchâteau

Moselle

Belfort

Vesoul

Dijon

Saône

Autun

Loire

Lyon

Rhône

Geneva

Grenoble

Avignon

Marseille

Toulon

Cannes

Nice

St. Tropez

Vosges

3

THE VOSGES ATTACK

November–December 1944

"Win the war by forty-four . . . stay alive by forty-five."
—Differing unofficial slogans of Seventh Army GIs
between Dec. '43 and Dec. '44

It was Thanksgiving Day 1944 when Haislip's XV Corps
started finally to move through the Vosges, heading for the
plain below and the Rhine. The night was stormy, with the
rain slanting down in the beams from the headlights. For although the US Army always drove blacked-out at night, the
commander of this division of Haislip's Corps had ordered
his drivers to roll with their headlights full on. It was the
only way, he knew, that they were going to conquer the narrow winding roads of the Vosges and surprise the Boche dug
in below.

Just like the men of Haislip's other two divisions, the
44th and 79th, already fighting on their flanks, they had been
given a piece of cold turkey, their Thanksgiving Day dinner.
But the great majority of the men of Haislip's armored division setting off on their desperate journey on this last
Thanksgiving Day of World War II turned their noses up at
such primitive fare. Their finely-attuned palates were used to
much better food than turkey and cranberry sauce. For although they wore the olive drab of the US Army and drove
American jeeps, Shermans and White scout cars, they were
not Americans. They were the men of General Leclerc's 2d
French Armored Division, some of whom had been fighting
the Boche since 1939.

There were, of course, some Americans among them.
Lieutenant Tony Triumpho of the attached US artillery bat-

talion, was one, and he had an important job. It was the lieutenant's task to set up a forward observation post for
Leclerc, who liked to direct his own artillery fire—from the
front! Now as the young officer's jeep wound its way up the
Vosges, while he gnawed a cold turkey leg and the rain came
belting down, he told himself "the plan was for the French to
get just over the other side of the Vosges and then wait for
the American infantry to come up for a combined attack on
Strasbourg." But as he admitted ruefully after the war, "The
French, of course, had another plan."

Back at Leclerc's forward command post, set up in a
commandeered chateau in the wooded foothills of the Vosges, the air was electric with tension and anticipation on account of that "other plan." Captain Chatel, who had joined
the 2nd from the Resistance, was attempting to snatch some
sleep on the hard wooden floor with the rest of the staff. But
he had little success, for as he recalled afterwards, the se-
vere-faced, mustached commanding general "kept coming
in and asking whether there was any news of the drive." Old
campaigner that he was, Leclerc was anxious and restless. It
was not simply that he wanted to cross the Vosges this
stormy winter night, with the rain lashing the tall windows
of the chateau and making them rattle; he wanted more.

He burned to fulfill that promise made so many years before; to take Strasbourg from the Boche—and, if his luck
held out, to give a French division the honor of being the
first Allied unit to cross the German Rhine.

"Mon General, here I can do no more. I ask your permission
to take my chance." Captaine le Vicomte de Hauteclocque,
son of an aristocratic French family renowned for its bravery
in battle, was asking his divisional commander for permission to desert.

On this 28th day of May 1940, with the heavy guns of the
permanent barrage rumbling in the distance and the long pathetic columns of shabby peasant refugees heading south before the ever-victorious Wehrmacht, the 37-year-old Captain
with the piercing blue eyes knew the French Army was

beaten. Soon it would lay down its arms tamely to the Germans. But not he. The scion of the de Hauteclocques would continue to fight the Boche wherever he could find an opportunity to do so. Thus, the man who would become General Leclerc left his division and attempted to rejoin the five French divisions still reported to be fighting near Lille. By the time he reached the northern industrial city, the fighting was over and those five divisions were on the run, too. Suddenly he found himself a fugitive in his own country, with his own countrymen refusing him food and shelter—in one case a priest turned him out—for fear the triumphant Germans might shoot them. Bitterly the fugitive reflected that he seemed to be the only man left in France who wished to fight the Germans.

At one stage in his flight, he was captured by the Boche, but he managed to talk his way out of the trap. On another occasion he was wounded by a dive-bomber and woke up to find himself in a hospital taken over by the enemy. Again he escaped.

Shortly after that second escape, he was one of the few Frenchmen who bothered to listen to a broadcast from London, given by a penniless fugitive from France. On that memorable June 17th, 1940, the voice from London thundered, "France is not alone. I, General de Gaulle, now in London, call on all officers and soldiers now in Britain or who come to Britain, with or without arms, to join me. . . . Whatever happens the flame of French resistance must not and will not go out!"

At last the fugitive knew what he had to do. Six weeks later, now bearing the nom de guerre of Leclerc to protect his wife and five children from any possible reprisals, he was on his way to French Africa to rally the French colonies there to de Gaulle. "Your immediate objective," de Gaulle had told him at their first meeting in London, "is to rally French Africa. Your long term policy is to free France."

One year later, Leclerc—helped by the British—had marched right across Africa at the head of a motley army of white colonial and native troops. He had come these 3,000 miles through jungle, barren mountains, and searingly hot desert to attack a fort which controlled the oasis of Kufra in the Sahara Desert.

For five days his men fought the Italians in the oasis until finally, on March 1, 1941, with only a handful of shells left for his guns, Leclerc saw the white flag being hoisted above the walls of the Beau Geste fort. The Italians had surrendered. That day Leclerc cabled de Gaulle the news that the Free French flag now flew above Kufra; it was de Gaulle's first victory. Leclerc ended his cable with the proud boast: "We will not rest until the flag of France also flies over Paris and Strasbourg!"

In August 1944, courtesy of the US Army, Leclerc had been allowed to enter Paris, thus fulfilling the first part of the "Oath of Kufra," as it had become known in Free French circles. But thereafter, there had been trouble. It was ordered that Leclerc's 2nd Armored Division should join General Lattre de Tassigny's First French Army. Leclerc refused categorically. "I will not serve with any commanders who previously obeyed Vichy and who I consider to be turncoats." By this Leclerc meant de Tassigny himself, who had served Petain's Vichy government loyally until 1942, when the Germans took over the unoccupied zone of France. General Patch tried to reason with the stubborn Frenchman but failed. He reported afterwards that Leclerc made it "distinctly clear" to him that "he did not want to serve with the First French Army." This was the first time that Patch had had trouble with his prickly French subordinates. But it wasn't going to be the last.

So Leclerc was left with Haislip's American XV Corps and in its burly, balding commander he found a sympathetic superior. Haislip had been a student at France's Ecole de Guerre, spoke fluent French and was by nature a francophile. "I never issued orders to Leclerc," he said after the war, "Whenever I wanted him to do something, I would say: 'Leclerc, this is what I am planning to do. It looks to me as though you could do this and that and so forth . . . I want you to go away and study it and tell me what you think.'"

So this November, while officially in reserve, and as the 79th and 44th Divisions slogged away at the Vosges, Leclerc had studied his maps very closely. As one aide remembered, "He searched for little entries, little narrow roads, or even tracks through which he might infiltrate his tanks. It was the same as he had done at Kufra."

Now in his chateau HQ, Leclerc waited impatiently for news of his column fighting its way through rain, snow and mud. Finally it came, just after dawn and it was good. One of his *têtes brulées* [burned heads] from his days in Africa, a Major Massu, had reached the little town of Dabo, on the other side of Vosges! After two months of hard slog, the first Allied troops had crossed the mountain range.

Leclerc leapt into action. He ordered an aide, Captain Chatel, to go to Haislip's HQ immediately. "Tell him," Leclerc snapped, eyes flashing, "I need one or two battalions of American infantry to clean up alongside the roads behind us and deal with all the prisoners. We don't want to be bothered waiting about to take prisoners. Bring me those battalions yourself, Captain."

Chatel woke the Corps Commander up from a deep sleep, but as the French captain recalled afterwards, "He was very nice about it." At first Haislip turned down the French request "because the armor had a bad habit of trying to borrow soldiers from infantry divisions to save getting their own infantry chewed up," which was exactly Leclerc's intention. In the end, however, he gave in. Leclerc could have one battalion from the 79th Division.

Just before Chatel left with the good news, the telephone rang. It was Patch. To Chatel, who understood English, it was evident that the Seventh Army commander was forbidding any drive to Strasbourg by Leclerc. Then he heard Haislip say, "Sir, we cannot take 'no' completely for an answer. Will you please confirm that it can be done?"

A great argument between the two generals followed,

while the rain lashed down the windows of the HQ savagely, making the panes rattle. In the end Patch relented a little, realizing just how emotionally important Strasbourg was to the French. Leclerc could patrol in the general direction of Strasbourg, but only when General Haislip gave the word.

Haislip hung up and told Chatel what Patch had said, adding "General Leclerc does know, of course, that he is only supposed to take the passes of the Vosges and not go further!"

Chatel rushed back to Leclerc with the news of how he would need to obey Haislip's restraints. By then, however, three of Leclerc's five columns had already reached the other side of the mountain chain and Chatel had barely time to swallow a quick cup of coffee before being sent back to Haislip with a request from the 2nd Armored's commander for permission to "patrol" towards Strasbourg. He got it. By ten that morning, Leclerc's Shermans were rolling toward the Alsatian capital.

The "patrolling" became a full-scale drive for Strasbourg. The French drove all-out for the Rhenish city. Phalsbourg was captured and the German commanding general caught completely by surprise. They halted to set up an ambush for German reinforcements going up to the Vosges front. The enemy hadn't even realized the French were through the mountains. One of the ambushers remembered: "It was an absolute massacre. We just let them come as close as possible and then shot them to bits—they were all sorts, lorried infantry, guns, staff cars, even the German Chief of Railways for the region. . . . With cannon and machine guns we poured fire into them until the roads were absolutely littered with burning vehicles."

Again the French barrelled on. Watching them go, British BBC correspondent Wynford Vaughan Thomas recorded, "The drivers drive with bare hands—the gloves can't grip the slippery wheels that whirl this way and that and move with every bump and pothole and everything slithering on the road. On they go, these endless, urgent columns crowd-

ing on every highway, debouching mud into the rough country tracks that are seething glaciers of mud."

Sergeant Bill Maudlin, formerly of the 45th Division,
now cartoonist with the *Stars and Stripes*, was so impressed
by the reckless and deadly way the French drove that last
week of November that he drew a cartoon for the Army paper. It showed a long line of disconsolate US truck drivers
being addressed by their lieutenant before departure. "Men,"
says the officer gravely, "some of you may never come back.
There's a French convoy on the road today!"

Whatever impact the French drivers had on their American counterparts is not known. What is known, is that the
French slaughtered hundreds of Germans, and French civilians too, who had sided with the Boche, on the road to the
Alsatian capital. Now as General Mencher, Haislip's Chief-
of-Staff, headed for Leclerc's CP with a direct order from
Eisenhower himself that the French General was not to drive
for Strasbourg, Leclerc went into hiding. He told Chatel, "I
don't want you to go back to Corps HQ because I don't want
you to bring me back any counterorders." Then Leclerc stationed staff officers along the road leading to Strasbourg
with instructions to head off any American soldiers bringing
orders to stop him driving for the great Rhenish city. Indeed,
by the time Mencher found Leclerc, the latter had already
taken Strasbourg.

At dawn on the morning of November 23rd, Leclerc gave
the order to attack by surprise. The Germans had a garrison
of 15,000 men there, and Leclerc knew that much of the
German-speaking local populace was pro-enemy. He would
have to catch the Germans off guard. He wanted no Alsatian
betraying his move to the enemy. They had to move fast.

Lieutenant Triumpho was one of three Americans to go in
on point that day. "We went roaring across the plain in our
jeep along with four or five light tanks and a few half-tracks
of infantry, about 70 men. We passed working parties and
groups of German troops . . . and they just stood open-
mouthed. When they saw it was French troops they were

scared to death, for they had heard that the French . . . did not take too many prisoners."

But the French were too intent on capturing Strasbourg to waste time shooting prisoners. Every minute counted now. At the point, the Frenchmen strained their eyes to catch their first glimpse of Strasbourg's famed Gothic cathedral. And then there it was. They had reached the city that Leclerc had sworn to capture way back in the desert three years before. He had almost fulfilled the "Oath of Kufra."

At 10:30 that glorious morning, the tanks of Major Rouvillois, head of the first column, barrelled through the narrow streets of the old city, firing to left and right like drunken cowboys shooting up some wild West township in a Hollywood "B" movie. But not for long. From over the Rhine some 600 yards away the German guns opened up. The Shermans scuttled for cover.

But they were there. As Vaughan Williams recorded for the BBC. There it was, "set against the rain-dark sky to the east, a looming outline of distant hills—the Black Forest, the western barrier of Hitler's Reich. We felt we'd come to the end of a long journey. . . . We'd got to the Rhine at last."

While Leclerc's 2nd Armored Division had been making the running for Haislip's XV Corps, the VI Corps (now commanded by General Brooks, as General Truscott had gone off to command the US Fifth Army in Italy), had also been attacking through the Vosges. They, too, were noticing the change in the inhabitants of the villages and small towns of the plain below which they were now "liberating." As one journal recorded, "From cities and villages that were predominantly French, we moved to cities and villages where speech, dress and customs were predominantly German." Now the VI Corps had to be wary of spies and German sympathizers, even snipers, and some of them women.

There was something else too. On the morning of November 26th, Corps HQ alerted a team to go and have a look at a strange sort of camp which had been found in the 3rd

Divisions' zone of operations at a place called Natzviller, eight miles away from the town of Rothau.

They found a rectangular enclosure surrounded by barbed wire fences, which could be charged with electricity. Two prisoners of the camp, who had escaped a couple of days before and informed the advancing Americans of the place's existence, helped the shocked investigators to understand the full horrors of Natzviller. Among the lethal equipment of the camp was a "shower room" where prisoners could by asphyxiated, and a crematorium with an elevator device to simplify the lowering of the victims into the furnace.

In essence, the Americans had discovered the first of the German concentration camps and the only one to be established on French soil. There, nearly 4,000 prisoners had been kept—Jews, homosexuals, priests, "socially unfit" individuals, "Bible students," and the like—while they were processed for death. On November 16th the camp had been evacuated and the SS had planned to blow it up. But the American advance had come as a surprise and had been too swift. So it was left as it had been as the SS fled, with their meals on tables, the ovens filled, and with the doctors, who had carried out the hideous experiments demanded by SS Reichsfuhrer Himmler, leaving their instruments and even their doctors' certificates on the walls of the operating theater, clear proof of their guilt.

Then, of course, the publicity machine cracked into full gear to detail this evidence of National Socialist inhumanity and the horror of the whole rotten Hitler system. But while the PR men displayed what the SS had done, in all its terrible gore and brutality, they conveniently forgot to explain to the shocked Western world who had put the victims into the camp in the first place. It would not have been very good politics to do so; there would have been a tremendous public outcry, especially in America. For the nation which had arrested these political prisoners, Jews, homosexuals and the rest, and delivered them to the SS to torture and murder so cruelly, had been France itself.

* * *

The military defeat of 1940 had seemed to millions of Frenchmen proof of the iniquity and perfidy of the politicians of the Third Republic who had taken France into the war against Germany. It was only explicable by treachery, the criminal negligence of the politicos and the abandonment of traditional French virtues.

As a result, the new Vichy Government under the leadership of the aged Marshall Petain—"the victor of Verdun"— came into being wearing a hairshirt and determined to cleanse French life of its corrupting influences. Petain had once purged the broken French Army of 1917 by breaking off the senseless slaughter of Verdun and then decimating the ranks of the mutineers by his own military police. Now in 1940, he was going to cleanse France, and, if necessary, he'd use force as he had done when he had "saved" the French Army.

Within days of taking power Petain's government started passing anti-semitic legislation. It required no spurring on by the Germans. There were plenty of anti-semites in France already. Jews were accused of having corrupted French youth, with their decadent art, books, and a flashy way of life.

In a letter of devastating irony, the head of the Paris bar and ex-senator Pierre Masse wrote to Petain directly after he heard that Jews would now be barred from becoming Army officers. "I would be obliged if you would tell me what I have to do to withdraw rank from: my brother, a second lieutenant in the 36th Infantry Regiment, killed at Douamont in April 1916; from my son-in-law, Second Lieutenant in the Dragoons, killed in Belgium in May 1940; from my nephew, J-F Masse, killed in Rethel in May 1940. Can I leave my brother his Medaille Militaire . . . my son, wounded in June 1940, his rank?"

Petain did not reply. Some people will never learn that sarcasm makes them no friends. Masse, the Jew, was arrested and sent to die in Germany like so many others.

Now it was Vichy's French police who rounded up 5,000

French Jewish children and handed them over to the Germans to do with what they pleased. It was French detectives who sought and captured French resistance workers for interrogation and torture by the "Butcher of Lyon," Klaus Barbie. It was the French paramilitary police, the hated Milice, which fought pitched battles with the Maquis in southern France in a vain attempt to stop them from aiding the advancing US Seventh Army.

Unknown to the ordinary foot-slogger of the Seventh Army, who was putting his life on the line in order to "liberate" France every day, a goodly section of the French population was totally indifferent to their being there—and a smaller number actually hated them. Petain had tried to "reform, to render more austere a Republic that we had made too easy," as the President of the French National Assembly had told Petain on the day he assumed power. Now here were these foreigners in their sloppy, dust-stained, olive drab uniforms undoing all his good work.

It was against this kind of background, a France obsessed with treachery, split among itself and growing anti-Americanism, that one must see General Patch's first serious spat with his French subordinates and comrades-in-arms.

Just after the discovery of Natzviller, the advancing elements of the weary 3rd Division had begun to enter Strasbourg. Their task would be to help Leclerc's tankers mop up the rest of the German resistance. For the enemy had dug himself in in some of the powerful 19th century forts which surrounded the Alsatian capital and had been incorporated into that celebrated white elephant, the French Maginot Line. But the 3rd's 7th and 15th Infantry Regiments were not the first US troops to enter Strasbourg.

General Devers at Sixth Army Group had already sent in a special task force, called "T Force." It contained combat elements of Brooks' VI Corps, but its main job was to supervise the change of control of the city from German to French hands. (Another smaller and very hush-hush task force within this main body also had the job of trying to discover whether the Germans had made any further progress in the production of an atom bomb. There were known links between the University of Strasbourg and leading German atomic scientists.) Four days after the "T Force" arrived, its commander reported on November 29th that the great city with its 200,000 citizens was in turmoil. The German-speaking Alsatians who had been full German citizens for the last four years deeply resented the French take-over. Already some of the French officials newly appointed by de Gaulle had been assassinated by local Alsatians. More would undoubtedly follow.

General Leclerc was not making matters easier either, the "T-Force" commander stated. He had had posters put up everywhere in the city, proclaiming he would have sharpshooters and those who sheltered them summarily shot without trial. He had also proclaimed that he would have five German hostages executed for every one of his own men murdered by the sharpshooters still lurking in the city.

General Devers was shocked. Orders like that were definitely against international law. Besides, it would look bad in the newspapers back home. You couldn't have Frenchmen shooting Frenchmen out of hand. It certainly wasn't something he wanted to be associated with.

The problem escalated. It was reliably reported that General "Iron Mike" O'Daniel, whose 19-year-old son had been killed with 101st Airborne in Holland the previous month, had been quoted as approving of Leclerc's orders. No one was going to shoot his "Rock of the Marne" soldiers and get away with it. Shoot 'em and be damned! O'Daniel was ordered to retract his statement. He did. But Leclerc was made of harder steel. When the French Military Governor of Strasbourg was commanded by Devers to proclaim to the city, by means of posters, that Seventh Army had always conformed to the Geneva Convention, Leclerc advised him to refuse to do so. And he did.

Leclerc was grateful to the Americans for his division and for the tolerance of his corps commander, but he felt that they simply did not understand France's present situation. The country was on the brink of the same anarchy that was currently afflicting Belgium and Greece, where soon British paras would be fighting the Greek Communist resistance. In the north, where the cities and infrastructure had been shattered by years of Allied bombing, the working class starved while the peasantry waxed rich from the black market. Thousands who had worked for the Germans or had supported Petain had been thrown into the jails and the Communist resistance was making great capital out of these rich and middle class "collabos," as they were called. Their ranks contained some of the most famous names in France: writers, painters, international movie stars with Hollywood reputations and one great female singer who, when accused of having worked "heart and soul" for the Germans, had replied in that tough Parisian manner of hers, "what does that matter, as long as my cunt belonged to France!"

Bitter and resentful, Leclerc hung on. But the pressure was too great. Leclerc and General Schwartz, the military governor of Strasbourg, were unofficially told that the Americans would totally cut off the vital supplies upon which they depended. It was a threat that Eisenhower was going to use against the French more than once in the months to come. So on December 10th Leclerc gave in and got on with the war. With his approval, General Schwartz agreed to give a newspaper interview which would be widely distributed, stating that the French would agree to the terms of international laws. The first crisis over Strasbourg had been solved—temporarily—but within a month it would be back again. With a vengeance.

While the top brass and the politicians argued and wrangled in their headquarters and chateaux way behind the front, the young men who paid the butcher's bill—the infantry and the tankers of Patch's Seventh Army—kept right on slogging. By now the three original divisions with which Patch had invaded France were becoming very weary. The Vosges and the Germans had taken it out of them. Losses had been mounting steadily. Not only in combat. Trench foot and diseases of the chest were becoming almost epidemic.

But by now, however, fresh infantry and armored divisions were flooding into France from the States and England. The 103rd Infantry and 14th Armored Divisions joined Brooks' VI Corps so that by the first week of December 1944, the Corps numbered these and the 3rd, 45th and 79th Infantry Division as its major units. Haislips's XV was not left out either. Now it was composed of the 44th and the new 100th Infantry Division and the 12th Armored—and there were more divisions on the way.

Now with the top brass still confident that the war would be over by Christmas—Monty had wagered Ike a "fiver" that it would—Eisenhower ordered Patch to attack towards the Reich in the Saar and along the River Rhine. While General Lattre de Tassigny's French Army dealt with the "Colmar Pocket," the 17,000 men of General Wiese's 19th Army still left on the French side of the great river in the general area of Alsace's second city, Colmar. With the French would be the 36th Division to help out when there was any particularly hard fighting to be done. For the First French Army was starved of equipment—and men. Wearing the cast-offs of at least three armies, the French, fighting on their native soil, were a forgotten army themselves.

As usual it was the "old hands" who led the attack. December 13th was the 365th day spent in battle by the US 45th Division ever since it had landed in Sicily the year before; and as usual the "Thunderbirds" were attacking. Using mules as transport like they had done in Italy, the division advanced through rugged country, fighting not only the terrain but also the weather in the shape of the first snows of that winter.

Despite the weather, the terrain, the stubborn German rearguard parties and the minefields, the men were in good heart. The Germans were falling back and the German frontier itself was only a few "klicks" away. Naturally all the "Thunderbirds" knew they were heading straight for the

Siegfried Line upon which the British had boasted they would hang "their dirty washing mother dear," so long before. But they were still throwing the enemy back onto his own soil.

On Tuesday, December 14th, 1944, Lieutenant Colonel Dwight Funk, commanding the 158th Field Artillery, telephoned Colonel Walter O'Brien, who led the Division's 157th Infantry Regiment. He said excitedly, "Colonel, from where we are now we can put a barrage across the border. Say the word and we can have a concentration into GERMANY!"

The other Colonel didn't hesitate a second. "What are you waiting for," he roared. "Fire away!"

Now the race started in the VI Corps to be the first outfit having the "honor" of entering Germany. In essence, it was between the "old heads" of the 45th and the "wet noses," or new boys, of the 103rd, nicknamed the "Cactus Division" from its divisional patch. The 45th, that lucky division, after a stiff fight for the villages of Lembach and Wingen, now had the advantage. For a sudden flanking movement by the "Thunderbirds" had so confused and disorganized the enemy that only isolated last-ditch German groups were able to oppose the triumphant division.

For the 103rd, the going was tougher, much tougher. On the same day that the 45th's artillery fired its first salvo into the Third Reich, whose master Adolf Hitler boasted would last "one thousand years," the 103rd's 411th Infantry Regiment was engaged in a fierce fight for the little township of Climbach.

Climbach was tough. It lay in a flat open valley with German heavy guns sighted on the two rugged wooded heights fringing the town and commanding all approaches. Inside the township itself, the enemy had the much-feared 88mm cannon, plus some Mark IV tanks. Then, scattered throughout the surrounding woods, there were well dug-in machine gun positions and mortars. Everything was ready for the advancing Amis, zeroed in.

To take Climbach, the 411th's regimental command set up a special task force. It consisted of a motorized rifle company, a platoon of engineers, a platoon of Sherman tanks and a platoon of towed three-inch tank destroyers from the 614th Tank Destroyer Battalion, under the command of Captain Charles Thomas.

The appearance of Captain Charles Thomas at the command post of the task force, which was led by Colonel Blackshear, caused something of a sensation. For Thomas was black, as were his men. These were America's "invisible soldiers," relegated to driving trucks and working in docks unloading supplies. Blacks were no use in combat, all the top brass knew that.

Patton, to whose army they had first been attached on arrival in France, thought differently. He told them, "I don't care what color you are as long as you go up there and kill these Kraut sons-of-bitches!" He added in typical Patton style, "There is one thing you men will be able to say when you go home. You may all thank God that 30 years from now when you are sitting with your grandson upon your knees and he asks: 'Grandfather, what did you do in World War II?' you won't have to say, 'I shovelled shit in Louisiana!'"

That pep talk had done it. "The invisible men," as they called themselves bitterly, were burning for action so that they could prove themselves. Now, as they were about to enter that strangely silent valley with the Germans waiting for them, Captain Thomas told Colonel Blackshear, "I would take it, meaning I would take my men into the valley first," Later he asked himself, "Why did I volunteer?" But he could find no answer to that overwhelming question.

"We felt naked," Sergeant Booker, one of them, said later. Now in complete view of the enemy, the ten-man crews manhandled their 5,000-pound cannon into position in knee-deep mud, waiting for the sharp crack and angry whine of an 88mm.

They didn't have long to wait. The enemy on the ridges opened up almost as soon as they were in position. Captain Thomas was hit, but he wouldn't allow himself to be evacuated and continued to direct the fire of his guns. Men started to go down everywhere. Within 15 minutes single soldiers were doing the work of a whole crew—loading, aiming, firing and then doubling back to the half-tracks under machine gun fire for more shells. Half an hour later after they had entered combat, there was only one gun, commanded by Sergeant Booker, still firing. Then it ran out of ammunition.

The little force's tanks were still bogged down to the rear, so three BAR men from the 411th Infantry volunteered to give the gun covering fire while something was done. The same men who had observed the blacks' arrival with disdain now risked their lives to defend them, as the Germans, confident of an easy victory, began to advance on the artillery position.

But help was on its way in the form of Private Phipps of the 614th. He sprang behind the wheel of his ammunition truck and rammed home first gear. "You can't go up there," he was told. "It's coming in too heavy." "The hell I can't!" he yelled above the roar of the gunfire. Before anyone could stop him, the black soldier was off, fighting the mud and the shelling. He was badly hit by a shell fragment. For a moment he thought he'd faint. Grimly he held onto the wheel and kept going. Finally he stuck fast in the thick gooey mud, some 25 yards from Booker's gun. Minutes later it was firing again and Private Phipps had won himself a Silver Star, as had Lt. Walter George Mitchell and Corporal Peter Simmons—posthumously.

The cost had been high. Half the company had been killed or wounded. But the black outfit, which was under fire for the first time that day and some of whose men were barely literate, had won itself the coveted Presidential Unit Citation at Climbach for "reflecting the highest traditions of the armed forces of the United States."

Now it is the turn of the 103d's white infantry, fighting their way doggedly through the shellfire and the mud and the icy rain. Twice the Germans threw in counterattacks, supported by tanks. Both times the enemy was repulsed.

They came to a battered graveyard. Everywhere the

strange, wrought-iron crosses of the area were broken and snapped off by shellfire, the stones pock-marked with shrapnel like the symptoms of some loathsome skin disease. But among the dead, which had lain there for centuries, there were the quick, too. The Germans had dug themselves in between the graves and behind the stone wall which surrounded the place. One by one they were flushed out.

A flight of P-47s was whistled up to hasten the process. But the fighter-bombers lost direction. Suddenly they were barreling out of the gray December sky, heading straight for the infantry. They had mistaken them for Germans. By now American planes had bombed and shot up their own troops so often that they were known as "the American Luftwaffe." But this time tragedy was averted at the very last moment. Some quick-thinking ack-ack lookout tossed out yellow smoke grenades. They burst and thick yellow smoke rose rapidly to warn the pilots that they were over friendly territory.

By one o'clock that Friday afternoon, it was about all over and Climbach, what was left of it, was in American hands. Now the 411th started advancing once more, slogging through the muddy forested Le Diebhalt Mountains until they reached the hamlet of Bobenthal, six kilometers west of the nearest large township, Wissembourg.

Here Company I, commanded by 1st Lt. William McCutcheon of St. Joseph, Missouri, followed a few minutes later by L Company under the command of Capt. Joseph Kasun of Bisbee, Arizona, crossed a little stream and then flopped down exhausted in the mud. They had been fighting all day and soon it would be dark in the forest. Now it was time for chow and there was a mail call. As one of them recalled that moment years afterwards, "The hills are deadly still. You read a letter, for the mail has come up at last. The letter is old, but you read and re-read it until it becomes soiled from the crusted mud on your hands. It is a letter from home. Home! You think of it the way a soldier does. That faraway dreamland of light and warmth and peace and love.

You wonder if you'll ever see it again.The lieutenant pants up the hill to the little group clustered around you.

"Boys, I want to tell you something," he says with a half smile. "This outfit was the first one in Seventh Army to cross into Germany today. Remember that little stream. That was a border."

"Good deal," someone mumbles. Someone else asks, "What's the date today?"

It is December 15th, 1944.

On that muddy lonely hillside, with the war settling down for the night and the flares sailing into the darkening sky at regular intervals, no one in that little company could have thought, even in the wildest of their dreams, that the US Seventh Army would still be in Germany nearly 50 years later.

In fact, that unknown Lieutenant was wrong. The "Thunderbirds" had beaten the 103d by exactly 20 minutes. For at 12:45 on that Friday, the 3d Battalion of the 45th Division's 180th Infantry Regiment began crossing into Hitler's vaunted "1000 Year Reich" north of Wingen.

Not that it mattered, nor was it noted by most of the "Old Heads." They had seen too much of war already; there was no glory left in it for them. Their old slogan of "Win the War by Forty-Four" had been replaced by a cynical new one, "Stay Alive in Forty-Five." For already on the morning of the following Saturday the 3d Battalion was engaged in fighting for the first German township to be taken by the Seventh Army, Bobenthal.

All day they battled there, as did the battered 79th Infantry Division which crossed over into Germany that Saturday and the advance units of the 14th Armored. Everywhere they were engaged, battling their way into the first defenses of the Siegfried Line.

It was no different in the sector held by the XV Corps. There the 44th and 100th Infantry Divisions were also fighting bitterly to overcome a line of fortification, pitting guts and frail human flesh against an invisible enemy, well entrenched behind a foot or two of ferro-concrete. Only this line of forts had not been built by the Germans, but by the French. They were attacking the Maginot Line, and the shells of the biggest cannon available—240mm caliber to be exact—were ricocheting off four-foot-thick walls like harmless ping-pong balls!

And all in vain. The Seventh Army would finally penetrate the Maginot Line this December, but it would take another bitter, cruel three months before they did the same to the Siegfried Line—and by that time most of the young men fighting this day would have died or disappeared.

For on this, the last Saturday before Christmas 1944, some 70-odd miles as the crow flies to the northwest, three massive German armies had smashed into the US First Army's thinly held front in the Ardennes at exactly 5:30 that morning. The Battle of the Bulge had commenced. Soon the fate of the Seventh Army itself would hang in the balance. Now it was to undergo the greatest crisis of its long history. Yet, just as with the landings in southern France, that crisis would be overshadowed by other events. The unknown second Battle of the Bulge, fought in Alsace by the Seventh Army, would hardly be noticed.

On Tuesday, December 19th, the top brass converged from every US command on the French city of Verdun. Verdun was an ominously evocative place, where in 1916 French and German soldiers had slaughtered one another in their scores of thousands. Adolf Hitler had been wounded on those barren heights. De Gaulle had been captured there. Sergeant Maginot, who had built that white elephant named after him, had lost his leg. Petain had shot French mutineers by the hundred in the same place. At Verdun, for a while, the fate of France in the Great War had hung in the balance.

Now on this cold gray morning with a hint of snow in the air, as the high ranking officers filed into the 18th century Maginot Caserne, the situation appeared little different. For three days the Germans had been attacking, sending the US divisions in the Belgian Ardennes reeling back in defeat. As the clock in the city's Vauban-designed citadel chimed 11:00, the Germans, 50 miles away, were racing for the

River Meuse. Beyond that lay their key objectives: the Belgian capital, Brussels, and the key Allied supply port, Antwerp. A sense of grave crisis, the greatest of the whole war in Europe, lay in the air.

Shivering in the squalid squad room, heated by a single pot-bellied coal stove, the officers took their places, their staffs behind them. All of them were important men who controlled the destinies of millions of men: American, British, Canadian, French, and a dozen other Allied nationalities. But on this Tuesday morning, as the bad news from the front came pouring in, they seemed powerless to act, leaderless, and at a loss to know what to do next. Everything now rested in the hands of the Supreme Commander, Dwight D. Eisenhower.

Many years later Sir Kenneth Strong, Eisenhower's British (but very loyal) chief of intelligence, remembered that day well: "The meeting was crowded and the atmosphere tense. The British were worried by events. As so often before, their confidence in the ability of the Americans to deal with the situation was not great. Reports had been reaching them of disorganization behind the American lines, of American headquarters abandoned without notice, and of documents and weapons falling intact into enemy hands. Stories of great bravery on the part of individuals and units did not change their opinion."

The "Verdun Conference," as it afterwards became known, marked the high point of Eisenhower's career as Supreme Commander, Allied Forces, Europe. His front had been torn virtually in half. Against all the predictions of his senior intelligence officers, who had been maintaining ever since September that Nazi Germany was beaten—"vying with each other for the honor of devastating the German war machine with words," as Robert Merrian of the US Ninth Army put it ironically—the enemy had launched the greatest counterattack in the West since the Normandy landings.

Of course, Eisenhower knew he was in trouble—serious trouble. He enjoyed powerful protection in Washington, but even General Marshall might not be able to save him if the

Germans did manage to cross the Meuse River. He was real-
ist enough, too, to know that he had powerful enemies in
Britain and in France, such as General de Gaulle. They
would demand his dismissal.

It was not surprising, therefore, that when he entered the
cold dank conference room, chain-smoking as always, his
customary ear-to-ear grin was absent. He was pale and
tense. He glanced around the waiting room. All the familiar
face were there—Bradley, Patton, Devers and the rest. The
sight gave him some return of confidence, for he forced a
wan smile and announced, "The present situation is to be regarded as one of opportunity for us and not one of disaster.
There will only be cheerful faces at this conference table."

As always, Patton was first off the mark. Eisenhower's
remark appealed to his flamboyant, pugnacious nature,
"Hell," he snorted, "Let's have the guts to let the sons of
bitches go all the way to Paris. Then we'll be ready to cut
'em off and show 'em up!"

The ice was broken and from that moment onwards, it
was Georgie Patton's conference.

While Eisenhower smoked yet another Lucky Strike,
Strong quickly sketched in the situation at the front. It was
bad. The Germans had already committed 20 divisions, five
of them armored, to the Ardennes, and intelligence knew the
enemy had plenty more divisions in reserve. The possibility
could not be ruled out that these reserve divisions might well
be used to attack elsewhere along the long Allied front
which stretched from Switzerland to Holland.

Strong ended by stating baldly that Bradley's front had
been effectively split. His First and Ninth Armies had been
separated from his Third and the Seventh to the south by
what was now being called "the Bulge." If Field Marshal
Montgomery to the north was not to be called—and all the
American commanders present feared that eventuality—
then Patton's Third Army must make a strong counterattack
into the Bulge from the south.

Following up the Scot's description with a few words of
explanation of his own, Eisenhower now turned to Patton

and said, "George, I want you to go to Luxembourg and take charge of the battle, making a strong counterattack with at least six divisions. When can you start?" "As soon as you're through with me," Patton answered in his usual cocky, brash manner.

According to General Strong: "There was some laughter around the table, especially from the British officers present." To them it seemed that Patton's reaction was rash and unrealistic. To achieve his aim, Patton would have to swing his Third Army round in a 90-degree angle from its present position in French Lorraine and Saar. This would mean, as it was later discovered, moving 133,179 motor vehicles over 1.6 million road miles in the worst winter Europe had experienced in a quarter of a century.

Patton was obviously undaunted by the prospect of this unprecedented move: "I left my household in Nancy [his HQ] in perfect order before I came here," he said triumphantly, obviously pleased with the impression he had made on the others. Eisenhower looked more kindly on the man who he had saved in Sicily the year before; now it was Patton's turn to save him. "When can you start?" he demanded.

Without the slightest hesitation, Patton answered, "The morning of December 22nd."

Colonel Codman, Patton's admiring aide, recorded later that the conference's reaction to that bold assurance was "electric." "There was a stir, a shuffling of feet, as those present straightened up in their chairs. In some faces, skepticism. But through the room the current of excitement leaped like a flame."

Eisenhower frowned. "Don't be fatuous," he snapped severely. Calmly, Patton lit one of those big cigars he favored and said, "This has nothing to do with being fatuous sir. I've made my arrangements and my staff are working like beavers at this very moment to shape them up."

Quickly he sketched his plan of attack, and then turning to the detested General Bradley, he exclaimed excitedly, "Brad, this time the Kraut has stuck his head in a meat

grinder." He clenched his fist around the cigar and raised it
aloft. "And this time, I've got hold of the handle!"

Now everyone laughed.

In all the accounts of that celebrated conference at Verdun,
which helped to determine the outcome of the most important battle the US Army fought in Europe in World War II,
most of the attention is focused on the star of the show, General George S. Patton. Everything he said that day was bold,
brash and belligerent. Later it would make excellent copy,
not only for the journalists, but also for the popular histori-
ans. But there was another three-star US general present
there that day, who went completely unnoticed. Yet it can be
argued he was to play an even more important role in what
was to come than Patton. For it can be reasoned that if his
troops had been defeated, not only would Patton's drive into
the southern flank of the Bulge have failed, but the whole
Western Alliance might well have collapsed. He was, of
course, General Devers, commanding the US 6th Army
Group, to which Patch's Seventh Army belonged.

Eisenhower did not like Devers. He was the only senior
officer in Europe not personally recommended by Eisenhower. Prior to the invasion he and Devers had clashed several times because Eisenhower thought the latter was
keeping generals back in the Middle East whom he, Eisenhower, needed for the battle to come in France. Later when
Devers led the four-month campaign into Alsace, Eisenhower complained he lacked command ability. Furthermore
he had allowed Wiese's Nineteenth German Army to escape
so that there were 17,000 German soldiers still on French
territory in the Colmar Pocket, another headache.

At the end of the war Eisenhower would be asked to rate
38 of his most senior commanders in Europe for employ-
ment in the future. Eisenhower placed Devers at number 24,
lower than several of his humble corps commanders. Worst
of all, Devers was the only officer of the whole 38 of whom
Eisenhower had something negative to report to Washington. He wrote Marshall that Devers was "often inaccurate in

statements and evaluations. . . . He has not, so far, produced among the seniors of the American organization here a feel-ing of trust and confidence."

Now as the celebrated conference started to break up, Eisenhower personally gave this general, whom he disliked and obviously distrusted, his orders for the future. The Sev-enth Army would break off its attack in the Saar against the Siegfried Line. Instead, its divisions would be used as a holding force, taking over the positions in Lorraine and the Saar which would now be vacated by Patton's Third Army. In effect, Patch's Seventh Army would be holding the front of two armies.

Of course, Eisenhower must have told himself angrily, if Devers had not let Wiese establish himself in the Colmar Pocket, Patch's men would have been very useful in an of-fensive operation in the Ardennes. But Devers had failed and now he had to waste Patch's Seventh in a strictly defensive role. It was very annoying.

Just before he left, Eisenhower gave Devers strict instruc-tions on what he was to do if his Sixth Army Group were at-tacked by those "missing" German divisions not accounted for by Allied intelligence. If his command was hit, he was to give ground slowly "on his northern flank, even if he had to move completely back to the Vosges." Eisenhower, however, stated categorically that Devers must not allow the "Ger-mans to re-enter those mountains [the Vosges] and this line was definitely laid down as the one that must be held on De-vers' front." The Supreme Commander could not afford an-other Ardennes debacle if he were to retain his post.

Thus, Eisenhower left in an armored car, surrounded by heavily armed out-riders. There were rumors that the Ger-mans had assassination squads out gunning for him behind the front, and his staff was taking no chances. Behind him he left a resentful and despondent Devers. Now he was to take over a front 80 miles long once held by two armies. Then, if he were attacked, he was to put up only token defense, giv-ing up ground which had been bought so dearly over these last weeks.

We can guess General Devers' mood that gray, cold day. Alone of the senior American commanders of World War II, he had still not found a biographer. But now as he overcame his first resentment at the way Patton had taken over the conference and Eisenhower's stern lecture, he surely must have realized just how little faith the Supreme Commander had in his abilities. Then, for the first time in the six-month-long campaign in Europe, the Supreme Commander had specifically ordered one of his senior commanders to withdraw if attacked. The US Army, which had always prided itself that it never gave up ground which it had "bought with its own blood," as Bradley had once phrased it, was now going to do so. And he, Jacob Devers, would command the shameful withdrawal. It could not have been a pleasant prospect.

As that fourth week of December 1944 started to draw to its close, with alarmist rumors flooding the Seventh Army's area—Montgomery's British were pulling back to the Belgian coast, Bastogne had fallen, Patton's 3d Army was virtually wiped out—General Patch hurriedly changed his disposition. Now his Seventh occupied an 84-mile front from a point a few miles west of Saarbrucken in Germany to the Rhine and then a flank position along that river north and south of Strasbourg. His VI Corps held the right from the Rhine to the French fortress city of Bitche, with the 79th and 45th Divisions in the line and the 14th Armored Division in reserve. On VI Corps' left flank, holding a front of ten miles with little more than a regiment, was Task Force Hudelson, named after its commander. On Task Force Hudelson's left flank, XV Corps held the line running westwards to within a few miles of Saarbrucken, using the 100th, 44th and 103rd Infantry Division, with the 106th Cavalry Group on its left flank, keeping a very loose contact with Patton's 3d Army fighting its way north to Bastogne. Along the Rhine itself, covering a front of 40 miles, were two regimental strength task forces, newly arrived in the ETO. These totally green soldiers, who had never been under fire for the most part, were known by the names of their commanders as Task

Force Herren (70th Division) and Task Force Linden (42nd Division).

It was an enormous front to hold, even for veteran soldiers—the equivalent of six divisions spread out over 84 miles of rugged terrain, facing the best soldiers in Europe, perhaps in the world. But for the most part Patch's soldiers weren't even veterans. Apart from the 45th and 79th they had seen little action. The 44th, the 103rd and the 14th Armored had been "blooded" in the last few weeks, admittedly, but the new boys of the 42d, 63d and 70th Infantry Divisions were still as green as the growing corn.

But there was no time to worry about that now. Things were moving fast. On a clear but freezingly cold December 26th, the Seventh Army was alerted for action. That day Brigadier General Eugene Harrison, G-2 of the Seventh Army, received a warning of what was to come from Devers' HQ. The message had come through the British Ultra, but that great secret could never be acknowledged. Instead Harrison noted in his diary: "Excellent enemy sources indicate enemy units building up in Black Forest area [which was just across the Rhine from the Seventh's positions] for offensive. Other indications for enemy action exist. Imperative that all defensive precautions be immediately effective."

That day both Patch and Devers moved their headquarters to the rear. Neither general wanted to suffer the shame of General Hodges of the First, who had been forced to make a run for it when his HQ was threatened by the Germans.

On that same Sunday, Devers went to see Eisenhower at his HQ outside Paris. He explained to the Supreme Commander that all indications were that he was going to be attacked in Alsace-Lorraine soon. Perhaps Devers' unexpected journey to Paris was motivated by a desire for some reserves—there were none. Or perhaps he thought "Ike" might change his mind and give him a more aggressive role in the battle soon to come. We do not know. All we do know from the Supreme Commander himself is that he repeated his orders of the 19th: "I told Devers he must, on no account, permit sizeable formations to be cut off and surrounded." The implication was clear. The Seventh Army was to put up to-ken resistance and then retreat to the Vosges. But what Eisenhower forgot was that if the Americans did this, it would mean that Strasbourg would fall into Geman hands again for the third time in 70 years. That would be some-thing that de Gaulle would simply not be able to tolerate. The German capture of Strasbourg, so recently liberated by Leclerc, could well mean the downfall of his Provisional Government. A major political crisis was beginning to brew.

Tension mounted in the huge area now commanded by Dev-ers. Because the Germans had made wide use of comman-dos, dressed in US uniforms, and paras behind the lines in the Ardennes, reports of German paradrops behind the Sev-enth and First French Armies' front came flooding in from all sides. They were reported dropping behind the US lines in the woods around Niederbronn. Others were said to be landing at Phalsbourg, which had been General Patch's HQ until Christmas. Some had been spotted floating down near the vital Saverne Gap in the Vosges.

General Lattre de Tassigny, the aristocratic commander of the First French Army, known behind his back as "King Jean" on account of his high-handed manner, was alerted by Devers' nervous HQ that "Parachute commandos have been dropped at various points to the rear of the Western Front." Devers advised him to find additional men to guard his rear lines of communication. It was thought that the German paras were trying to cut his communication below the Col-mar Pocket through the vital Belfort Gap in the Vosges.

In Paris, de Gaulle hastily organized what he could in the way of help for de Tassigny. But although there were young men enough, there was a terrible shortage of arms and equipment. General Dody, the overall French ground com-mander, noted that some units were going into the line "still in civilian clothes and merely had sky-blue overcoats [the pre-war French army uniform] unrecognized by the Allies."

In the end de Gaulle managed to scrape together some 50,000 men for rear-line duties, guarding crossroads, railroad installations, bridges and the like, whom General Dody thought were really "not fit to fight." In addition, a new infantry division was sent to fill out the line surrounding the Colmar Pocket. But the French 10th Division's sole contribution to what was to come was not exactly calculated to enhance Franco-American relations. On the way to the front, one of their troop trains stopped at a station just outside the town of Laon. Here the bored and hungry soldiers came across an American train, laden high with parcels meant for US troops at the front. They didn't hesitate. They systematically looted the gifts from the "folks back home" for "our boys at the front." The incident caused quite a stir at the time, though it was immediately hushed up.

Closer to the front the rumors grew in intensity and frequency. For the divisional commanders had not been able to fool their men that everything was quite normal; that this was just a temporary lull in the attack on the Siegfried Line. That last week of December 1944, one GI of the 103rd Division recorded how a runner from company headquarters came crawling up to their foxhole position and hissed excitedly, "Get your men alerted for a Heinie attack."

The GI was not impressed. "That damned messenger is always as important as if he is commanding the whole Seventh Army and you smile scornfully."

Next moment the smile was wiped off the young soldier's face abruptly, for the messenger then added, "Here are your gas masks, too." "Gas masks!" the startled GI exclaimed, suddenly feeling frightened. Their burdensome gas masks had been the first things they had thrown away when they had gone into the line back in November. Were the Krauts going to attack using poisoned gas?

On the 29th the whole of the new 100th Division was also issued with gas masks. It appeared intelligence had recently discovered that all American prisoners of the Germans were being asked a new "standard set of questions about gas masks and gas training," as the divisional history recorded. For months Hitler had been threatening new secret weapons to follow the V-1s and V-2s currently raining down on battered old London. Was he now going to use some terrible new poison gas?

"Nervous Nellies," as they were called contemptuously, spotted German patrols in the rugged, wooded front-line areas all the time now. Captain Donald Pence, newly arrived with the 70th Infantry Division, recalled how his men sighted enemy patrols everywhere (though there weren't any); and how they worried about the "Krauts just over the hill" from the company positions, getting "loaded up on schnapps for their next attack."

The chronicler of the 100th Division recorded how "while unloading a chow truck, Tec 4 William H. Bailey was surprised to see two Jerries walk out of the woods. They explained they had been sweating out dinner call for several hours."

On December 28th a general alert was supposedly sounded—at least the nervous GIs up the line thought it was. It was reported that Alsatians who had fled with the retreating Germans back in November were flooding back into Alsace by remote mountain paths known only to them. All suspicious persons wandering around the area were to be rounded up. In particular, the GIs were—supposedly—to be on the lookout for Polish DPs (displaced persons) currently working on the land. They weren't in fact Poles deported from their homeland to work for the enemy; they were German agents disguised as Poles, who reported back to their spymasters by radio.

The truth was that the Germans had strictly limited their patrol activity in the Alsace area because they feared that some captured German might give the game away. Besides they knew all they needed to know about the American positions and dispositions. As SS Colonel Linger, commander of one of the assault formations, the 17th SS Panzer Grenadier Division, who was later captured in Alsace, told his interrogators: "When the breakthrough in the Ardennes had been stopped by the Allies, it was realized that several American divisions had been sent to aid the Americans in their defense. It was, therefore, decided to launch an attack against what we felt sure to be a weak position."

Indeed, German information was good about the movements and dispositions of the Seventh Army on the day before Patton launched his great attack into the Bulge, as Eisenhower had ordered. Hitler commanded German Army Group B to exploit the new situation in Alsace-Lorraine. On that day Hitler ordered that the German forces in the Saar would attack the Americans, sweep through the Saverne Gap in the Vosges to link up with German Nineteenth Army, now reinforced, in the Colmar Pocket. In this way, the Seventh Army would be trapped.

Forty-eight hours later, German shock troops would cross the Rhine to the north and south of Strasbourg. In the meantime Wiese's Nineteenth Army would break out of the Colmar Pocket, cut through the First French Army, and head north to link up with the bridge-heads and their other troops coming through the Saverne Gap.

In essence, it was to be a classic German pincer movement, that would eventually destroy the US Seventh Army and give German morale in the Reich a tremendous boost by capturing Strasbourg.

With luck, the Germans reasoned, the destruction of Patch's Seventh Army would bring all American offensive action in the Ardennes to a stop. More importantly, if Alsace was re-taken and Strasbourg fell, then de Gaulle's shaky Provisional Government in Paris would tumble. The Communists, still armed from their resistance days, would definitely attempt to seize power—there might even be fighting or civil war as in Greece this December. But one result would be sure. The whole of the Allied supply system in France would be thrown into total disarray, just as the German one had been the previous summer when the Resistance had revolted. In fact, the Germans told themselves, the great Allied coalition in the West would collapse just as the one against Frederick the Great had collapsed back in the 18th century when everyone had thought "Old Fritz," the Prussian king, was finished. Victory might well belong to the Germans after all.

As New Year's Eve approached, the tension mounted even more. On the night of December 30th, unidentified small arms fire was reported from a dozen spots on the Seventh Army's front. At the hamlet of Lichtenberg an "American" officer appeared and ordered that the village concert scheduled for New Year's Eve should be stopped. Why? What did this strange American officer know, the puzzled, apprehensive villagers asked themselves. Suddenly they were scared. In Wingen the fireworks hoarded for New Year's Eve celebrations exploded and blew up the main road nearby. Were they really fireworks—or had some secret German sabotage unit mixed high explosives with the fireworks? At another hamlet not far away another "American" officer appeared and in fluent German told the inhabitants that they had better evacuate the place. "It wouldn't be long now!" What that "it" was, he didn't explain. In nearby Heideneck, although as yet not a single shot had been fired, the whole village started trudging westwards, pushing their laden carts and tugging the Bollerwagen through the snow. Among the new refugees were the priest and the mayor, the two officials most likely to be arrested by the Gestapo if the Germans returned. Who had told them to go? What had they heard? Afterwards, when it was all over, no one could answer those two overwhelming questions.

On New Year's Eve, when far away in the States, the civilians prepared for the usual ritual of "Auld Lang Syne" bellowed in a drunken chorus in Times Square, General Patch visited his two corps commanders, Brooks and Haislip, at the latter's command post at the village of Fenestrange.

Patch knew from Ultra that an attack was imminent. He even knew the German dispositions. Eight thousand reinforcements had been ferried across the Rhine at night to General Wiese's Nineteenth Army; the German 21st Panzer Division, a veteran outfit which had fought in North Africa and Normandy, was moving south along the river, and the

17th SS Panzer Grenadier Division would kick off the German attack. Yes, he knew everything.

He knew, too, that his division had prepared defenses in depth. Back at the eastern foot of the Vosges, positions were being readied as stop lines if the Seventh really did have to retreat that far. Eisenhower was in the picture as well. As soon as American divisions could be released from the Ardennes, which was now going in the Allies' favor, they would be hurried south to the Alsace Front. All had been considered, planned, prepared for. But Patch had been in France in that terrible summer of 1918, when the Allied generals had been well aware that the Germans were going to attack the Western Front, yet it had still been a damned close thing. The Germans had nearly beaten them, although the Allies had known they were coming. What was to be the outcome this time? In the heady days of non-stop victories back in the fall, the top men, Eisenhower and Montgomery among them, had thought World War II in Europe would be over by Christmas. The Ardennes had changed that. In a few short hours it would be 1945 and instead of being beaten, the Germans were attacking furiously.

Now a worried Patch, facing his two senior commanders around that rough wooden table in that remote border village, warned Brooks and Haislip they would be attacked in the early hours of New Year's Day 1945. The actors were in place, the stage was set. The drama could commence.

4

COUNTERATTACK

January 1945

"I count upon you to enable me to announce to the Führer in a few days' time that the swastika flag flies again over Strasbourg Cathedral."
— REICHSFUHRER SS HEINRICH HIMMLER
Order of the day to the Army of the Upper Rhine,
Jan. 5, 1945

IT was now nearly midnight on this last day of the old year, Sunday, December 31, 1944. The snow had ceased falling. Now the two young officers, Lieutenants George Bradshaw and Richard Shattuck, decided that someone ought to celebrate the advent of 1945 in the 44th Division's Fox Company. In spite of the freezing cold, the two young officers were in high spirits as they clambered out of their snowbound foxholes.

For the last 48 hours the 44th Infantry Division had been dug in between the French border industrial town of Sarreguemines and Rimling along the River Blies at the extreme left of Seventh Army's 84-mile-long front. Nothing much had happened in that time—a bit of patrol activity, a mortar barrage. It was all too good to be true and the men knew it.

Of course, the top brass had not told the weary infantrymen holding the line in the snow what was soon to come their way. That would have been demoralizing—bad "man-management." But the frightened looks on the pale faces of the few civilians who had remained behind in the area and the snappy anxious manner of the staff officers who had visited the line these last two days told them all they wanted to know. Soon the "shit was going to hit the fan," as the parlance of the day had it. Why else should they stand to every night with twice the normal number of men in the line? On the previous night they had felt their forebodings were to be realized. In the small hours of the night they had been startled out of their uneasy sleep by the sound of one of their own booby traps exploding. It had been followed by another and another. In all, five of the deadly devices had gone off. For the rest of that night they had tensed over their weapons, fancying every new shadow on the snow was a German creeping toward them. But on the morrow they had discovered—to their relief—it had been a false alarm. Two dead rabbits lay sprawled out in their own blood. Well, at least they made a welcome addition to the rations. Better than "shit on shingle" (chipped beef on toast) any day.

Now, despite the tension that had been building up these last two days and was soon to come to a head, the two young officers stood in the snow, carbines raised. On the stroke of midnight, they would fire a "feu de joie" to celebrate the new year. In the freezing foxholes, the GIs grinned at the crazy antics of their two high-spirited company officers.

"Two minutes to go," Bradshaw called to Shattuck. He clicked off his safety catch and prepared to fire. His comrade did the same, carbine raised.

But they were not fated to fire their salute to 1945. With startling suddenness, machine gun slugs started to kick up the snow all around Bradshaw. Out of the moonlit sky a fighter plane came hurtling in, dragging its monstrous black shadow behind it in the snow, angry flame rippling the length of its wings, as it shot up Fox Company. An instant later it was gone, roaring away in a tight right curve. Shakily the two officers, who had dived for cover, rose to their feet, patting the snow from their uniforms.

"What the hell's going on, Dick?" Bradshaw called to his buddy.

Shattuck didn't answer. His head was cocked to one side as he listened hard. Already he could hear the rusty squeak and rattle of tank tracks to their front. Instinctively he knew this was it. The long expected German counterattack was on its way.

Roughly about the time that the lone German fighter shot up the positions of General Dean's 114th Regiment, Sergeant Luther Ott of its sister regiment, the 71st Infantry, was trudging through the snow on patrol. Like the two officers, his mind was half on the patrol and half on the fact that it was New Year's Eve and he was far from home.

Just before midnight he topped a small hill and what he saw below drove all thoughts of New Year from his mind. Later he recalled his astonishment at the sight: "It was the biggest swarm of Krauts I'd seen in my life! They were all in white, moving in a kind of triangle formation with the base of the triangle heading right for my company."

The Sergeant didn't hesitate. He knew he could be overrun by the Germans at any moment. All the same he paused there and radioed his commanding officer, Captain Robert Sindenberg, what he had just seen. The company had to be warned in time.

That job done, he was off, floundering down the hill in the deep snow, with his men chasing behind him. A wild volley of excited firing broke out from the white-clad Germans and then they were panting and cursing their way up the hill, knowing now that they had lost the advantage of surprise. The XII SS Corps had commenced its attack.

By one o'clock that Monday morning, the Seventh Army's flank division was under desperate attack everywhere, for the Germans knew it was imperative to drive a wedge between the Seventh and Patton's Third Army to the north. On Dean's left, his 114th Infantry Regiment beat off determined SS efforts to exploit a bridgehead they had managed to secure across the Blies River. In the end a massive bombardment by the whole of the divisional artillery managed to pin the white-clad assault infantry down near the river.

In the center, the fighting on the 324th Infantry Regiment's front was even more intense. Three times the Germans came screaming and shouting across the River Blies and three times they were thrown back—just. But the most serious threat of all to the 44th was on its flank held by the 71st Regiment. Here the Germans attacked in full strength and with the utmost determination. Screaming "Yankee bastards!" or "Come and fight, Yankee gangsters!" as if they were drugged or boozed, they smashed into the American positions.

Here there was no stopping them. A five-company German assault north of Rimling curled round the right flank of the 71st's First Battalion. It reeled back a thousand yards. Hurriedly the Third Battalion counterattacked. To no avail! Already 600 Germans had advanced through the First's position and occupied the snowbound forest to their rear. Confused fighting broke out everywhere.

The Third was ordered to change its objective. It was now to clear the forest. It didn't get far. In the thick gunfire, knee deep in snow, companies broke up into disorganized platoons and platoons soon became squads. A reserve battalion of the 324th was thrown in to help their comrades of the 71st. But the heavily outnumbered SS troops held out stubbornly. They were used to fighting in forests; the Americans weren't. Time and time again, the white-clad Germans held off the Americans until finally the latter grew weary of the carnage and the hopelessness of their attacks. The two battalions gave up. They dug in and sealed off the forest, while the Germans continued to attack the 71st's last remaining battalion, the Second.

Now as the winter dawn cast its harsh gray light on the battlefield, it was obvious that the 44th Division's flank bordering on that of its neighbor, the 100th Division, was beginning to crumble. But that was not the only problem facing the "Century" men, as the 100th was nicknamed. To their right, the paper-thin line of the task force, named after its commander Colonel Hudelson, was beginning to break under severe attack. For Task Force Hudelson was being assaulted that dawn by elements of two whole German divisions. The fear which Eisenhower had expressed to Devers the week before looked as if it might well be realized. The 100th Division stood a definite risk of being cut off.

Task Force Hudelson, which consisted of the 62d Armored Infantry Battalion, the 117th Cavalry Reconnaissance Squadron, some combat engineers, mortar crews, a tank destroyer outfit, and the 94th Cavalry, had been preparing its link-up position between the 100th and 45th Divisions for two weeks now. But Hudelson knew his position was hopeless. He had to defend a front of 10 miles with less than 2,000 men. The Germans could feed whole platoons through his positions without his men even noticing them. He knew, too, that his defensive positions would be an ideal spot for the Germans to break through. Indeed the attackers placed so much importance on the penetration of the Hudelson Line that they gave the attack a special codename. It was "Tenth May 1940." It was a date of historic significance for the Wehrmacht. For on that day, five years before, the victorious German assault on the West had commenced.

Matters were going to be made worse by the fact that on this Monday morning, the 62nd Infantry Battalion, the Task Force's main component, was to be relieved by the "new boys," the soldiers of the 70th Division's 275th Infantry Regiment, most of them suffering from the dysentery which would plague them for most of the coming battle. "Sure hate to be relieved in this sector," Captain Trammell of the 62nd told Captain Long of the 70th's advance party. But there was going to be no relief this day and suddenly this was no longer a quiet sector—it was now the hottest part of the whole Seventh Army's front.

The first unit of the Task Force attacked was 94th Cavalry Reconnaissance Squadron in the center of the 10-mile line. It hadn't a chance. It was shattered almost immediately and all that the helpless recon soldiers could do was form small groups and, as the Divisional History put it euphemistically, "effect an escape by flight."

Rapidly the Task Force began to break down. Its 117th

The newly born Seventh Army wades ashore at Red Beach, between Gela and Scoglitti in Sicily, July 12, 1943.

Reinforcements coming ashore, including an AA gun on the right. Note discarded life-rings in foreground.

The pride of France: a Free French partisan group posing with American, British, French and German arms in 1944.

Fighting amidst the rubble of a bombed-out village. The Seventh Army would see a great deal of this.

This cavalry patrol has abandoned their jeeps, and this is only the Low Vosges. It gets steeper after this.

Willy, Joe and a friend having a smoke: 79th Division takes a break in the Parroy Forest in October 1944. It was ordinary Americans like these who beat the Wehrmacht.

General George Patton, Lt. Gen. Alexander M. Patch, and Lt. Gen.
Jacob L. Devers. From the flamboyant Patton to the steady Patch,
the Seventh had some of the best commanders in the war.
Gen. Devers commanded the overall Army Group.

Gen. Haislip, commander of the XV Corps, Gen. Brooks, commander
of the VI Corps, and Gen. Milburn, commander of the XXI Corps,
all of the Seventh Army.

Lt. Eugene Inzer of the 70th Division was cut down while leading an attack outside Saarbrucken. Repeatedly wounded, he survived for two days under enemy fire and artillery barrages from both sides. A year after the war medals were still coming in, including the Bronze Star with Oak Leaf Cluster.

Company L, 142nd Regiment, 36th Division, pulling back in the snow for hot food and some rest before the next phase of the assault.

The conditions at Dachau concentration camp sickened the liberating troops, although they were touched by this homemade American flag.

20th Armored Division tanks fording the Inn River, the bridge at left being deemed unsafe. Salzburg lies ahead.

101st Airborne paratroopers approach Berchtesgaden by the narrow mountain road leading to Hitler's mountain retreat.

Seventh Army trooper watching Berchtesgaden burn, after the SS lit it on fire as the Americans swept into the mountains.

Through the ruins and rubble, past snipers and booby traps, the "forgotten army" held true, and fought some of the hardest campaigns of the war—not in the spotlight, but always at the sharp end.

Cavalry Reconnaissance Squadron was soon virtually surrounded. Its 94th Squadron disappeared. Captain Trammell, who hated to leave this "quiet sector," called back to his C.O., Colonel Myers, to report that "My men are being cut to pieces."

There was nothing the harassed Colonel could do but pray. The 62nd was fighting for its life, retreating from the frontier down the winding little road that led to the single street village of Philippsbourg, where the 70th had just begun to arrive.

In the village of Bannstein, up the road from Philippsbourg, everyone was chased out of their houses in a vain attempt to stop the advancing "People's Grenadiers" of the German 256th and 361st Volksgrenadier Division. Cooks, clerks, drivers—they were all given rifles and bazookas and ordered to hold the Krauts at all costs. A cook-sergeant manned a mortar on his own—firing, loading, reloading, the lot. For a while he held off 30 German soldiers who were trying to get down the steep embankment and outflank the village. He was wounded in the foot, but refused to be evacuated. The cook's brave efforts, however, were to no avail. The Germans kept on coming.

Ammunition started to run out, as did troops. Colonel Hudelson threw in his last reserve—a company of the 125th Engineers. They went forward, grumbling they weren't infantry, but determined. They passed the wire they had put up two days before. Now they found it "hanging with dead and dying Germans. Some were hanging limply, some moved, and some lay and screamed. They were covered with a light coat of new fallen snow." Up at point, Sergeant William Godfrey was just muttering about "One hell of a way to start off the New Year," when his half-track was ambushed. Angry fire erupted from the trees on both sides of his platoon. Something hit him like a sledgehammer. He blacked out. When Godfrey regained consciousness, he found himself stripped naked, save for his pants, his legs trapped beneath the five-ton White half-track. Around him lay the four members of his squad. All were naked and very dead. The man next to him had a bullet hole right through his skull between the eyes. Perhaps he had been killed after capture, Godfrey didn't know.

But he was still alive and he could hear Germans talking not far off. The Krauts were not going to finish him off that way. He found his trench knife. Desperately he started to dig himself free. He worked frantically until he was bathed in sweat and there were blisters on his hands. Finally he managed it. Somehow he struggled back to his own lines: one of a handful of the brave engineers who survived . . .

By now the survivors of Task Force Hudelson were in full retreat. Everywhere there was chaos and confusion. Infantrymen, cavalry, engineers, tankers, gunners, all using the same narrow slick roads, skidding and sliding dangerously as the tracked vehicles tried to climb the many steep slopes of the area; and all the time the frightening knowledge haunted them that the victorious enemy was just behind. As the Divisional History described the "big bugout," it was "like walking in a nightmare."

Now the task of holding the area was left to the 70th Division, which a month before had still been in training in the States. It was a division that had never heard a shot fired in anger, led by a commander whose last dose of combat had taken place in 1918. A potential disaster seemed in the making. But for the moment the division's 275th Regiment were more concerned with a "new enemy—the dysentery germ." As the 70th's Divisional History records: "History books don't list this bug along with the facing German divisions, but it inflicted . . . more damage than did the intermittent shelling and small arms fire." Soon things would change.

By noon that terrible Monday, it was clear that the Seventh Army's front was definitely cracking. "The feather merchants" and the "canteen commandos," as the service and supply troops were known contemptuously to the front line troops, had already begun pulling out immediately when the first German attack had been reported. As the chronicler of the 45th Division's 179th Regiment recalled afterwards:

"Rear echelons . . . Seventh Army HQ, 12 TAC HQ, huge trucking and ordnance outfits, all packed and fled." Leaving food uneaten on the table, they "partied" and never stopped until they had reached Luneville (Seventh Army HQ) . . . "The rear pulled out as if the end had come." But it was not only the rear echelons that were pulling back. Now it was clear that virtually all Patch's forward units were under attack by eight German divisions and some of them were in serious trouble. Part of the 44th had been forced to withdraw. Because of that and the near disintegration of the Hudelson Task Force, the 100th Division was becoming increasingly isolated and in danger of being encircled.

That afternoon the situation grew even worse. An unknown officer of the 117th Reconnaissance Cavalry Squadron on the 100th Division's flank called in and said, "We're falling back a little."

"How far is a little?" he was asked.

"About 2000 yards," was the reply.

"Do you have to fall back that far?" came the anxious query from the 100th Division.

The answer was a click on the telephone. The unknown cavalryman had hung up. When next heard from the 117th Cavalry had retreated to Wingen, some nine miles to the rear. There it found the enemy already in place and it fled once again. After that, the 117th Cavalry disappeared from the combat zone altogether. There'd be work for the Inspector General's branch of the Seventh Army once this particular battle was over . . .

So far the Supreme Commander had had a bad Monday. That morning the Luftwaffe had caught the Western Front totally by surprise. Between six and ten o'clock that morning over 1,000 German fighter-bombers had come zooming in and had bombed and shot up every major Allied field in the ETO. By the time it was over, 27 Allied bases had been knocked out and 350 Allied aircraft destroyed. Even Montgomery's personal Dakota had been wrecked (Eisenhower had to give him another one later). Immediately Eisenhower had issued a claim that the Allied defenses had destroyed over 300 German aircraft (which was not true) and ordered a cover-up. Free French fighter ace Pierre Clostermann, who himself came from Alsace, later wrote: "The American censorship and press service, in a flat spin, tried to present this attack as a great Allied victory by publishing peculiar figures. We pilots were still laughing about them three months later."

But that wasn't Eisenhower's main problem that day. Alarming news was coming from Devers' Army Group. About three of his divisions were in serious trouble. In particular, the situation of the "Century" Division worried him. Back in mid-December the US 106th Division had allowed itself to be encircled in the Ardennes and most of the division had surrendered: the biggest defeat of American arms in Europe in World War II. He didn't want that kind of thing happening again in Alsace. That afternoon Eisenhower summoned his fiery chief-of-staff, Bedell Smith—"somebody's got to be a sonovabitch about this headquarters"—and told him to tackle Devers. The Sixth Army Group Commander was not following his instructions. "You must tell Devers," he informed Bedell Smith angrily, "he is not doing what he was told to do, that is to get VI Corps back and to hold the Alsace Plain with recce and observation elements."

His chief-of-staff, who felt Eisenhower dithered like an old woman and changed his mind all the time, informed him that Devers should either try to hold or fall back completely. There was no half-way solution. For once, however, Eisenhower was adamant. "The bulk of VI Corps must come back!" he snapped. "But from this force, mobile elements must be sent out to give warning of the enemy advance."

What Eisenhower, the "political" general par excellence, seemed to forget when he gave this order was the position of Strasbourg. After Paris, the Alsatian capital ranked second emotionally in French hearts. Here, Rouget de Lisle had composed the Marseillaise in 1792. It was here in Strasbourg that Alphonse Daudet had set his touching little story La Derniere Classe, about a French schoolmaster's last lesson in French before the new German authorities imposed the German tongue on the whole of Alsace. It was the story that all French children learned before they were ten. Now the question was how long Strasbourg was going to remain French, and, as Eisenhower was to write in his book *Crusade in Europe,* it was an issue that "was going to plague me throughout the Ardennes battle."

On that same January 1, General Juin, Chief of the French National Defense Staff, reported to de Gaulle that plans were afoot to withdraw from Strasbourg. Already the American 42d Division, which had taken over from the Third Division at the great city, was beginning to pull out. It was a shock for de Gaulle. Afterwards he wrote, the abandonment of Strasbourg would be "a terrible wound inflicted on the honor of our country and its soldiers, a terrible curse for the Alsatians to the despair of France."

De Gaulle acted with dispatch. He drafted a signal to Lattre de Tassigny stating, "Naturally the French Army cannot consent to the abandonment of Strasbourg. . . . In case the Allied Forces retire from their present positions north of the French First Army lines, I order you to take matters into your own hands and to ensure the defense of Strasbourg."

Then de Gaulle wrote a letter to Eisenhower, declaring that the "French Government, for its part, obviously cannot let Strasbourg fall into enemy hands again without first doing everything possible to prevent it. . . . *Whatever happens,"* he concluded, *"the French will defend Strasbourg."* [Authors's italics.]

That done, de Gaulle wrote his last communication on that eventful Monday. It was a telegraph he sent both to Churchill and President Roosevelt, drawing their attention to the "extremely" serious consequences of any withdrawal in Alsace and stressing his opposition to any such move.

All the elements of a serious political row were brewing, making this Monday, January 1, 1945 one of the worst days in Eisenhower's career as a "political" soldier. But the events of that Monday would also have a lasting effect on de Gaulle and France. De Gaulle had always suspected the

Americans of double-dealing as far as his beloved France was concerned. Now, it seemed to him, he had clear proof that the Americans would not defend French territory if it did not suit their purpose to do so. And he drew his own conclusion from that realization when he finally had firm power in his own hands. In 1958, when he had achieved almost dictatorial control as French President, he took his country out of the American-dominated NATO and kicked the US Seventh Army out of their bases in France, over the frontier to the land of their one-time mutual enemy, Germany. At those very same places, which the soldiers of the Seventh Army and their comrades of Patton's Third had captured with their own blood—Etain, Metz, Phalsbourg, Toul, Nancy, and others—they were evicted hastily, lock, stock and barrel, and all traces of their ever being there were speedily removed. It was as if they had never come this way nor paid their share of the bloody butcher's bill for the liberation of *la belle* France.

Now, as Patch prepared to withdraw as Eisenhower had ordered, an attempt was made to shore up the sagging front before it cracked completely and the withdrawal became a rout. The task was given to General Frederick. He was just the man for the job. The former commander of the "Black Devils," the Provisional Airborne Division, and now the hard-pressed 45th Division, was whipcord tough. Once, just after the war, he was having a drink in a West Coast bar when a cop walked in and asked for his identification. He apparently didn't believe that such a young man could be wearing the two stars of a major general. Frederick handed the policeman his ID card. The cop wasn't satisfied. He dropped Frederick's ID card on the floor and asked for further proof. A suddenly angry Frederick asked him to pick it up. The cop refused. Frederick didn't hesitate. He pole-axed him with a single blow.

Now this tough ex-paratrooper threw everything he could find to bolster up the line. He threw in the new boys of the 12th Armored Division—"the Hellcats," as they called themselves; engineers and infantry from the veteran 79th Division; and yet more men from the untried 70th Infantry Division. Anyone who would and could fire a weapon was hurried into the line. For General Frederick knew that the vital Saverne Gap through the Vosges to his rear had to be held at any cost. For if the Germans managed to loose their armor through it, the ordered withdrawal would be purposeless. Further, with enemy panzers driving through the gap and then southwards to link up with other German troops attacking out of the Colmar Pocket, the whole of the Seventh Army could be cut off.

One of those "new boys," Don Docken, a BAR man with the 70th Infantry, who would one day become a church minister, remembered many years later his First Squad digging in outside the little village of Philippsbourg and waiting for the Germans to come. "Everything seemed quiet, but we began to get anxious when we saw people fleeing down the road with all their possessions stacked high on horse-drawn wagons and hand-pulled carts. We saw fear in their eyes but they were in a hurry and did not stop to talk."

After the refugees there came the sudden roar of a motorcycle side car. It barrelled straight past the positions of the First Squad. A little while later it returned, going flat out and the new boys were "so surprised we didn't have time to attempt to stop it." It was followed some time later by a black German staff car. Again they were caught off guard and it got through.

But now the First Squad were very wide awake. To their front was the boom of artillery and the obscene howl of the German mortars. Over the hills tracer zipped back and forth in a lethal morse. Their baptism of fire was about to commence.

As the future clergyman recalled so many years later: "Fear gripped us as the 88s came nearer and finally were right on top of us. It is a very helpless feeling, not knowing whether the next shell will have your number on it. . . . Many times during the night we could hear the cries of fear and terror, but the men held fast. . . . My Christian faith strength-

ened me and calmed me at the time. . . . Many prayers were
uttered that night."

But for many their prayers didn't help. By the time the
70th would come out of the line after it was all over, the new
boys would have lost one third of their number killed,
wounded or captured; and by then they would be "new
boys" no longer.

On the same Tuesday that the 70th Division underwent its
bloody baptism of fire, the crisis over Strasbourg had nearly
come to a head. That day de Gaulle sent the head of the
French Army, General Juin, to see Eisenhower to "confirm
that France alone would defend Alsace with all the means
she had at her disposal, if the American Seventh Army withdrew from the province."

Juin, a small stocky man, had been dealing with the Americans for two years. Indeed, he had been in charge in North
Africa when the Allies had landed there in 1942. As a result,
some 1,000 British and American soldiers had been killed by
the very people they were supposed to be "liberating."

Soon thereafter, he had gone over to the Americans and
had fought with them in Tunisia and Italy. By now he had
the measure of the Americans. Writing from Italy, he stated,
"I have a feeling that we will only make our mark here by
showing tact and discretion. The Americans are not a people
one can hustle. . . . They like us a lot, but they are also im-
bued with their sense of omnipotence and with a touchiness
you can hardly imagine. . . . The French always seem a little
excitable to them and it is important for me to first gain their
confidence."

This day the Frenchman was going to see just how
"touchy" the Americans could be.

Juin didn't waste time. He told Eisenhower's chief-of-
staff, Bedell Smith, that the line must be held at all costs.
There would be a blood-bath in Alsace when the Gestapo returned. If Strasbourg were recaptured, it would be a tremendous propaganda victory for Les Boches. Then the
Frenchman laid it on the line. "General de Gaulle," he an-

nounced, "has ordered de Lattre to take responsibility for the defense of Strasbourg."

Smith's famed and feared temper, fueled by a grumbling ulcer, flared up at once. "If that is so," he rasped, sticking out his jaw pugnaciously, "it is bordering on insubordination, pure and simple, and the French First Army will not get a single further round of ammunition or a gallon of gas."

Now Juin grew excitable, just as he had warned that Americans thought all Frenchmen were. "All right," he retorted, "in that case General de Gaulle will forbid American forces the use of French railroads and communications."

Bedell Smith must have felt shocked at that moment. He realized immediately the full implications of what Juin had just said. If France cut all the supply routes from the Channel ports and Marseilles, all hell would be let loose. That would cause a major political row at the very top. He backed off immediately. He agreed de Gaulle should meet with Eisenhower personally to discuss the matter on the morrow. Afterwards, when Juin had departed, he told a worried Eisenhower, "Juin said things to me last night, which, if he had been an American, I would have socked him on the jaw . . ."

That Wednesday, some Frenchmen were still prepared to fight with the Americans without restrictions. Frederick had called upon Leclerc for aid and the tough little Frenchman had agreed to send elements of his French Second Armored Division to help the hard-pressed Americans. Just before he left his CP to lead the desperate attack, he was handed an official-looking envelope. Colonel Chatel watched as he read its contents and then threw back his head "and laughed and laughed and laughed."

As Chatel recalled afterwards, "But it was bitter, cynical laughter." Without a word Leclerc handed the letter to his aide. It was from the French Supreme Court. It stated that Leclerc had been reprieved of the death sentence passed upon him by his own nation when he had joined de Gaulle back in 1940. "Despite all the magnificent things Leclerc had done for France, despite all the honors he had won," Chatel remembered, "the new regime in Paris had found it necessary to proceed through official channels and lift the death sentence. . . . This was the reason for the bitterness of the joke as he saw it."

It was against this kind of background—the bitter division of the French people, the fears of a Communist insurrection, the possibility that his government might fall—that de Gaulle went to meet Eisenhower that Wednesday.

The Supreme Commander kicked off by explaining the problems he had in the Ardennes, the threat of the Colmar Pocket and his lack of manpower, especially in the infantry. "That is why I have ordered the troops to establish another, shorter line further back," he said.

"If we were at a Kriegsspiel," de Gaulle retorted, "I would say you were right. But I must consider the matter from another point of view. Retreat in Alsace would yield French territory to the enemy. In the realm of strategy this would be only a maneuver. But for France it would be a national disaster. At the present moment we are concerned with Strasbourg. I have ordered the First French Army to defend the city. It will, therefore, do so in any case. But it would be deplorable if this entailed a dispersion of Allied forces, perhaps even a rupture in the system of command. That is why I urge you to reconsider your plan and order General Devers to hold fast in Alsace."

Eisenhower frowned when he heard the interpreter utter the delicately phrased "rupture in the system of command." He knew what it meant. France might be prepared to go it alone without America.

"You give political reasons for me to change military orders," Eisenhower objected.

Loftily de Gaulle retorted, "Armies are created to serve the policy of states. . . . And for the French people and the French soldiers, the fate of Strasbourg is of extreme moral importance."

Winston Churchill, who had come over specially for this

meeting (though he had made it seem that it was only a casual visit) now joined the discussion. He knew that a grave threat was looming on the horizon. If de Gaulle went his own way, as he was clearly stating he would, the whole Allied coalition might fall part. He said to Eisenhower, "All my life I have remarked what significance Alsace has for the French. I agree with General de Gaulle that this fact must be taken into consideration."

Eisenhower was stubborn. He attempted to blackmail de Gaulle, stating that he might be forced to cut off the French Army's supply of ammunition and gasoline. De Gaulle wasn't impressed. He repeated his threat that he would forbid the use of the French communications system by the American army. Finally, Eisenhower gave in. He telephoned Devers to cancel the general withdrawal. General Brooks' VI Corps would make only a partial withdrawal but it would continue to cover northern Alsace and thus Strasbourg, which would be garrisoned by the First French Army. That night Eisenhower wrote to his boss Marshall, "All my life I have known what significance Alsace had for the French. I agree with de Gaulle that this fact must be taken into consideration."

As always, Dwight D. Eisenhower learned fast.

On the night of January 4/5, those elements of the 42d Infantry Division, the famous World War I "Rainbow Division," recruited in New York and New Jersey, started to pull out of their positions around Strasbourg as de Lattre's Frenchmen moved in. It was bitterly cold. The roads were icy and refugees with their pathetic bits and pieces piled onto hand-carts were leaving Strasbourg in their thousands. They had no confidence in the French soldiers. Besides, they knew from their own sources what was soon going to happen on the Rhine. The "Rainbow Division," which after the Old War had movies made of its exploits, whose fame had been sung by America's number one poet-soldier, was now a shadow of its former self. Its men were completely green and not particularly highly rated by the powers-that-be. Yet now these "new boys" were heading straight into the heart of a new battle.

That icy gray dawn, the Germans started crossing the Rhine at the small village of Gambsheim. The first patrol of the 12th Armored Division running a routine checking mission along the west bank of the great river, which divides France and Germany, disappeared without a trace. Another patrol was sent out by the 12th's 94th Mechanized Reconnaissance Squadron. Hastily the 94th's armored cars and half-tracks came racing back with their tails between their legs. "The Krauts were across"—"there were SS and infantry"—"huge tanks too" —"Beaucoup Krauts, indeed." In truth, that dawn the Germans, despite the fact that the American Top Brass had been warned by Ultra what the enemy were up to, had succeeded in ferrying across two battalions of SS Panzergrenadiers, supported by artillery and mortars and 20 tanks and self-propelled guns.

Now this force bumped right into the men of the Rainbow Division. The "new boys" did their best. "Everyone kept shooting, trying for a lucky hit on the wheels or in the engine," one sergeant explained afterwards. "The tanks just came up and fired point blank at the men, but they didn't retreat. . . . Finally an officer leaned out of his turret and shouted, 'Surrender, surrender you damn fools!' A fellow next to me answered with a blast from his BAR which tore his arm off."

North of Gambsheim, the Germans attacked the Rainbow Division's positions at the tiny hamlet of Herrlisheim. They had artillery and infantry, but no tanks. But the outcome was the same, as one of the survivors recalled: "They came at us in a straight line, just walking toward us with their rifles held at port arms. They seemed to want to keep their lines straight for some reason or another. Whenever it would begin to sag or to show gaps where we had hit men, they would send up a flare, stop, straighten up the line and then come forward again. All the time their machine guns and mortars were firing at us. There were so many of them that we couldn't stop them. They encircled us in the towns."

It was the same at Gambsheim. There was no other alternative for the "new boys" of the 42d Division but to surrender.

But the "old heads" of the 45th Infantry Division, in even a worse position further north, refused to give in. They knew what happened to men who surrendered, that is if the Krauts allowed them to surrender. They fell apart. They forgot honor, self-pride, discipline. Once they were "in the bag," it seemed, it was every man for himself.

Thus it was that the 45th's "Lost Battalion," as it later became known throughout the "Thunderbirds," battled on, although there was so little hope for them.

"The Lost Battalion" was some 700 men who had been trapped near the village of Reipertswiller on what the Army knew as "Hill 348," a wooded red sandstone hill, now rapidly being transformed into a lunar landscape by the German artillery and mortars.

The 45th's deliberate withdrawal, in accordance with Eisenhower's order, had come to a sudden halt as the "Thunderbirds" were struck by the 6th SS Mountain Division, the best of all the assaulting German formations. They had come straight from Finland for the attack and were well experienced in fighting under the kind of conditions now pertaining in that area. As Colonel Sparks, commander of the 157th's Third Battalion, commented after the war: "They were the best men we ever ran into, extremely aggressive and impossible to capture. There was no driving them out for they fought until they were killed."

The SS had done their job well. Using the expertise they had gained in the rugged terrain of the Finnish tundra, they had swiftly encircled five companies of the 45th on Hill 348. But the "Thunderbirds" had refused to surrender. Desperately they had hung on, taking a terrific pounding from German artillery and mortars, hardly daring to leave their foxholes even during lulls in the bombardment. For SS snipers were everywhere. Men fought, slept, ate, defecated—and died—in those freezing holes.

As each new dawn revealed that desolate landscape, with its fir trees snapped off like matchsticks, the smoking shell craters, the crumpled bodies of the dead, the weary survivors hoped for relief. But none came.

Once a brave young officer, Lt. Willis Talkington, volunteered to get supplies through to the Lost Battalion. He found a light tank, armed only with a 37mm cannon, loaded it with ammunition, food and Red Cross supplies and set off into the unknown. The terrain was terrible and the noise the tank's engines made grinding up the steep slopes of the area soon alerted the SS to its presence. Doggedly Talkington and his men fought their way through, the machine gun bullets pattering off the tank's steel sides like heavy tropical rain on a tin roof. Somehow he made it. But next morning when the tank set off back for further supplies, the SS mountain troopers were waiting. A round from a Panzerfaust slammed into the tank's side. It rocked wildly on its boogies and came to a sudden halt, smoke pouring from the turret. The whole crew had been killed outright and Talkington badly wounded. Somehow he managed to struggle back to his own lines. But that was the last attempt to supply the Lost Battalion by direct means.

On the 18th the SS attacked in force. G Company was overrun. Only 30 men escaped capture or death. Hurriedly the SS rushed in their mountain artillery and started mercilessly pounding the defenders' flanks. Later one of the two survivors of the Lost Battalion reported to his C.O., "The enemy artillery and mortar fire out there was the worst I'd ever seen. At least three quarters of the men on the hill had a wound of some kind or other and a few had two or three. Until the last day we placed the wounded in holes with the other unwounded, so that the men who weren't hurt could guard them and give them aid. We had no medical supplies, no food and no heat to melt the snow for water. Once we found a box of rations underneath an ammunition pile. We gave the rations only to the wounded."

The 157th's First Battalion was ordered to break through to their trapped comrades. They had hardly jumped off when they came under heavy artillery fire. They started to withdraw in some disarray. The SS, always quick to take advantage of the enemy's failure, rushed in six heavy machine guns. When the Americans attacked a second time, they ran into a solid wall of steel as the German MG 42s opened up, firing a terrifying 1,000 rounds a minute. The attack just fizzled out. Now there was no communication with the Lost Battalion save by radio. Over it the survivors asked for artillery fire to protect their perimeter, bringing it down to within 20 yards of their own foxholes. Now the divisional artillery commenced firing a staggering 5,000 rounds a day to help their trapped comrades.

A desperate General Frederick asked for another attempt to relieve the Lost Battalion. Somehow the 157th Infantry managed to throw together a composite force of heavy machine-gunners and anti-tank men and push them into the attack. They didn't get far. As one of them, Sergeant Fleming, a squad leader, recalled afterward: "My squad was in a ditch with three enemy machine guns on us. I asked for a volunteer to get aid. He got only 50 yards when a machine gun killed him. I asked for another and he got about ten yards before he was shot through the legs. I went out and dragged him behind some cover, then yelled to the others that I was going to the rear myself. I don't know how I made it, but I did."

There, the NCO reported to Colonel Sparks, who commanded the Lost Battalion, but who had not been trapped with it. A desperate Sparks commandeered a tank, and single-handedly drove it to Fleming's trapped squad. Reaching them he fired a staggering 5,000 rounds of machine gun ammunition to ward off the Germans, while the wounded were loaded.

Still the cruel slaughter went on. That night the Second Battalion of the 411th Infantry Regiment was brought up. On the morrow it would attack and relieve the Lost Battalion. Hastily they were briefed, and prepared for the slaughter to come.

The slaughter came. Setting off in a blinding snowstorm,

they ran straight into well-prepared German positions. As the regimental history laconically states: "They were cut down." Somehow the battalion was reorganized and they set off again, leaving the dead behind them in the snow, lying crumpled like bundles of abandoned rags. Again the Germans were waiting and they didn't stand a chance. As the regimental history reports yet again, "They were stopped cold."

After that General Frederick gave in. He ordered Colonel O'Brien, who commanded the 157th Infantry Regiment, to which the Lost Battalion belonged, to withdraw what was left of his regiment. O'Brien was in despair. He felt he had failed his poor trapped soldiers. He knew the survivors hadn't a chance, but he ordered them to make a breakout to their own lines. At 3:30 that snowy afternoon, a faint radio signal was received from the Lost Battalion. It read: "We're coming out. Give us everything you've got." (They meant covering artillery fire.) Firing every weapon they still possessed, the unwounded and lightly wounded men tried to break through. The SS were waiting for them. They were mown down mercilessly. In the end only two survivors reached the 157th's lines.

Even the hard-bitten SS mountaineers, who had been through the horrors of the bitter campaign in Russia where no quarter was given or expected, were impressed. As they rounded up the survivors of the Lost Battalion, they found, according to the divisional history of the Sixth SS, "456 enlisted men and 26 officers of the 45th Division, most of them wounded. Over 200 dead were found and buried. Our own losses were 26 dead, 127 wounded and 12 reported missing."

The battle of the Lost Battalion was over.

While the Lost Battalion had fought and lost its lone battle, every other division in the Seventh Army had been engaged in heavy combat. Their losses had been heavy and morale had not been improved by the rugged terrain and the terrible weather. Whole battalions had been wiped out, such as the

Second Battalion of the 79th Division's 314th Regiment, which was annihilated by the SS at Drusenheim by the Rhine on January 19.

That third terrible week of January, reviewing the situation, a worried Patch had to conclude that his battered divisions were in no fit state for offensive action. With average casualties of 15 percent per division (the 70th Division would claim 58 percent), Patch rated the combat efficiency of his divisions as generally low. Of the six regular divisions of Brooks' VI Corps, for example, he felt that only two, the 36th and 103rd, were "very satisfactory." The 45th and 79th Infantry Division and the 14th Armored were listed as "satisfactory"; while the 12th Armored and the Task Force Linden (42nd Division) and Task Force Herren (70th Division) were categorized as "unsatisfactory." Both the task forces needed, in his opinion, "additional training," something they were definitely not going to receive at this particular moment, with the enemy massing for yet another attack. Accordingly, he informed Devers that his VI Corps would not be able to withstand another serious assault.

So it was that Devers gave the order that Eisenhower had demanded he should give back in December. It was that the VI Corps should withdraw to a new line along the River Moder. The Moder flows out of the High Vosges and along the southern edge of the Haguenau Forest down through the plain to the Rhine. The VI Corps would dig in along this front, which curved to the south between the villages of Bischwiller and Weyersheim, where the VI Corps would link up with de Lattre's First French Army.

Patch was relieved when he heard Devers' decision. Although Patch observed to General Brooks that "I think he (the enemy) is getting tired, I think we will be able to hang on all right," he knew in his own heart that the Krauts still had plenty of fight in them. It was wiser to get the troops out while there was still time. The fate of Strasbourg was not his concern, although a German prisoner had boasted that the Alsatian capital would be in German hands again by January

30th, the 12th anniversary of Hitler's take-over of power in 1933. His responsibility was primarily to his army and the men under his command.

So the withdrawal commenced. Among the fighting men, emotions were mixed when they heard the order to go. "There was relief but not real relief," said the History of the 14th Armored. "Behind them were their friends and comrades, in the rubble of those towns and on those fields, and more of their friends and comrades were in the hospitals. . . . They felt a little as if they were giving up, as if they had fought and suffered and died in vain . . . and it was a bitter night, that night, a night of tears in the soul and it snowed."

Some of the fighting men were ashamed that they were pulling out, leaving those civilians loyal to the Allied cause to their fate. As more and more Germans dressed as Americans began to probe the 103rd Division's forward positions, the men noted, "The people of Alsace became strangely quiet. . . . The shining joy was gone from the eyes of this liberated people. . . . Tears welled in the eyes of the young and old. Alsatians who had given up half their home to the Cactus (103rd) Division asked hopefully, "Vous nix parti?" (You're not going?)

Most of the 103rd soldiers, unwilling to break the news that they were leaving—besides they were under orders to say nothing—lied, "No, no," they said, "just shifting troops."

But the locals seemed to know what was going on. Those who had served with the Resistance or had fled to avoid being called up into the German Army told the embarrassed GIs it would be death for them and their families when the Germans returned.

In their turn, the GIs grew angry. "Why pull back?" they asked, "Why leave these people to the mercy of the SS? Besides, won't we have to take back all this ground in the spring?"

But it was no use. Orders were orders. Like thieves in the night, they began to pull back out that dark afternoon, hampered by Germans dressed as Americans, so that no one trusted anyone. It was recorded that as they did so, "the children, always a barometer of native feelings, began to hurl icy snowballs at the troops." The soldiers didn't care much. "We deserve it," they thought.

It was no different in those frontier villages so hotly fought over by the men of the 70th Division. Jean Beck, then a youngster in the village of Niederbronn, now a professor at the University of Arizona, recalled how after they had gone, "All Sunday long there was not one soldier left in the town. However, during the night we heard shooting. On Monday at about 10 a.m., the Germans came. . . . In front were a few cars pulled by horses, the Germans being out of gas. Then came a cannon pulled by horses. Everybody else was on foot. We could not understand why the Americans had retreated."

Thirty years later those bitter memories of 1945 still linger in the hill villages. One group of veterans of the 70th Infantry Division attempting to visit the iron foundry at Niederbronn where they had been billeted that year were turned away in 1979. The factory guard explained to the old gents that it was because of the "January 1945 American abandonment of Niederbronn."

Some units did attempt to take endangered French civilians with them. The "Hellcats" military police evacuated civilians under fire at the village of Rohrwiller and were the last to leave the area save for the final rearguard. Others hadn't time to bother themselves with the ethics of the move and what might happen to the local civilians. They were too busy saving their own skins. The 222nd Regiment of the hitherto unlucky 42nd Division, for instance, was just about to move out at 7:30 on that Saturday night when the Germans burst through their final skirmish line. Swiftly the surprised infantrymen doubled for their trucks, while others turned and fought back. In the end that wild windy night, with the snow falling as if it would never stop again, they held the Germans.

Thereafter, the regimental commander ordered that each company should drop off a squad at each stopping place on their move back to make as much noise as possible to convince the Germans that the "Rainbow Division" was still in the line. "For the sake of propriety and for the salvation of what the Japanese call 'Face,'" wrote the chronicler of the 222nd Infantry Regiment, "it was a withdrawal. But in the minds and consciences of the men it was a retreat."

"It was cold that night, a bitter cold that ate into our bones. It snowed that night, a blinding blanket that wet us to the skin. We retreated that night, a retreat that hurt our minds. But worse than all these things was what our eyes told our soul. Our eyes saw people, newly liberated French people, trudging down those snowbound roads with their houses on their backs and despair in their eyes. Hordes of civilians who had trusted us, moving once again to escape the imminence of a German advance."

Then they were gone, the raging blizzard wiping out their tracks, as if they had never been there.

On the night of January 24/25, after the Americans had three days to dig themselves into their new lines on the banks of the River Moder, the expected German attack was launched. Six whole German divisions struck the river line in three prongs. The worst hit, as usual, was the 42nd Division's 222nd Infantry Regiment. It was struck first of all by a tremendous artillery bombardment all along the three-mile length of front it held.

"We waited," the regimental history records, "Sweat. THEN! All bammed and clattered, streaked and crashed around us until 2000. Shapeless blobs started to poke up out of their positions, moved around and started towards us. Onrush. Spit on your muzzle, sweetheart, here comes the devil!"

The "devil" came in the form of a five-division German attack against 3,000 Rainbowmen. Easily they forded the shallow Moder. Desperately the defenders sprayed the ranks of the advancing Germans, their bodies outlined a stark black in the light of flares shooting into the sky everywhere. But still they came, "half drunk, spurred on by desperate and gutteral commands."

Communications began to break down. Frantic battalion commanders could only guess where their outfits might be. A company was surrounded. The companies withdrew of their own accord. The surrounded company fought its way out and joined the other two to form a new battle-line. All night and into the next day the 222nd slogged it out with the Germans until they were exhausted and it became "an effort to squeeze a trigger or to move, either forward or backward."

But in the end they held the Germans and, as the regimental history records, "proved something to ourselves: 1. War is hell. 2. We were no longer green. 3. Americans could fight with a cold passion and fury even without that unlimited supply of matériel which so many believed is responsible for American success in battle." Yes, the Rainbow Division was living up to the tradition of their fathers in the Old War now!

The 103rd Division was also hit that night. Troopers of the Sixth SS Mountain Division rushed their positions, "yelling, cursing in English, screaming like madmen." German intelligence was good. They knew every weak spot in the American line. First they hit a battalion message center and then the battalion HQ. The US main line of resistance broke.

Something akin to a panic broke out. Men were running for the rear. A young officer, Lt. Leonard Doggett, scraped together an emergency squad. He threw it into action around the battalion aid station, fighting off the SS until the wounded and the medics could escape. One of this squad was a "happy-go-lucky" kid named Dennis Bellmore. He and four other men were ordered to guard a crossroads with a BAR. The Germans rushed them. The gun jammed. It was frozen solid by the icy night air. The SS were less than 40 yards away. The other four turned to make a run for it. Not

Bellmore. The sergeant in charge spotted him kneeling in the snow, pistol raised as if he were back on some stateside range.

"What's the matter, kid?" he yelled above the snap and crackle of small arms fire.

"I'm hit," Bellmore answered. "You guys take off!"

There was no time for arguments. The Germans were almost on to them now. The other four ran for the safety of the aid station. As they ran they could hear the regular spaced-out shots from a .45 pistol, followed by the hysterical high-pitched burr of a German burp gun. There was one last shot. Then silence. Dennis Bellmore "had paid with his life for 10 minutes of time . . . precious time during which the aid station and the remainder of the American defenders left the village."

While Brooks' VI Corps held the Moder River Line that third week of January, the US XXI Corps, attached to the First French Army, was attacking southwards into the Colmar Pocket. At last Eisenhower was going to "run the last German soldier" out of France for good. As always the 3rd Division was in the forefront of the attack. It had been fighting now since North Africa and its commander, "Iron Mike" O'Daniel, wanted to be in at the kill.

The newly commissioned Second Lt. Audie Murphy was there, too. By now he had won the Bronze Star, the Silver Star (twice), the Croix de Guerre and the Distinguished Service Cross, and also gained a nasty wound in October which had kept him out of the line until early January. Now he was back with his old outfit, the 3rd's "Can Do" 15th Infantry Regiment, looking for trouble. This day he found it. On that cold January day, Audie Murphy was the new C.O. of Company C, with not one single man, besides himself, left in the company from when he had joined it in North Africa in 1942. The night before he had slept in the forest near the Alsatian village of Riedwihr and it had been so cold that his hair had frozen to the ground. With two tank destroyers he was now advancing to the next hamlet of Holtzwihr. But the company—what was left of it—did not get too far. For the Germans spotted the Americans and opened up with mortars. The deadly little eggs came hurtling out of the gray winter sky, exploding in bursts of angry flame, throwing silver-gleaming fragments of red-hot metal everywhere. The company went to ground, clinging to the earth, hands clasped fearfully over their helmets.

Murphy had been through it all before—too many times. He set to work getting his men organized. Springing to the cover of a drainage ditch behind the two tank destroyers, he set up his "command post." He called the commander of the second tank destroyer and told him to move; he was in full view of the Germans in Holtzwihr. The tank destroyer C.O. refused. He felt safer with the infantry. Murphy accepted his decision and settled down to wait with his survivors. They had been in the line for 48 hours now. Fresh infantry would be taking over from them soon.

He waited all morning. In vain. Nothing was coming forward and his own men were becoming increasingly jittery. They were urinating all the time; a sure sign of nerves. Time passed leadenly. The wind rattled in the skeletal trees. The very air seemed heavy with tension. Finally Murphy had had enough waiting. He talked the situation over for a minute or two with the young artillery observer, Lt. Walter Weispfennig, and then contacted his battalion CP by field telephone. "What orders?" he whispered.

The answer was cold and dogmatic. "No change . . . Hold your position." That was that. No explanation. The waiting continued into that freezing January afternoon.

At 2:00, as Murphy himself wrote afterwards: "I see the Germans lining up for the attack. Six tanks rumble to the outskirts of Holtzwihr, split into groups of three and fan out towards either side of the clearing. Obviously they intend an encircling movement, using the fingers of the trees for cover. I yell to my men to get ready."

The tank destroyers opened up. Solid white armor-piercing shot hurtled toward the advancing German tanks. One shot struck the side of a Panzer and howled off like a ping-pong ball. The German tank did not even "falter," as Murphy recorded.

Now the Germans opened up, with their long overhanging cannon. 75mm shells ripped the air apart, howling flatly toward the tank destroyers. The first tank destroyer driver panicked. He tried to back off in reverse, but missed the track and went slipping helplessly into the drainage ditch. In virtually the same moment, the second tank destroyer was struck a great blow. It shuddered to a sudden stop, its commander and gunner killed outright. The rest of the panicked crew baled out madly, as thick smoke started to belch from its open turret.

Abruptly Murphy's men realized that they were without their armored protection and 200 German infantry dressed in "spook suits" and yelling their heads off like men demented, were running straight for their positions. Murphy sprang into action. He ordered his men to fall back to a prepared position some half a mile to the rear. Then while they did so, he withdrew together with Weispfennig. He said he would try to contact the artillery over his field telephone. Later he'd write that the reason he sent his men back was because he "couldn't see why all had to get killed when one man could do the job that had to be done." And it was up to him to do it.

Now he was all alone, with Weispfennig posted some 100 yards or so to his rear. There Murphy waited, armed only with a battered carbine and a field telephone, a baby-faced 20-year-old who would go down in the history of the United States Army as its "greatest fighting soldier." Audie Leon Murphy's hour of destiny had come.

One wonders why Murphy did what he was now to do. America had done little for Murphy in his 20 years of life. His native Texas had provided him with little, save as he remarked cynically in later life, "free advice—and malnutrition." Son of a dirt farmer who had abandoned his houseful of kids and sickly wife when it had gotten too much for him, Audie Murphy's schooling hadn't gone beyond fifth grade. Even now, as a newly created "officer and gentleman," his

spelling was terrible as he made mistake after mistake in his
letters home. Why, as he proudly informed his sister Corinne
back in Texas that winter, he had been awarded "the Distgh
set Cross" (he meant the Distinguished Service Cross). No,
Murphy owed his native country little. He could have withdrawn with his men. But he didn't. Perhaps, simply, his Irish
dander was up.

Now he stood his ground as the 60-ton enemy tanks rumbled closer, carrying out what an admiring Weispfennig later
declared was "the bravest thing I had ever seen a man do in
combat."

"Kraut tanks rumbled up to Murphy's position, passing
within 50 yards of him and firing at him as they went by.
They did not want to close in for the kill because they
wanted to give our tank destroyer, which was burning but
not in flames, as wide a berth as possible."

Murphy, however, was not going to let them pass and
massacre his men to the rear. He called for instant artillery
fire. Battalion CP did not seem to understand. How close
were the Krauts? Murphy's famed Irish temper flared.
Above the noise he yelled angrily, "Just hold the phone and
I'll let you talk to one of the bastards!"

Moments later shells started to howl above his head and
fall in the fields to his right. Now Murphy decided to tackle
the German infantry. With all his carbine ammunition gone,
he retreated to the smoking tank destroyer and clambered up
its steel deck. There he grabbed the tank destroyer's .50 caliber machine gun and began spraying the Germans with
lead. An awed Weispfennig reported later, "He was completely exposed and silhouetted against the background of
bare trees and snow, with a fire under him that threatened to
blow the destroyer to bits if it reached the gasoline and ammunition."

Fortunately for Murphy the stalled German infantry
could not figure out where the fire was coming from. No one
could be firing from the smoking wreck of the tank destroyer, so they milled around in bewilderment, taking casualties all the time.

The German tankers, however, spotted the source of that deadly fire. They started to turn. As Weispfennig recalled, "The enemy tanks . . . returned because Lt. Murphy had held up the supporting infantry and they were apparently loath to advance without infantry support." They joined the fight. Back at Battalion HQ they could hear the boom-boom of the German cannon over the field phone and there one excited NCO cried, "Are you still alive, Lieutenant Murphy?" Murphy, his clothes already black and smoking, carried away by the crazy logic of combat, yelled back "Momentarily, Sergeant . . . And what are your post-war plans?" The tanks and infantry now closed in. Weispfennig reported later that Murphy "was enveloped in clouds of smoke and spurts of flame. His clothing was torn and riddled by flying shell fragments and bits of rock. Bullets ricocheted off the tank destroyer as the enemy concentrated the full fury of his fire on this one-man stronghold."

"The German infantrymen got within 10 yards of the lieutenant," one of his company, Sgt. Brawley, recalled afterwards, "who killed them in the draws, the meadows, in the woods—wherever he saw them. Though wounded and covered with soot and dirt that must have obscured his vision at times, he held the enemy at bay, killing and wounding at least 35 during the hour."

Now Murphy resorted to one last desperate measure. He called down an artillery barrage on his own position. As he explained later, "I figured that I could luck out the barrage— if those goddamned Germans could. With those shells bursting all around me, they couldn't even hear the machine gun, much less locate it." But in that same instant the phone went dead and the artillery didn't fire.

Thereafter, one of those inexplicable lulls which occur in combat took place. It was as if both sides were winded and wanted to take five to regain their strength. But that lull was the saving of Audie Murphy, of whom President Truman would say, "I guess he was the best soldier we've had since George Washington." For during it the gray clouds parted momentarily and the American fighter-bombers, cruising around above the clouds, spotted the melee below. They came zooming down, cannon and machine guns blazing. The Germans fled. It was all over and Murphy had won himself America's highest award for bravery in the field, the Congressional Medal of Honor.

As for Murphy, as he refused medical help and led his company into the attack in Holtzwihr, he recorded in his autobiography, "Except for a vague pain in my leg, I feel nothing, no sense of triumph, no exhilaration at being alive . . . Existence has taken on the quality of a dream in which I am detached from all that is present . . ."

Understandably, all the young men still fighting in Alsace that last week of January 1945 were numb, feeling little, with existence taking on "the quality of a dream," as the battle went on and on. Farther north the Battle of the Bulge had officially ended with the link-up of the First and Third US Armies at the Belgian town of Houffalize. Now the Top Brass up there—Eisenhower, Bradley, Patton, Hodges, Montgomery—were slapping each other on the back and telling one another just how smart they had been after all. No one seemed to know—or care—that the second battle of the bulge was still raging down south in France, with hundreds of young men being killed daily.

Admittedly some of the formations released from the fight in Belgium were trickling into the Seventh Army's firing line to fill the gaps. But they were in poor shape themselves. There was the battered 28th Infantry Division, for instance, which had lost one whole regiment in the first two days of the Bulge; or the "Bloody Bastards of Bastogne," as their calypso-singing PR man liked to call them—the 101st Airborne had held Bastogne, or "Nuts City," as it was now calling itself, for nearly two weeks against everything the Germans had been able to throw against it. Now, the "Screaming Eagles" received 467 infantry replacements from the Seventh Army—men who had never even seen the inside of an airplane, much less jumped from one—and were sent back into the line yet once again, to bolster up the Moder Front.

Weary as they were, their officers were as cocky as ever. When told that the VI Corps, to which they now belonged, was opposed by seven or eight divisions, while the VI had only five depleted divisions, Major Lew Schweiter, the 101st's G-2, said scornfully, "What the hell are you worried about? The 101st alone can lick five German divisions simultaneously. We just did."

As always, the 101st did not wait for the enemy to come to them; they went to the enemy, with each regiment sending aggressive, large patrols across the Moder to seek and destroy the Germans.

But occasionally these daring patrols went wrong, such as the one led by cocky Lt. Jones, straight from West Point and very "gung-ho." Coming back across from the far bank of the Moder, the patrol ran into heavy mortar and artillery fire. The paras doubled for the cover of a lone house. The Germans must have spotted them in the glowing darkness, with the flares hissing into the night sky every few minutes, for a self-propelled gun rumbled up and joined in the firing.

The paras became rattled under the strain. One of them, his face blackened with grease and gleaming with sweat in the light of the candles, screamed at the two German prisoners they had taken earlier on, "Lemme kill 'em . . . lemme kill 'em!" He was stopped from doing so only after he was wrestled away from the captives.

Then a "little fellow . . . who had been wounded in the head by a German hand grenade," started screaming as the shells dropped outside, "Kill me . . . kill me! Somebody kill me . . . I can't stand it, Christ! . . . For God's sake someone kill me!" He began to sob hopelessly as the blood streamed down his ashen face, "Please kill me . . . "

One of the paras, who felt that it was "like a scene from a movie," couldn't stand the strain any longer. He went upstairs and took a spell as guard-lookout, fascinated by the falling shells and flames everywhere. Spellbound, he started to become aware of a weird gurgling noise coming from the direction of the Moder.

It was the wounded German they had abandoned earlier on, after one of the patrol had to be stopped from shooting him there and then because 'he "wasn't worth bringing back."

The moaning and groaning of the man dying out there all alone unnerved the lookout, a veteran of Normandy and Holland. He decided to swim the stream once more and knife the German to bring his suffering to an end. But a sudden German mortar barrage made him change his mind. Instead the veteran crouched in the darkness, listening to the "ghastly wheezes" of the dying German. "I pitied him, dying all alone far from home, dying slowly without hope or love on the bank of a dirty little creek."

Just before the dawn another veteran para spotted the dark writhing shape and threw a grenade to put the German out of his misery at last. As the chronicler put it, "Dawn came. The cold yellow sun shone through the gray mist on the dead German, a monument to war and the achievement of man."

The German counterattack was over.

5

STORM TO THE RHINE
February–March 1945

> "Life, to be sure, is nothing much to lose. But young men
> think it is, and we were young."
>
> —A.E. HOUSMAN

ON Wednesday, January 31, 1945, the US Seventh Army
shot Private Eddie D. Slovik, Serial Number 3689415, dead.

It had snowed heavily during the night and the little Alsatian mountain village of St. Marie aux Mines, where the execution took place, glistened with the new snow. Slovik had
been brought up the slick, winding mountain roads to the
village from the stockade in chains. Now the chains were removed and the officer in charge of the execution read to him
the court martial order stating that Slovik was to be shot by a
firing squad from his own outfit, the 109th Infantry Regiment of the 28th Division. Thereupon, Slovik, who was
wrapped in an army blanket on account of the biting cold,
was asked if he had any special requests. He answered "no"
and the officer in charge noted that Slovik was "exception-
ally calm and resigned." Of course, Slovik had never expected to be shot for desertion. Even when he refused to go
into action the second time and had walked away from the
firing line, while his comrades of the 28th Division, "the
Bloody Bucket," as it was so aptly named, were dying in
their hundreds and finally in their thousands, he had never
thought it would come to this.

As one of the judges who convicted him, Benedict B.
Kimmelmann, recalled 43 years later, "I am inclined to believe, as did the reviewing authorities and some who were
his guards in the stockade, that he deliberately sought a

guilty court-martial verdict to avoid serving as combatant. He was sure he would never make it on the line. He was not afraid of prison, having served time, and someday, when the war was over, he would come out alive and unharmed. He would have had no reason to fear execution; he believed that had never happened."

Why should he? Before him some 40,000 deserters had been apprehended in the ETO, of whom 2,864 had been tried and sentenced to anything from 20 years to death. Of the 49 American soldiers currently waiting for their death sentence for desertion to be carried out, why should Eisenhower pick him?

But he had—*pour encourager les autres*. Eddie Slovik was confessed by Father Cummings, the Catholic chaplain. With tears in his eyes, the skinny little deserter handed the chaplain a bundle of letters he had received from his crippled wife back in Detroit and said, "The only break I ever had in life, Father, was this girl. But I've lost her now. Everything we had will be gone. They wouldn't let her be happy."

Outside they waited for Eddie in the walled courtyard of the big house, shielded from the curious eyes of the locals: the Top Brass from XXI Corps and the 28th Division, the firing squad of 12 combat-experienced 110th infantrymen, several chaplains and a colonel carrying the black hood they'd slip over Eddie's head before "it" happened.

Now the execution procession moved into the courtyard. There must have been something tragically beautiful about that little scene at Number 86 Rue de General Bourgeois that morning: the snow-covered Vosges all around, the caw-caw of the rocks in the skeletal trees; the knowledge that all these men present would be taking part in the last attack into Colmar Pocket on the morrow, perhaps to die; and the little man in the field jacket with no insignia, with his hands now tied behind his back, who was going to die violently soon at the hands of his fellow countrymen.

General Cota, the burly divisional commander of the 28th, black swagger cane clasped beneath his right arm, opened his mouth, his breath fogging on the keen icy air, and yelled, "Attention!"

The hollow square of official spectators snapped to attention as the procession halted. Again the charges were read out to Eddie Slovik by a Major Fellman, who asked: "Private Slovik, do you have a statement to make before the order directing your execution is carried out?"

"No," Eddie mumbled.

Now the Catholic chaplain asked, "Do you have a last statement to make to me, as a chaplain, before your death?"

Again Eddie said, "No."

Fellman barked: "Prepare the prisoner for execution!"

Swiftly the execution party tied Eddie, who was calm and didn't struggle, to the waiting pole, strapping him around the knees, ankles and shoulders so that he wouldn't fall when hit. Then came the hood. His face disappeared beneath it. He had seen the world for the last time. Lieutenant Koziak, in charge of the firing squad, snapped an order. There was a crunch of heels on the snow. Fellman commanded, "Squad . . . ready!"

Up flashed the M-1s. The infantrymen socked the butts hard into their shoulders and squinted through the sights at the blindfolded man tied to the pole in the snow.

"Aim!"

They caught their breaths, white-knuckled fingers curling around their triggers as they exerted first pressure.

"FIRE!" Fellman yelled.

As one they did so. Some of the spectators gasped. Others jumped, startled. In angry protest the birds rose from the naked trees squawking. One of the firing squad reeled back. His rifle had been dirty. The blast had nearly smashed his collarbone.

At the pole Slovik's hooded head fell forward. There were sudden scarlet patches on his jacket. But he wasn't dead—yet. Slowly the doctor crunched over the snow towards him. The spectators could hear that solemn, steady crunching as he fingered the stethoscope.

The Medical Officer applied the instrument, automatically noting that Slovik had been hit by all 11 bullets (by tradition one rifle had been loaded secretly with blank ammunition). He listened, the heartbeat was faint, but it was still there. He guessed, however, that Slovik wouldn't need a second volley. So he played for time.

Behind him Fellman gave the order to reload. Angrily the Catholic chaplain snapped, "Give him another volley if you like it so much!" Fellman, however, was not listening. He wanted the damned thing over with quickly. He called to the MO to pronounce Slovik dead or to stand aside for the second volley.

The doctor straightened up, putting away his instrument. "The second volley won't be necessary," he said quietly. "Private Slovik is dead." Later General Cota, the 28th's divisional commander, would recall: "That was the roughest fifteen minutes of my life . . ."

But Slovik had served his purpose. One of the firing squad, a Private Morrison, knew instinctively why the little man, one of thousands who had committed the same military crime, had been shot that morning. He stated later, "I think General Eisenhower's plan worked. It helped to stiffen a few backbones. When the report of the execution was read to my company formation, the effect was good. It made a lot of guys think about what it means to be an American. I'm just sorry the general didn't follow through and shoot the rest of the deserters instead of turning them loose on their community."

As ex-Captain Kimmelman observed truly so many years later, "Over a six-and-a-half-year period, then, reasons were found by those in higher authority to void the death sentence of 48 men found guilty of desertion. Slovik, guilty as many others were, was made an example—the sole example, as it turned out. An example is a victim. His execution was an historic injustice." Kimmelman, of course, is right. But that January, as Eisenhower's armies set about fighting their way back into Germany, there had to be an example—a victim, if you like—in order to stop the rot.

* * *

The US Army had undergone its baptism of fire in North Africa at the disastrous rout of the Kasserine Pass in February 1943. There, up to 34 percent of all casualties were "mental." Worse still, only three percent of the soldiers who had broken down with "shell shock," as it was still called, ever returned to the firing line.

In Italy in one period of 44 days, the US First Armored Division's psychiatric casualties amounted to a startling 54 percent of all losses. In northwest Europe it was no different. By January 1945, nearly 100,000 men had been diagnosed as suffering from "combat fatigue," as it was now named. In the bitter fighting of the Huertgen Forest—"the death factory," as the GIs called it—whole companies, even battalions, had broken down and refused to fight or had fled. Battalion commanders had collapsed and wept. Even a regimental commander was diagnosed as suffering from "combat fatigue." Divisional commanders were forced to set up their own psychiatric centers—"rest centers," they were called officially—to deal with the flood of soldiers who had broken down. There they would be drugged and allowed to sleep for three days before being sent back into the line. The idea was that once these men suffering from combat fatigue got as far back as the general hospitals they would never be returned to field duty. In any event, those who were returned from the "rest centers" usually broke down again.

But the rot was not only confined to the problem of combat fatigue. There was also that of desertion from the firing line, self-mutilation, and absence without leave. In that winter of 1944/45, an infantry company commander might check his front at night expecting to find a hundred-odd soldiers manning their positions, only to discover that half that number were present. The others had simply walked away and hidden themselves somewhere to the rear.

Some got out of front-line duties by throwing away their false teeth—a man who can't eat, can't fight. Others rubbed diesel oil into their chest to produce an incurable skin complaint. Some exposed their feet to the winter elements in order to get those nice pinky, pulpy toes which meant "trench foot" and a spell in a rear-line hospital. There were even those who made pacts with another man to shoot off each other's big toes with their rifles, shielding the muzzles of the M-Is with loaves of bread so that the tell-tale black mark of a self-inflicted wound would not be there. A few, it was rumored, even had themselves infected with syphilis in order to get a spell in the "pox hospital" and away from the front.

But those offenders detested by the top brass the most (and by, it must be stated, their comrades who did stay in the line and sweat it out, too) were those who went "over the hill" back in the fleshpots behind the line on one of those, so precious, 72-hour leave passes. In the line they led short brutal lives. If they were junior infantry officers, they survived, on average, three weeks. Enlisted men could expect twice that long in combat before they were killed, wounded or broke down. So when they were lucky enough to receive a furlough in Paris, Brussels or Liege, their wants at first were simple: booze and dames. The "feather merchants of the COMZ"—"One man in the line and five men to bring up the Coca-Cola"—might offer them movies, USO shows and pretty Red Cross girls serving "java and sinkers." But that kind of fare could not help them to eradicate the horrors and misery of the front. They wanted stronger medicine.

But "Pig Alley" (Place Pigalle) in Paris and the "Roo Nerve" (Rue Neuve) in Brussels, with cheap women and even cheaper booze, proved too tempting for some. When the regimental "deuce and a half" turned up to transport the leavemen back to the front, they were simply not there waiting for it, hung-over, happy and broke.

They had lost their nerve and gone "over the hill," as that phrase which dated to the Civil War had it. Now until they were caught, they lived off their wits. Some took to armed robbery. One gang hi-jacked a whole trainload of cigarettes bound for the front, worth a fortune on the black market. Others lived off what they could steal from Allied "open messes" to be found in every big city behind the lines, selling the margarine, corned beef, cans of apricots and the like

to the locals. Some took up with B-girls and amateur prosti-
tutes and simply existed on their earnings.

But before every big offensive that winter the number of
these deserters increased by the thousand, just as those of
the combat fatigue did and the men who got "lost" in the
line. It was something that the top brass could not tolerate.

They, the products of the hard discipline of the "Point"
and devotion to "Duty, Honor, Country" could not understand the weaknesses of their wartime soldiers. Those reluctant heroes had had a different concept of the war. Before
they had been inducted into the Army, their idea of what battle would be like was based mainly on the products of Hollywood and the New York publishing industry: a jolly, patriotic
mish-mash which had little resemblance to the harsh reality
of army life. It had been the Andrew Sisters belting out the
"Boogie-Woogie Bugle Boy of Company B"; Brian Donlevy
in "Wake Island" responding to a Japanese invitation to surrender, with "tell 'em to come and get us"; John Marquand's
oddly moving "So Little Time"; Gary Cooper as Sergeant
York, replying when asked how he had captured 132 Germans single-handed, "I surrounded them," etcetera.

The reality as they had now learned—those who had survived into 1945—was totally different. "Tinseltown" had
not been able to even hint about the short-lived, degrading
brutality of the average soldier's existence in the front line.
Neither had the popular war novels of the time. The shock of
that realization had been too much for some of these
wartime soldiers and they had voted for another easier way
of life, with their feet. Now, however, as the army prepared
for the attack on the Siegfried Line which barred their way
to the Rhine, Germany's last great natural bulwark, its Seventh Army, in common with all the other US armies involved in the drive, was no longer prepared to show mercy.
For anyone who broke and ran now there would be little tolerance. Supplies of riflemen were running out. Every man
who could hold and fire a rifle was needed at the front. There
would be no further shirking.

As General "Dutch" Cota told Huie, the author of the *The Execution of Private Slovik* after the war, "During the Second World War, I was privileged to lead 36,000 Americans into battle and I saw many of them die for the principles in which we believe. Given the same conditions of those hours, I do not see how I could have acted differently in the Slovik case and remained faithful to my responsibilities." Now the young men who would fight the coming battle would be expected, if necessary, to "die for the principles in which we believe . . ."

One minute after midnight on February 17, 1945, the 70th Division's 276th Infantry Regiment moved out of its positions in the woods and shattered villages of the frontier and began its drive for the German town of Saarbrucken. The Seventh Army's offensive had commenced. By now the winter snows had begun to melt and those of the "Trailblazers," as the 70th was nicknamed, who had been out on patrol in the area previously were shocked to see that they had been walking over hundreds of the dreaded schu-mines. They seemed to be everywhere and, together with the thick black mud, they hampered the division's progress much more than the enemy's fire. Doggedly, however, the Trailblazers pushed on, up and down the long steep ridges of the area, their armor bogged town in the mud, braving the 88mm artillery and the machine gun nests which were everywhere. Second Lieutenant Eugene Inzer was typical of many who fought and fell in that bloody third week of February as the 70th Division edged its way ever closer to the Reich. Formerly an NCO, he had just been granted a field commission. Now this newly created "officer and gentleman" was ordered to take his platoon forward and occupy a ridge some 500 yards to his front. Almost immediately he and his men stirred up a hornet's nest. "The whole area was being raked with machine-gun fire," he recalls nearly 50 years later. "One could hear, feel and even smell the slugs there were so many."

Going to ground in a little hollow, he heard one of his men call out, "Inzer, I've been hit," followed by a soft moan.

The officer called back, "How bad?"

His answer was a strained laugh and the wounded man replied, "I've been hit in the butt . . . what will my friends think?"

For another hour the small arms battle on the hillside raged, with the pinned-down Americans fighting back the best they could. Then, completely unexpectedly, the Germans started raising white flags pinned to the muzzles of their rifles.

Some of Inzer's replacements, who had had little more than basic training back in the States, fell for the old trick. They clambered out of their foxholes to accept the German surrender. Immediately the enemy opened fire, felling three GIs. Inzer and the rest weren't fooled, however. As the Germans came out of their holes now to inspect the Americans writhing in the mud, they loosed off a violent salvo of fire. Eleven Germans dropped, dead before they hit the ground.

But Inzer's career as the newest "second looey" in the regiment was not going to last much longer. Advancing further, he and his men spotted what they thought were troops wearing German helmets to their front. He was just about to order his platoon to open fire when a sergeant ran up, crying, "Don't shoot . . . they're Americans!"

As Eugene Inzer recalled long afterwards, "This was a mistake and so was my next move." He called out the day's password. His answer was a burst of rifle fire and the first struck was himself. "The slug penetrated the center of my chest and exited from the lower chest wall, taking half of my lung and leaving the other half collapsed with sections of four ribs missing."

Badly wounded, Inzer fell to the ground—and safety, so he thought. Again he was wrong. Somewhere a German machine gun opened up and six slugs slammed into his right thigh, breaking it. But his ordeal wasn't over yet. The next volley "landed several more slugs in my right arm, mangling the humorous and elbow."

All day the wounded officer lay in the open with the Germans all about him. They looted his body, taking what candy they could find and then left him presumably to die.

Another day passed and another, with the wounded man suffering under 10 or 12 barrages, both German and American, before the Germans withdrew and he was found by a Private Harris, who was so shocked by the officer's appearance that he did not speak a single word when Inzer called to him. Inzer wasn't surprised. As he recalled afterwards, "I shall never forget his facial expression. I had bullet-shredded clothes, blood over a goodly portion of my body and face, as a result of bleeding profusely through the nose and mouth, mingled with a week's growth of beard. No wonder he did not believe what he saw."

Inzer survived, but many didn't as the 70th slogged it out with the enemy. Two days after the offensive had started, one of the division's companies set about capturing the ancient, ruined castle of Schlossberg, which dominated the area and which they believed the Germans were using to direct their artillery fire.

Stealthily, nerves ticking electrically with apprehension, the hundred men or so approached the red sandstone pile with its ten-foot walls through the woods, waiting for the first high-pitched hysterical burr of a German MG 42. None came. To the soldiers' surprise, they scaled the castle walls without a shot being fired to find the place empty. Puzzled and feeling strangely uneasy, they spread out to search the ruin, but they found nothing. The Germans, if there ever had been any up there, had vanished. Trouble started for the new owners of Schlossberg Castle just after dark. Without any warning, an 88mm shell streaked across the sky with a tremendous roar like the sound of a giant piece of canvas being ripped apart, and exploded inside the castle. It seemed to act like a signal. Almost immediately other German guns

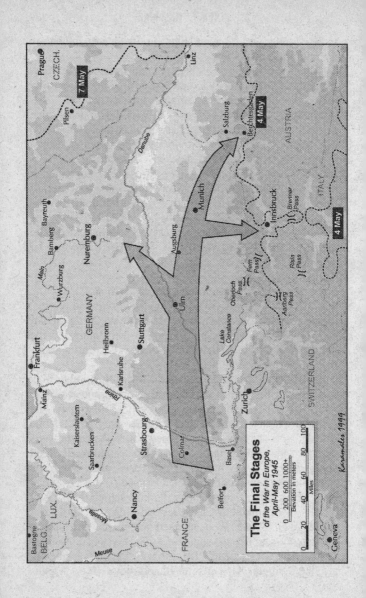

The Final Stages
of the War in Europe, April–May 1945

0 20 40 60 80 100
Miles

0 200 600 1000+
Elevation in meters

Kaumelis 1999

Cities/Places: Bastogne, BELG., LUX., Bastogne, Nancy, Kaiserslautern, Saarbrucken, Strasbourg, Belfort, Geneva, Frankfurt, Mainz, Karlsruhe, Heilbronn, Stuttgart, Colmar, Basel, Zurich, Prague, CZECH., Pilsen, Linz, Bayreuth, Bamberg, Wurzburg, Nuremburg, Ulm, Augsburg, Munich, Salzburg, Berchtesgaden, Innsbruck, SWITZERLAND, GERMANY, FRANCE, ITALY, AUSTRIA

Dates: 7 May, 4 May, 4 May

Rivers: Meuse, Moselle, Main, Rhine, Danube

Passes: Fern Pass, Oberjoch Pass, Arlberg Pass, Resia Pass, Brenner Pass

Lake Constance

joined in and mortar bombs started to howl down from the heavens. Five minutes later German infantry began to infiltrate the company positions. Company I of the 70th's 276th Regiment had fallen into a well-prepared enemy trap.

The barrage stopped, leaving behind it a loud echoing silence which ran round the circle of darkening hills. Immediately the Germans rushed the American positions, coming in from all sides. The defenders fired at them furiously, bowling many of the Germans over "like rabbits." But still the rest came on. Frantically they cut their way through the wire of the US outside-perimeter and raced for the castle walls themselves.

Now the Americans played their ace. They called down their own artillery. Within seconds the 884th Field Artillery began pouring down fire just short of the walls. It stopped the Germans dead. They broke and ran back the way they had come, leaving their dying and wounded sprawled everywhere.

By now the "Trailblazers" were approaching the Spicheren Heights just to the south of Saarbrucken, a grim high plateau, which had played a role in Franco-German history right from 1870 when one of the decisive battles of the Franco-Prussian War had been fought there. In 1939, this tip of Alsace had seen no less a person than the Führer himself walk cautiously a thousand yards across the border into newly captured French territory. Thereupon, he declared the heights "Germany's holy ground." A heroic monument was erected there in 1940 when France finally fell, and right throughout the war special excursion rates were offered to inland Germans so that they could make "pilgrimages" to the place.

Now it was up to the 70th's 274th Regiment to clear the heights—at double-quick time—for General Patch was impatient to get to the Rhine before Patton and his Third Army did. And Patton was going all out to reach that great river.

At the sharp end, the capture of Spicheren Heights proved to be tough, very tough indeed. "The tanks were advancing up the road and the tank gunners were firing point-blank at single men," ex-PFC Ralph Crawford recalls 44 years later. "There was screaming and terror—the terror of a man fighting a machine in a battle he feels he cannot possibly win. . . . The panic was on and the men were running pell-mell through the forest, tripping and falling."

Another member of that same outfit, Lee Miller, remembers helping to defend a 57mm anti-tank gun in the woods when "there was a lot of shooting and hollering and a BAR man came running back. He said the rest of his outfit had been wiped out by a tank and he was the only survivor. He was worried about being shot for desertion. A Kraut tank came up the trail and the 57mm stopped it about 65 feet from us by knocking a track loose after bouncing several rounds off its side."

Just after that a Major Cahoon came up and was shocked to find just how few men were still in the line. He said he'd send aid, and as one observer noted, "It really hurt our guys to see him run from cover to cover while the enemy was firing. He was behind a tree when he was hit, slumped over and didn't move again."

Lt. Harry Durkee, who was soon to be wounded too, recalls: "Jerry foot soldiers are right behind the tanks. Some hand-to-hand fighting ensued, in which most of my men are taken prisoner. Our few survivors remain where they have hidden while the enemy, with the POWs riding tanks, pull back." Thereafter the few survivors, hiding in ditches, were plagued most of the day by a concealed sniper. Every time anyone raised his head he was hit. At dawn it was Durkee's turn. "I climbed out of my foxhole and the sniper's bullet, which seemed like an 88mm round, hit me squarely in the forehead," and that was the end of his fighting career. In the end Spicheren Heights fell and the way to Saarbrucken was open. But by that time many of the companies engaged had lost most of their officers, the first to be killed and wounded, so that in two cases the skeletal companies were commanded by first sergeants.

One of the survivors, then a machine gunner and later a full colonel in the Army, Cornelius Cremer, commented long afterward about the performance of the men who fought to take the Heights: "There were those of us who went where we had to and tried to get the job done; others loved the adventure of war and killing; others were cowards."

Be that as it may, it had taken them, valiant and cowardly alike, eleven days to do it. The cost was 1,662 young men dead, wounded, and missing.

On Monday March 5, 1945, the Western Allies were elated by the tremendous news that General Hodges' First US Army had captured a bridge across the Rhine intact. It was, of course, that celebrated railroad bridge at Remagen, which for a while became the "most famous bridge in the world." The rest of the fighting on the long western front from France to Holland was totally forgotten, while the media concentrated their attention on that single division—the US 9th Armored—trying to preserve the only bridge across the Rhine that hadn't been blown up by the enemy.

But on that same Monday something even more momentous was taking place, for on that day Eisenhower and Patton flew to Patch's HQ at the little picturesque Lorraine town of Luneville to coordinate the combined Third and Seventh Armies drive to the Rhine.

Patton was full of himself. Five days before he had captured the key Moselle city of Trier, using the 10th Armored Division of SHAEF's reserve without authority. Thereupon, thumbing his nose at Eisenhower ("our future president," as Patton liked to mock him), he signalled SHAEF HQ: "Have taken Trier with two divisions . . . What do you want me to do? Give it back?"

Now as they flew to Luneville Eisenhower praised Patton and his Third Army excessively. "George," he told the man whom in the past he had compared to a "burr under the saddle," "You are not only a good general, you are a lucky general. And as you well remember, in a general, Napoleon prized luck above skill."

Patton was well pleased with the praise. He was riding high this March, not knowing that Eisenhower would fire him within six months and that he would be dead by the end of the year. He laughed, showing his dingy sawn-off teeth and said, "That's the first compliment you've paid me in the two and a half years we have served together, Ike."

Eisenhower smiled and assured him it wouldn't be the last.

At the great 18th century palace at Luneville, which had once been the summer home of the French kings, and which now served as Patch's HQ, Eisenhower and Patton listened as the Seventh Army Commander explained his plan for the attack through the Siegfried Line to the Rhine. Codenamed "Operation Undertone" it envisaged a three-corps assault into what was now being called the "Saar-Palatinate Triangle": a three-sided industrial area, bounded by the Rhine to the east, the Moselle River to the northwest, and the Lauter-Saar River's line on the south and west.

Patch's three corps, the XXI, VI and XV, would attack in line abreast, using all those divisions which had become veterans during the great counterattack, plus the new 63d and 71st Infantry Divisions, and two really veteran outfits, which Eisenhower had allotted to the seventh. These were the 4th Infantry— "The Ivy League Division"—which had landed on D-Day and suffered a 300 percent turnover in personnel due to casualties since then; and General Grow's Sixth Armored which had been in combat almost constantly since August 1st, 1944.

Eisenhower nodded his approval and then, taking off his reading glasses, he indicated that while "Sandy" Patch's men had not succeeded in breaking through the Siegfried Line in the Saar, "Georgie" Patton's Third had already achieved its breakthrough. Eisenhower asked if it would be all right with him if Patton attacked across the northern section of the Seventh Army's zone of operations. In this manner Patton could cross the Moselle, cut through the Palatinate behind the Siegfried Line and dash for the Rhine.

Patch, always unassuming and eager to cooperate, did not hesitate. "Sure, Ike," he agreed. "We are all in the same army."

Thus the matter was settled. While Patch's Seventh

would continue to batter against the Siegfried Line, fighting their way from house to house through the grimy industrial towns and villages of the Saar steel-and-coal basin, Patton would barrel through to the Rhine on what was little more than a motorized road march. Patton, in due course, would grab the newspaper headlines once more, while as usual, America's Forgotten Army's costly battle would be barely noticed.

No wonder Patton was well pleased with the day when he flew back to his headquarters. For although he had been granted a slab of the Seventh's future territory, he had no intention of working together with Patch. As he wrote at the time, "There was some talk of trying to coordinate the plans of the Third and Seventh Armies, but since the Seventh Army could not jump off until the 15th, I determined to attack as soon as I could, as I felt that time was more valuable than coordination. In fact, it is my opinion that coordination is a very much misused word and its accomplishment is difficult." Besides, Patton thought ex-infantryman Patch was a "plodder," and there was no place in Patton's book for "plodders."

Now as Patton started his attacks across the Moselle at half a dozen points between Koblenz and Trier, Patch's men readied themselves for the attack on the Siegfried Line soon to come. In the sector, where the new 63d Infantry Division would kick off the whole Seventh Army assault, Hitler's Westwall appeared very frightening. As the Divisional History records: "It consisted of two belts about a mile apart, each composed of a line of dragon's teeth which were three staggered rows of concrete pyramids about three feet high. Before the line of dragon's teeth were one or two anti-tank ditches, each eight feet deep and twelve feet wide. On every knoll and through all paths in the woods were concrete pillboxes so situated so that each one was supported by fire from one or more of the others. For every three to six pillboxes there was a key or central pillbox which contained a control point for the others. The line itself was about 500 yards in depth, though well camouflaged pillboxes dotted knolls and rises for miles. Most of the fortifications were covered with earth and overgrown with vegetation." Without doubt, the 63d's first major assignment was going to be a tough nut to crack.

But that prospect didn't faze the division's gung-ho commander, General Hibbs. Three days before the attack was scheduled to kick off, he issued a spunky (some thought vainglorious) order-of-the-day, telling his men, "Beyond the Siegfried Line lies crumbling Germany, the Rhine and final victory. Your immediate task is to open the gate for our armored divisions. Yours is the honor and the glory . . . take it. Pay dirt lies ahead. Blood and Fire [the Division's nickname] drives in for the kill. The world will be watching you. Strike hard, fast and viciously . . . victory comes by outfighting and out-lasting the enemy." Patton would have loved it.

General Barnett, commanding the 63d's left-hand neighbor, the 70th Infantry Division, was not so sanguine. On the day before the great attack was due to start he had lost a whole patrol probing for weak spots in the Siegfried Line and he didn't like the idea of a frontal attack on the fortifications one bit. He told Patch to his face that an assault of that kind would needlessly cost the lives of many young men. Patch urged him to push his division harder and get across the River Saar into Saarbrucken, to which Barnett replied, "Not until I can stand on the river bank and smoke a cigarette." Patch gave in, and thus the uncharismatic, somewhat indecisive commander saved the lives of many young men.

Commanders like General Barnett were worried, too, about the quality of the reinforcements used to fill up the gaps that had resulted from the battles of January and February. Many had no experience in the use of infantry weapons save their own M1 rifles and no idea how to conduct themselves in combat. Indeed, the week previously Barnett had been forced to send out several platoons of replacements to get some marksmanship practice in the front line. The "practice" hadn't lasted long because the Germans on the other side of the valley interpreted the firing as an imminent attack and had commenced replying with artillery. The replacements fled.

The 12th Armored Division, readied to exploit any breakthrough made by the infantry, was also not pleased by the quality of the replacements it received just before the battle, even though their replacements had been forwarded to the "Hellcats" by the Army Commander personally.

On the very day that the 12th convinced Army HQ to rid it of the black 827th Tank Destroyer Battalion, which had inadequately trained under inadequate officers, and had fallen down on the job during the January fighting, the division received twelve black platoons of infantry. All the men were volunteers from the supply services and some of them had taken cuts in rank for the "privilege" of becoming a combat soldier. But they had received very little training as infantry and none at all as armored infantry, who needed to engage in the tricky business of providing close support to tanks. Prejudiced by the poor performance of the 827th, 12th Armored was convinced that black replacements would fail. So it was that the blacks were placed in outfits which didn't like them under officers who expected the worst; and the prophecies became self-fulfilling.

So the huge army prepared for the assault to come. Bridging equipment was brought up to the front and concealed behind a permanent smoke screen. Field hospitals were moved just behind the artillery which was lined up gun next to gun for the massive bombardment that would start the offensive. Engineers were alerted on the River Saar to be on the lookout for enemy "battle swimmers" and floating mines. Every field was filled with armor. Along each road and track leading to the front there were huge piles of ammunition and supplies. All was controlled confusion, hectic but orderly, as the hours ticked away to D-Day; and all the while the grim-faced somber men of the Graves Registration details played their cards and drank the cheap French "dago red," waiting for the call to come. Soon there would be work—in fact, more than enough—for them to do.

* * *

At midnight on Thursday, March 15, 900 Lancaster bombers of the Royal Air Force came thundering in to bomb the main German communication centers at Homburg and Saarbrucken. As the great glowing identification signals—"Christmas Trees" the Germans called them—of the Pathfinders came floating down turning night into day, heralding the bombs to come, divisional artillery groups everywhere on the Seventh Army's front opened up. Suddenly the March night was hideous with the howl of the bombs, the crump of artillery shells exploding and the thump of German anti-aircraft guns vainly trying to ward off the bombers.

Manned by teenagers, many still in the uniform of the Hitler Youth, they tried their best. Indeed one of them, a gangling bespectacled youth of 15, Helmut Kohl, would boast nearly 50 years later to the *Wall Street Journal* that he had helped to shoot down American bombers. But there was little hope for the youthful fanatics this night. The odds against them were overwhelming.

Now everywhere along the American front, the whistles shrilled and that old familiar, frightening cry came floating down to the waiting platoons, "All right men, move out!" Up they rose and started walking forward, bent slightly like men braving a strong gale, bodies laden with equipment, hands suddenly damp, hearts fluttering with tension and apprehension. This was it.

For some, it was surprisingly easy. The veteran 45th Division had four companies across the River Blies within the hour. An hour later, two footbridges had been built over the water, and by daylight the 45th Division was back in Germany in force, for the first time since December 15, 1944. The 3rd Division was just as lucky. It deserved its luck, for by the time the war was over it would have experienced the most casualties of any unit in the ETO and would have won no less than 35 Congressional Medals of Honor. Just before the veteran formation jumped off through the positions of the 44th Division, "Iron Mike" O'Daniel told his troops, "The attack will be pressed with the ruthless vigor that has routed every enemy formation opposing the 3rd Division. All men will be brought to the highest possible offensive spirit prior to the jump-off. Bayonets will be sharpened!" In the event, bayonets weren't needed. Within 30 minutes of starting their attack, the 3rd was over the German border and rolling up the forward German positions.

The 100th Division's attack also went well. Back in December 1944, the 100th's first real mission had been an assault on the formidable French fortress town of Bitche. Then it had failed. Now, Century men took the town in their stride before the day had finished, their commander General Burress being granted the award of "First Citizen of Honor" in the 18th century community's history. Behind them the new boys of the 71st Division took over.

All the divisions of Brooks' VI Corps also achieved tactical surprise. Without too much difficulty, the four infantry divisions, the 42nd, 103rd, 36th and the 3rd French Algerian, supported by the 14th Armored, pushed forward and by the end of the first day had gained most of their objectives.

General Barnett's 63rd also did well. Despite their commanding general's fiery outpourings before the attack, they had been circumspect, outflanking the Siegfried Line positions wherever possible and thus suffering few casualties.

Having beaten off one German counterattack without too much difficulty, the division's forward companies now found themselves right in the middle of Hitler's vaunted "Westwall." There was only one catch, however. Their training stateside on how to tackle an enemy pillbox simply didn't work. The accepted method was to close up enemy firing ports by pouring a hail of fire at the slits while a bold soldier armed with a "polo charge"—20 pounds of TNT tied to a long stick—placed it next to the concrete. In theory this should blow a big hole in the stuff. But it didn't and the "Blood and Fire" men were puzzled. How were they ever going to get through this mass of pillboxes?

It was now that "The Private Who Cracked the Siegfried Line" made his appearance. First, however, an unknown corporal approached the CO of the Third Battalion of the Division's 254th Infantry. He said, "Sir, see that open pipe vent sticking out of the top of the pillbox? How about me dropping a grenade down it?"

"Best idea of the day," the Colonel agreed. So while the machine gunners poured fire at the slits of the nearest pillbox, the corporal worked his way forward with his grenades and dropped the first one down the vent. He was out of luck. Just like one of those devastating scenes in a pre-war Hollywood cartoon, the grenade came rolling out of the vent and landed directly at the corporal's feet. He fell down wounded and the attack stalled yet once again.

Now an ammunition carrier, bearing a Bangalore torpedo—a five-foot long drainpipe packed with TNT—approached the Battalion CO. "Sir," he said, "this won't roll out. Let me try with it."

Again the Colonel agreed. The private doubled forward as the machine guns cracked into angry life once more. He crawled behind the nearest pillbox, covered by the thick concrete from both enemy—and friendly—fire and slipped home the Bangalore torpedo, which the British had invented back in the 18th century for their colonial wars in India. It worked like a charm. As the 63rd Divisional History records: "The rear door of the bunker opened slowly like the door of a bank vault and two German soldiers staggered out; one had a burned face and other was bleeding from the nose. "Our comrades will have to be carried out," they said. And that was the truth of it.

As the infantry commander said jubilantly afterwards, "The private had done it! He had found the 'key' to the strongest part of the 'Westwall' . . . with a drainpipe filled with nine pounds of TNT."

Within the next 30 minutes five other bunkers were cracked and the 63rd was through. And the unknown "Private who cracked the Siegfried Line" had become a minor footnote in the history of World War Two.

The "Blood and Fire's" left neighbor, the 70th Division, was not so fortunate. They were running into a lot of trouble.

Brought to a halt by the minefields and the pillboxes of the Siegfried Line, they were pounded mercilessly by German artillery for which they presented a perfect target: hundreds of men caught out in the open with very little cover.

"Artillery, mortars, rockets . . . everything the Kraut possesses was thrown at us," Colonel Wallace Cheves, a regimental colonel, recalled after the war. "The earth was ripped apart and torn and the whole area pockmarked with shell holes. The trees were sheared down to shattered trunks. All along the lines we laid into the ground, trying to escape the flying shell fragments. A thick, dry, black, suffocating curtain of smoke hung over the whole area. Every few seconds, another shell would explode with a murderous red flash and send death-dealing shrapnel shrieking among the prostrate troops. It looked for a while as though the attack would end before it began."

But the troops held their ground, both the replacements and the veterans of "Operation Northwind." There was no panic. Like their fathers in the Argonne back in 1918, they stuck it out, knowing it was more dangerous to break and run over open fields, than to stay where they were.

A company armed with flame throwers and white phosphorous grenades rushed forward to aid their stalled comrades. But they, too, were hit by the murderous German fire. They flopped to the ground, panting hard. Lt. Wilson, in charge of the company, cried to his second-in-command, Lt. Beck: "Beck, this is costing us lives! We'd better keep moving."

As the lethal black eggs, mortar bombs, fell out of the sky all around them, they pushed on, blundering through some trees which were being snapped off by the explosions like matchsticks. Beck was hit by a red-hot piece of shrapnel. It set off the phosphorous grenade attached to his belt. It hissed into furious frightening life and ignited. Beck's whole body was enveloped instantly in a sheet of dazzling white flame. Men fell all around him. But Wilson could spare no time for the dead and dying. He had to save the living. He led the survivors across an open fire-break. They slammed through some barbed-wire entanglements and collapsed, lungs heaving like a cracked leather bellows, in the trees on the other side. Behind them the German mortar barrage continued to throw up an explosive curtain. They had got so far. But still the German line wasn't broken.

"I emptied my medical pouches that day," T/5 Jimmie Owen, a medic, recalled afterwards. "I tried to take care of the worst cases first, but there were so many, I hardly knew which ones needed help most. As soon as possible I got a line of walking wounded started back up the hill to the aid station. It was almost impossible to evacuate the serious cases. The casualty collecting point was in the edge of a wood all the way at the top of the ridge. About two trips up that hill with a litter was all a guy could stand."

Many straggled back of their own accord, faces blanched with shock, eyes wild, wide and unseeing. Some trembled and mumbled meaningless sounds. Others stared, as if angry at their torn limbs, wondering why this bloody indignity had been inflicted upon them. A few were brave beyond words. Medic Monroe Gable recalled later meeting Master Sergeant Lewis Ripley staggering up that steep hill to the aid station, "a crude bandage wrapped around a hole as big as an egg in his elbow. His face was ashen gray and he could hardly walk. But he refused to let me give him first aid or a shot of morphine. He told me to help the other boys first."

The slaughter went on. Tanks were thrown in to help. But the Germans, already knowing that their rear had been cut off by Patton's armored, fought back desperately. As Sergeant McNeely, who was with Lt. Wilson, recalled later, "Mortar and artillery rounds were coming in as fast as they could be shot out of guns. We wondered how long they could keep it up . . . and how long we could stand it. I knew we must be in closer now. Long bursts from our light machine guns and BARs cracked nearby—followed by answering bursts from enemy burp guns. There were a lot of pillboxes in front of us to be blown and a squad of engineers was following close behind us loaded down with high explosives. If one of their shape charges was ever hit, it would have cleaned up an area of about a hundred yards"—and the rest of what was left of Lt. Wilson's company. Patch applied more pressure on General Barnett, the commander of the 70th Division. It was three days now and the 70th had still not crossed the Saar River. Barnett responded by throwing in more men. Advancing with these new men, Sergeant Robert Kirk saw the casualties of the first attacks streaming back on foot or being carried on litters, moaning softly. "The sight of them was enough to take the heart right out of a guy," he recalled long afterward. But they pushed on all the same, hoping against hope that the Germans wouldn't spot them.

They did. As one of them, Private Tice, remembered, "It was then that the Krauts saw me. I knew it was coming as soon as I heard the croak of the Screaming Meemie off in the distance. Everybody else heard it, too, and just stopped in his tracks and wondered if it was coming our way."

It was.

"Then it hit. The first rounds struck a trench where the second squad was sitting . . . The whole squad was nearly buried alive in the eruption of earth." And so the slaughter went on.

Most of the men of Lt. Wilson's company called their executive officer "Little Boy Blue" behind his back. He seemed so young and such a textbook soldier, always correct, doing the right thing: military perfection itself. Now accompanied by Yale-educated PFC Corrigan, he attacked a German-held house and "the young Krauts poked a white flag out of the window," as Corrigan wrote afterward. "When the guys saw it they only got sore. Everyone was for moving in and cleaning them out."

But Wilson wouldn't have it. He wanted the Germans alive. So they called out for the Germans to surrender and they came rushing out: "Three of the most frightened men I have ever seen."

Now Wilson's survivors advanced on the next house. The

officer told Corrigan, "I want you to holler in there and tell them to come out and give themselves up."

Corrigan did so, but there was no answer. So they rushed the place, only to find that it was empty. Puzzled, the dirt-grimed, weary GIs tried to figure out where the firing was coming from. Just then Sergeant McNeely ran towards them. Two shots rang out. McNeely slammed to the debris-littered ground, blood pouring from his nose and mouth.

Now the GIs spotted where the firing was coming from. It was a small pillbox built into the side of the next house so that it was hardly noticeable. Wilson decided to attack. But how? The sniper in the pillbox, who seemed to be armed with a machine pistol, had them zeroed in perfectly. He was picking off every man who tried to get in or out of the house they held. Even as Wilson racked his brains for some form of an attack, one of the remaining combat engineers (Wilson had started off with 12) was hit in the hip and sank to the floor groaning.

In the end Wilson decided he could get a better picture of the situation from an upstairs window. Together with two GIs of his company, he clambered up the battered stairs only to see some unsuspecting soldiers from another unit beginning to dig in below. Ignoring the danger to himself, he leaned out of the window and shouted to them to run for the cover of the house.

Suddenly he jerked violently. He staggered back from the window. "My God, I'm hit!" he cried, voice full of disbelief. Abruptly he thrust out his legs, as if he were trying to brace himself, in a last desperate attempt to fight off death.

"Slap my face," he commanded, "Slap my face!"

A soldier dropped his rifle and struck him across the cheeks. It was no use. "Little Boy Blue" fell to the floor and with his last burst of energy slammed his boots against a heavy table, kicking it right across the room.

"When I went upstairs," Corrigan, who would never forget the "Little Boy Blue," recalled, "it was all over. I opened his shirt and found two small bullet holes just above his

heart. There was not a trace of blood on the outside. He must
have bled internally. I realized that sooner or later he would
have been killed but now that it had happened none of us
could quite believe it. I took the codes and overlays from his
pockets and looked at his AGO card. He was only 21 and as
he lay there he didn't look anywhere near that. His hair was
cropped close and he had no beard at all. He was just a kid,
yet he proved himself to be the driving factor of the whole
company. He was everything that could be expected of an
officer and soldier. When he died the spirit of the company
died with him . . ."

Just after midnight on March 20, 1945, the 70th Division finally started crossing the Saar River. Saarbrucken was
within grasping distance now. The men in the flat-bottom assault boats were tense and nervous. As the Divisional History records: "The silence grew eerie. The enemy was
obviously waiting to get their American targets within un-
missable range. Each man wondered: What to do when the
defenders opened up? No ground to shrink into . . . And if a
soldier fell or was thrown into the river, what were his
chances of survival?" Cautiously the first troops started to
land, waiting for the trap to be sprung. Nothing happened,
and "It took long, long minutes before the men realized that
there was no enemy there . . ." The advance patrols found an
empty pillbox and then they knew that the birds had flown.
Patton's bold dash for the Rhine had had its effect. The German High Command had ordered a general withdrawal from
the Saar-Palatinate Triangle before it was too late.
    The 70th Infantry Division had fired its last shot in anger.
Now it all ended in a note of farce as Lt. Theodore Heck,
who had been the first man to cross the Saar, returned to the
American side crawling along the wreckage of a bridge half-
submerged in the river. The staff of the 275th's Third Battalion were waiting for his report on the bank and one extended
a carbine to Heck to help him up the side. Accidentally it
went off and Heck reeled back wounded, but not seriously.

Just as he had been the first man to cross the Saar River, now he was the last man in the whole of the 70th Division to become a battlefield casualty.

But during its three months in combat the "Trailblazer Division," as it liked to call itself, had suffered a total of 8,201 casualties, 58 percent of its total strength.

Now General Patch's divisions were running wild in the Saar-Palatinate. On the same day that Saarbrucken fell to the 70th, the "Hellcats" of the 12th Armored Division were ordered to "Keep going. When you hit the Rhine, search for a bridge at Ludwigshafen intact." The race for the Rhine was on.

On that same day the 3rd Division captured Zweibrucken. A day later its old running mate, the 45th, captured Kaiser-lautern, eventually to become the US Army's biggest overseas garrison outpost: "K-Town," with its "GI bars" and five dollar whores, as it would become known to succeeding generations of GIs. By that time the 42nd, 103rd, 36th and 14th Armored Divisions had slugged their way through the last of the Siegfried Line; though on that day, March 21st, it took the 36th all day to eliminate eight German strongpoints. The Texans saturated the obstinate pillboxes with grenades, rockets and burning gasoline. To no avail. Finally the engineers resorted to special explosive charges on the roofs known as "beehives." They did the job and it was just hard luck to the Germans that they had not surrendered while they had the time.

The state of the Saarland cities shocked even the hardened veterans of the war in Italy and France. In Zweibrucken, the 3rd found the entire business district had been razed to the ground by the years of bombing. Only 5,000 of the pre-war population of 37,000 still remained, hiding in cellars and basements. Rubble and ruins were everywhere. There was no water, gas or light. Sewage was taken care of by open pits. Everywhere there were "displaced persons," armed for the most part, eager to take their revenge on the Herrenvolk, raping, looting, destroying.

Homburg was even worse. There, fires still raged. There were dead horses and human beings on all sides. Frauleins impatient to be "raped" importuned the GIs on all sides. "For an extra bar of chocolate I could have had her mother too!" they boasted, these young conquerors, whose rations of coffee, cigarettes and candy now became the new German currency, buying anything, including honor.

As General Frederick of the 45th Division stated in a message to General Barcus, commander of the XII Tactical Air Force which supported the Seventh Army, "It is difficult to describe the devastation which . . . the fighter bombers have wrought. So intense has been the attack that scarcely a man-made thing exists in their wake; it is even difficult to find buildings suitable for CPs. This is the scorched earth." It was and it would take the United States several billion dollars in the form of Marshall Aid to start something growing on that same scorched earth. But that was in the future. At present in this third week of March 1945, the Top Brass was not concerned with the destruction of German cities and the plight of the German people. Their eyes were fixed firmly on the Rhine, as everywhere the Seventh's divisions began to close up to that river. Of course, they all knew that the main attack across the Rhine was to be under the command of Field Marshal Montgomery, leading the Second British and Ninth American Armies further north at Wesel. But they knew, too, that such consideration didn't bother Bradley and, in particular, Patton. The two generals wanted to commit as many US troops on the other side of the Rhine as possible. They feared the possibility of Montgomery being in sole charge of the final offensive on the far bank of the great river. If they could cross they would do so whether it fitted into the grand strategy of the war or not.

Patton burned to put one over on that "little fart" Montgomery, who had been anathema to him ever since Sicily. Now while the Seventh reorganized, he did just that. On the night of March 22/23, completely without Eisenhower's approval, he crossed the Rhine at the little wine-growing township of Oppenheim. With a force of six battalions (at first

Patton had thought of sending his infantry across in twos in the Army's Piper Cub spotter planes; fortunately he changed his mind in time) he caught the German defenders completely by surprise. At first light he was pouring troops across, again without approval from higher headquarters.

Now Patton felt like a mischievous child who sensed he ought to be punished for having done something naughty. For hadn't he spoiled the impact of Monty's great set-piece crossing of the Rhine, which would be attended by Eisenhower and no less a person than that old war-horse Churchill himself?

Thus it was that he decided to telephone Bradley at breakfast time to let him know what he had just done. As Bradley, who was drinking his morning coffee, listened, he said in an unusually subdued voice for him, "Brad, don't tell anyone, but I'm across."

Bradley nearly choked on his coffee. "Well, I'll be damned!" he exclaimed. "You mean the Rhine?"

"Sure am," Patton replied. "I sneaked a division across last night. But there are so few Krauts around there they don't know it yet. So don't make any announcements. We'll keep it secret until we see how it goes, eh?"

Bradley agreed.

But the "secret" lasted exactly two hours. At the Third Army's morning briefing for the Press, Colonel Stillman of Patton's staff told the assembled newspapermen, obviously referring to Montgomery's tremendous preparations for his own crossing yet to come, "Without benefit of aerial bombardment, ground smoke, artillery preparations and airborne assistance, the Third Army, at 2200 hours, Thursday evening, March 22, 1945, crossed the Rhine River." On the same day that Montgomery's attack was launched at Wesel, Patton himself crossed the river on a pontoon bridge near Oppenheim. On the other bank he appeared to slip, steadying himself with both hands. When he rose again, those hands were filled with German earth. "Thus William the Conqueror," he proclaimed for the benefit of the watching

correspondents, and explained that the Norman King had
made the same significant, symbolic gesture when he had
first set foot on English soil in 1066.

The general certainly knew his history. But in his private
story he recorded a more earthy comment for that day.
"Drove to the river and went across on the pontoon bridge,
stopping in the middle to take a piss in the Rhine . . ."

So the Seventh Army lost out again. It would be the last of
the four American armies in the ETO to cross the Rhine, and
once more that crossing went virtually unnoticed.

General Patch, however, got on with the job of planning
the crossing, as he usually did, without fuss and without any
apparent resentment at the fact that the efforts of his men
would go totally unsung. On the same day that Patton "took
a piss in the Rhine," he ordered his two most veteran formations to prepare for the assault crossing. His 45th Division
would force a crossing north of Worms, while his Third Division would do the same to the south of the medieval town,
where Martin Luther had once stood up against the might of
the Catholic Church.

As soon as the veterans were safely across and had
formed a bridgehead, they would be followed by the 63rd
Division, which would join up with the 45th, and the 44th,
which would assist the 3rd. The 106th Cavalry Group would
also be attached to the "Rock of the Marne" Division.

By this time intelligence had worked out that the Rhine at
the places selected for crossing was 1,000 feet wide and
some 17 feet deep. The current was swift and there was little
cover on the American-held bank. Hence all troops had to be
moved up under the cover of darkness.

Intelligence, however, had little idea of enemy strength
on the other side. Remnants of an estimated 22 German divisions were believed to have escaped over the Rhine in the
area, but intelligence guessed there could be no more than
50 men per river-front kilometer and few guns except those
of the flak used in a ground role. This seemed confirmed by

a bold patrol carried out by four men of the 45th's 180th Infantry Regiment. They paddled across the Rhine at midnight on March 24/25 and spent half an hour on the enemy shore. They found no mines, no wire and no gun emplacements. There were enemy troops in the vicinity who they thought had spotted them but the Germans did not fire. The news encouraged Patch. He ordered that D-Day would be March 26. The two divisions, the 3rd and 45th, would make their assault at 2:30 in the morning.

While all this was going on, General de Gaulle in Paris fretted at all the glory being earned by Britons, Canadians and Americans on the Rhine. Once in the 18th and 19th centuries, the Rhine had been France's own river, used as a border between *la belle* France and the Boche. Now, it seemed, France had no part to play in its conquest. That was something which could not be tolerated. That day he signalled Lattre de Tassigny, whose forces had been on the Rhine now since November 1944, "My Dear General, you must cross the Rhine even if the Americans are not agreeable and even if you have to cross it rowing boats. It is a matter of the greatest national interest. Karlsruhe and Stuttgart await you—even if they do not want you."

Sensitive about his own and France's prestige and position in the world, de Gaulle wanted the world to see that he and France were playing a full part in these world-shaking events. True, he had once stated privately that the Anglo-Americans should be allowed to do the fighting against the Germans and be killed, if necessary, doing so; France would need all the soldiers she could muster to deal with the problems of the post-war world. But now he was prepared to sacrifice French lives for the sake of the publicity a crossing would gain for France.

De Gaulle's order placed de Lattre in a quandary. Devers, the Sixth Army Group Commander, had been reluctant to have the French First Army getting in the way of the assault on the Rhine. Accordingly he had issued neither bridging equipment nor boats to the French. Besides, Stuttgart was in the zone of operations allotted to Patch's Seventh. Devers wanted no repetition of the problems that had occurred over Strasbourg. Stuttgart would be taken by Patch's men.

Wondering how the problem could be solved, "King Jean" handed it over to one of his corps commanders. He was portly, heavily-mustached General Monsabert, whom de Lattre ordered to attempt a crossing opposite the small German town of Speyer. Two years before, Monsabert had loyally supported Petain in his post as a divisional general in North Africa; he had rallied to the Anglo-American cause only when it seemed the former were about to beat the Germans. Thereafter he had fought in Italy and now in France. Like so many of his fellow senior commanders in the French First Army, he was not a dedicated Gaullist. He suspected that de Gaulle was something of an upstart. But Monsabert was French and he knew the importance of a French Rhine crossing for France. The problem was—where was he going to get the assault boats he needed?

In the end, Monsabert turned to General Patch and was promised that he would soon receive a number of rubber dinghies. They had no outboard motors, no steering and were not as sturdy as those used by the Americans. But they were boats and they could be paddled across—when they arrived. Now Karlsruhe and Stuttgart awaited the French, it seemed, and another major Franco-American clash was in the making.

Under a scudding moon, obscured every now and again by fleeting clouds, the 3rd Division moved up the Rhine, lugging the heavy assault boats with them. At regular intervals, German mortar bombs landed with a thud and burst of angry red flame among their tanks. For the enemy had already spotted what was afoot. The 3rd was not going to be lucky like Patton's 5th Division, which had crossed virtually unopposed three days before. The 3rd would have to fight its way across.

At precisely eight minutes to two, the whole of the divisional artillery opened up. With a great baleful, banshee-like howl, a couple of hundred shells sped across the glowing water right onto the German positions. For the next 38 minutes the cannon would fire an amazing 10,000 shells at the enemy; more shells than the whole of the US Army had used in an average year before the war.

Still the Germans continued to fire back. One German incendiary shell hit a barn in the vicinity of the 7th Infantry Regiment's CP. In an instant the whole area was alight. Night was turned into day. Unfortunately for the 7th Infantry that lucky German shell illuminated their crossing point. Now the men and the boats were outlined a stark black against the lurid flames. The 7th were sitting ducks.

As H-Hour approached, the infantry crouched at the water's edge with their boats being pounded by heavy German fire. Shells exploded everywhere. Mortar bombs flung up huge spouts of wild water. Tracer zipped across the river in a lethal Morse code. Many of the assault boats were shot to pieces even before they could be launched. But the men persisted. When the whistles shrilled, they rushed forward and slapped the boats into the water. The engineers started the outboard motors and they were off.

Boats capsized. Here and there motors died on the engineers and the men had to paddle frantically with their hands or rifle butts, trying to find their way through smoky, murky gloom; and all the time the Germans kept up their barrage.

The survivors of the first wave struggled ashore to run straight into a heavy concentration of mortar fire. Here and there in the bright moonlight that now illuminated the fields ahead, they could spot lurking German self-propelled guns. Still the men of the 3rd pushed on, heading for the high bank of the *autobahn* to their front, men falling wounded and dying all around, as the German MG 42s dug in on the embankment swung back and forth mowing the GIs down. On the 3rd's sector of the Rhine, a full-scale battle was developing.

The 45th was luckier. As they started to cross, a heavy spiralling fog descended upon their area, covering the moon and concealing the hundreds of men milling around the assault boats. But as soon as the boats started up, the Germans were alerted. They commenced probing the mist with machine guns. All the time flares shot into the air, trying to find the oncoming Americans.

But on the whole the "Thunderbirds" were lucky until they reached the opposite shore. Here the flak guns, used in a ground role, found them. They walked straight into a glowing wall of 20mm incendiary shells pumped at them from the quadruple flak guns at a tremendous rate. Hurriedly the GIs spread out, dashing to left and right, carving out a bridge-head with their bayonets and BARs.

By daylight, in spite of the fact that the engineer battalion lost half its boats in the crossing, one battalion of artillery and two thirds of the 45th's combat troops were across. Hastily the Tac-Air Force came to the aid of the infantry. Every 20 minutes now a section of eight planes appeared over the bridgehead. Controlled by radio from below, they bombed and covered the advancing infantrymen for 20 minutes before being relieved on the second by a further flight of eight fighter-bombers. They were assisted by a massive force of 1,500 bombers from the US 8th Air Force's airfields in Britain. The Liberators and Flying Fortresses were ordered to knock out 18 German airfields in the Frankfurt region from which the feared German jets were known to operate. Covered by British fighter-planes, they did just that. Thus, the Luftwaffe, which in these last weeks of the war was becoming more daring, even suicidal, knowing that their jets could outfly and outrun every known Allied fighter, was kept at arm's length.

By the evening of that first day, the 45th had taken all its objectives and had reached the line set down for it by Corps HQ before D-Day. But the 3rd continued to find the going tough. Indeed it would be three days before the 3rd felt its crossing points were secure enough to remove the smoke screen which had covered them during that period. Tanks were sent to help the hard-pressed infantry, but only half of them reached the other side.

But the American pressure was telling and more and more troops were beginning to cross after the first waves. By the 27th, the 44th and 12th Armored had crossed unopposed.

Two days later the 63rd and 10th Armored were over, too, to be followed on the last day of March by the 4th and 42nd Divisions.

By that time it was clear that the Seventh Army was over the Rhine in force and that it was there to stay. Already Patch's staff were beginning to work out the problems that would face them in the future when they attacked all those river-lines which lay in the Army's path—the Main, the Neckar, the Danube, etc.

But while the Seventh's staff considered the future, General Monsabert worried about the present. All that day, the last day of March 1945, the portly commander with his flowing moustache waited for the promised rubber dinghies to arrive. The formation which was to make the crossing once the boats arrived, the 3rd Regiment de Tirailleurs Algeriens, knew that not only were the eyes of their corps commander upon them but those of General de Gaulle himself. He would not brook much more delay.

In the end the Americans appeared. With them they brought one single rubber dinghy! The reaction of the hard-bitten colonial soldiers is not recorded. But honor had to be satisfied. The whole of France was waiting for a French crossing. So a certain Sergeant Bertout and nine of his dark-skinned Algerian riflemen clambered into the boat and laboriously rowed themselves across the Rhine. It is doubtful whether the Germans were even aware that the French were crossing the Rhine for the first time since the days of Napoleon. Or perhaps they didn't take the "invasion" seriously. At all events they did not react until daybreak. Then they started shelling a second French crossing at the small town of Germersheim.

There the crossing turned into a near-tragedy. Only three boats reached the opposite side of the Rhine and the "bridgehead" of 50 meters by 150 meters was held only because French artillery managed to pound German positions all day long and prevent the Boche from counterattacking.

Eventually the neighboring American corps commander, General Brooks, took pity on the French. He agreed to let 20

French vehicles cross the Rhine, using the US bridge at Mannheim.

The wheel had nearly turned the full circle. The scruffy bunch of one-time "collabos," renegades, ex-Maquis and North African colonial soldiers had managed to do what that haughty aristocratic Leclerc had failed to do back in November 1944. They had crossed the Rhine; aptly enough the date was April 1, 1945—April Fool's Day.

Some time later the French at Speyer, while their comrades were burning and plundering their way through the Black Forest heading for Stuttgart, started to erect a monument to Sergeant Bertout and his nine North Africans, who had crossed the Rhine in that lone rubber dinghy. It was in the form of a stone pillar, the height of a man. It bore the palm twig of the French Army, a curved scimitar and some letters in Arabic, perhaps to symbolize French and Algerian cooperation. Chiseled into the belly of the stone was the inscription:

Le 31 mars 1945 le 3d Rgt de Tiralleurs
Algeriens franchit le Rhin
L'operation fut executee par le group Franc
du Regiment le Ier Battaillon et les Sappeurs
de la 83 I Cie

It was to be a lasting tribute to the glory of France, and naturally, in addition, to General Charles de Gaulle.

That March thousands of Britons, Canadians and Americans had died in the attempt to cross the Rhine. Yet for their effort and self-sacrifice there is no single monument save for those rows and rows of white headstones in those quiet green cemeteries, such as the ones at St. Avold and Epinal dedicated to the dead of the Seventh Army. Along the whole length of the Rhine there is no trace of their passing, those young men of 50 years ago. Only at Speyer does that one pillar exist. Of all the nations involved, the French, ironically enough, are making sure that "la gloire de France" will be remembered when all else is forgotten.

6

END RUN

April–May 1945

"Observe, you glorious men of the Seventh Army, our efforts and exploits are not unrecognized in our country. To you, who have done the fighting, I send my deepest and most patriotic thanks."

— GENERAL ALEXANDER PATCH, May 1945

IT was a crazy time. The British called it "swanning"; the Americans called it that "rat race." Both phrases meant that Allied armor had an almost free run on the other side of the Rhine. The Shermans and the new US Pershing tanks, which finally had a gun to match that of the German tanks, no longer fanned out over the countryside as they had done in Alsace. Instead they went straight down one or two parallel roads, bypassing towns and villages, leaving the infantry to mop up behind them. And if the infantry couldn't do so without too many casualties, TAC fighter-bombers or the artillery were whistled up to blast the Germans to smithereens. If innocent civilians got hurt in the bombardment, then it was just "tough titty."

For Patch's tankers of the 10th, 12th, 14th and the veterans of the Sixth's Armored Divisions, this type of tactic involved the reconnaissance elements crawling forward, "daring" the enemy to reveal his position by firing at them. At the point there would be a lone tank or armored car, linked by radio to another one half a mile behind, which in turn was in visual contact with the armored infantry in their half-tracks a little further back. Sooner or later the unfortunate handful of men at the point would run into a roadblock covered by mines, panzerfausts, the deadly one-shot German rocket launcher, and machine guns. Sometimes there might even be some fanatical last-ditch flak crew using their 88mm in the ground role.

Then the fun would start, and the men at the point would die. Immediately, the second tank would alert the armored infantry. While it fired at the road block, they would hurry up in their half-tracks, roll expertly over the sides of their vehicles and fan out left and right for the assault. As the BBC correspondent with Patch's Army commented, with typical British understatement, "Being in the lead tank is one of the war's most uncomfortable jobs."

But "swanning" or the "rat race" brought with it problems too. There was, of course, the ever present problem of supply: how to get fuel, food and ammunition up dangerous roads, where bunches of fanatical Hitler Youth teenagers and stragglers from the SS would ambush any "soft" vehicle they spotted, especially if it were on its own.

Control was a headache, as well. By now superior commanders had lost contact with many of their far-ranging subunits. Previously the men had mostly lived and fought in empty countryside, their bed for the night a hole in the ground or at the best a shattered barn. Now they were in German villages and towns, surrounded by the locals who did not want to or didn't have the time to flee. Here, in enemy territory, they did just as they pleased. The only control now was in the hands of noncoms and junior officers.

As US General Franklin Davis, then a combat major, wrote long afterwards, "There were new benefits to being victors. They were conquering enemy territory now instead of liberating the countries of the Allies. They often slept in houses, apartments, taverns, hotels, even sumptuous villas. Once a town fell to them, their billeting parties had only to select a good spot, tell the German inhabitants 'Raus!' and they were in."

Discipline became difficult. Many GIs violated the orders against looting. They stole and mailed back home cameras, silverware, assorted bric-a-brac. Some of the more knowing and astute sent to US addresses fortunes in easily saleable treasures, such as old masters and the like. Incidents of rape began to mount, totalling 500 a month from March onwards, though there were, of course, many more which never came before a court martial.

Many of the young soldiers were naturally sickened by the behavior of the minority, who looted, wrecked and seduced, using their cigarettes, coffee and candy to entrap impoverished German women.

In Private Atwell's section of medics, for example, there was a supply sergeant, Joe Mortara, who constantly was trying to tempt German women to go to bed with him. Holding out a half a bar of chocolate he would murmur enticingly, "schlafen . . . schlafen . . ."

"Now that's a goddam shame," protested Phil, one of Atwell's buddies, "to tempt women with little kids who haven't enough to eat."

One morning—the same morning that it was announced that there would be a fine of $65 for any GI even speaking to a German outside the line of duty—the medics lined up to receive an orange each, the first fresh fruit they had seen for months. They were watched by a thin, sickly woman holding a skinny baby in her arms. Phil took his precious orange and gave it to the woman, saying, "They want to fine me, court martial me, let them. I don't care who they are and what they've done. It's a woman and a child and they're hungry."

Later that same day when the supply sergeant tried his old trick with the chocolate, Phil exploded. He wrapped a bundle of goodies and gave them to the skinny woman.

Joe Mortara was not pleased. "Hey," he exclaimed, "what's the matter with you? Here I am, I got the chocolate bar all ready and you come along and spoil everything."

"I'm sorry Joe," Phil answered, "but I'm going to continue spoiling it for you. If they want to go with you voluntarily, well and good. That's their business. If it's through hunger, no!"

Mumbling to himself, Mortara put away the half of the Hershey bar, as Atwell noted, "for use some other time . . ."

At first it seemed all too easy. Wine, women and song. On March 30, elements of the 63d Division moved into "Old Heidelberg," one of them, George Powles, singing a song he had learned at his mother's knee. "Oh Heidelberg, dear Heidelberg. Thy name we'll never forget. That golden haze of student days, will live with us yet." Hitler had not allowed the old university town to declare itself an "Open City," although it housed 30,000 German wounded. But its citizens no longer had a desire to die for "Folk, Fatherland and Führer." They negotiated a surrender with the Americans who advanced through the medieval university city, doing a little bit of looting and sightseeing at the historic red sandstone castle with its students' jail and huge wine barrel, which could hold, so it was said, 50,000 gallons. Unfortunately it was empty, but there was word that up at the road at Neckargemund there was a huge warehouse which contained case upon case of champagne. A little sniper fire and the odd machine gun were brushed aside hastily and the men of the First Battalion, 253d Infantry, who discovered the warehouse, declared the champagne was the best "lemon soda pop" they had ever drunk.

That night the 862d Field Artillery Battalion heard about the Neckargemund warehouse. Hastily they filled up an ammunition trailer with bottle after bottle of champagne and rolled on to their next frontline position. En route the convoy was shelled by the Germans and unluckily one shell struck the trailer carrying all the champagne. Those in the convoy who didn't know there was no ammunition but booze in the trailer dived frantically for cover, waiting for the huge explosion that had to come. But no, only a "gigantic mound of foam and froth," as the Divisional History records, "served to mark the previous location of the trailer." The battalion went dry that night.

By now the road from Heidelberg to Neckargemund had become known as "the champagne trail" and it wasn't long before divisional HQ was informed. The commander, General Hibbs, acted decisively. That very night divisional HQ was to move from Heidelberg to make room for the headquarters of the Seventh Army, and Hibbs was determined that the "canteen commandos" of Army HQ were not going to get their hands on his "boys' booze." He decreed, therefore, that every enlisted man should receive one bottle of bubbly and every officer two.

Shortly, thereafter, the divisional HQ moved out, heading for Aglasterhausen, and as the Divisional History records: "The route from Neckargemund to Aglasterhausen, where the division was headquartered, was clearly marked by empty champagne bottles along the side of the road."

But it wasn't all "frowleins," loot and "lemon soda pop" as March gave way to April. Here and there groups of Germans, military and civilian alike, stopped running and made a fight of it. By the last days of March, the 45th and the 3rd Divisions had crossed the next river line in their path, that of the River Main, quite easily. But the city of Aschaffenburg on the other side proved a very tough nut to crack for the 45th. So far in their rapid 57-kilometer advance from the Rhine, the Division had encountered only tame German civilians, "dead-faced women and old men who glared with unfathomable bitterness or simply looked blankly, while the great serpentine stream of American men and vehicles passed." But at Aschaffenburg, the civilians, old men and young boys, joined in the actual defense of their town.

For six long, hard days the whole division was engaged in house-to-house fighting, encountering not only enemy soldiers of the 36th German Infantry Division but also "boys of sixteen and seventeen, thoroughly indoctrinated with the theory that it was glorious to seek death for the Fatherland." When the 45th granted them that "glory," they refused to surrender and had to be killed in their foxholes.

On the second day of the assault, men of the Division's 157th Infantry actually faced a German counterattack. It took an hour of bitter hand-to-hand fighting before they were beaten off and the GIs could push on, using the bayonet and hand grenades in the ruined streets as their principal weapons. Artillery and tanks were of little use in the grim street fighting that raged in Aschaffenburg.

As one GI who took part remembered, "House cleaning always means sudden death for somebody. It means kicking in a door and lobbing in a grenade and then running in to see who's still alive and who wants to surrender and who wants to die. Then it means yelling upstairs for the bastards to come down and give up. If nobody answers, it means creeping upstairs to double check, throwing up another grenade, praying like hell that there isn't another Jerry with a waiting grenade hiding in the bedroom or the closet or the toilet.

"And then one house is cleared, there's another house and another house and another . . ."

There were indeed. Major von Lambert, the German commandant of Aschaffenburg, now organized old men, women and girls to fill out the thinning ranks of the defenders. They hurled grenades from rooftops of the second stories of the shattered houses at the Americans advancing cautiously below. The "Thunderbirds," hardened now, their hearts full of hate, shot them down just as they would have done any soldier in enemy uniform.

A frustrated General Frederick, commanding the division, asked for air support, in an attempt to blast the stubborn defenders from the rubble. The commander of the P-47 fighter-bomber squadron said he would have a go, but due to the close proximity of American troops in the shattered burning town he was only prepared to use 50-caliber ammunition, not bombs.

The attack didn't work. So this time the P-47s picked out specific targets, such as the town's Gestapo HQ, which the 45th believed was being used to direct Aschaffenburg's defense, and went in with rockets and light bombs, braving a wall of angry white 20mm flak to pinpoint their target. For the very first time napalm, which hitherto had been reserved for the Pacific war against Orientals, was employed against white German civilians. It was indicative of just how serious the situation was in the city on the Main River. Indeed, earnest consideration was already being given at Eisenhower's HQ to whether civilians found bearing weapons should not be shot out of hand without trial. In the event, they were. Men, women and children, especially when they were acting as snipers, were mercilessly eliminated by angry GIs.

Confirmation that the town was going to be held to the last round and the last man was given by prisoners taken by the 45th. According to these POWs, when individual groups of the defenders attempted to surrender, their leaders were strung up in the streets by the SS from the nearest lamp-post. Thereupon, a placard was placed round their chest bearing such legends as "Here Died a Defeatist" or "Death to All Traitors." One Hungarian POW stated that when he and some comrades had attempted to bolt from the death trap, most of the group had been mown down by SS on the lookout for those trying to flee. Right to the very end, Hitler's "New Order" was living up to its chilling reputation for cold-blooded cruelty.

On the third day of the assault on Aschaffenburg, General Frederick gave up. He ordered two of his regiments to continue their advance, while his third, the 157th, was left to maintain what now amounted to a siege of the town.

By now the 45th's veterans of the Italian campaign were calling the place "Cassino-on-the-Main," after that bloody Monte Cassino in Italy which stopped the Allied armies dead for nearly three months. But the end was in sight. On Easter Sunday, a "Thunderbird" soldier who had been captured earlier on, returned through enemy lines accompanied by a German captain. The latter bore a note from Major von Lambert.

The fanatical commander was weakening. He said in his note that he would negotiate a surrender if the Americans would send an emissary to his headquarters.

Colonel O'Brien, the commander of the 157th, refused to bargain. He had had quite enough of von Lambert. He told the German to tell his superior that if Lambert did not immediately have white flags waved over his HQ the artillery bombardments and aerial attacks would be intensified at once. Surrender of the garrison at Aschaffenburg would be unconditional. The glum captain went back the way he had come and a few minutes later white flags were being flown over the battered castle which had been Major von Lambert's HQ. Aschaffenburg had fallen and the six-day siege was over. But the Germans' resistance had shaken the American top brass. Even the Secretary of War, Henry L. Stimson, was informed of the siege and told the press that "There is a lesson with respect to this in Aschaffenburg. These Nazi fanatics used the visible threat of two hangings to compel German soldiers and civilians to fight for a week." He commented that he must now warn the enemy that "their only choice is immediate surrender or the destruction of the Reich city by city."

By the second week of April, 1945, the rat race had ceased and it seemed that Stimson's grim warning was going to be put into effect. German resistance appeared to be stiffening. Virtually every larger town in the path of the Seventh Army, as it plunged deeper into southern Germany, was defended, some of them to the last.

Heilbronn was held, for instance, by the usual mixed-bag of Wehrmacht, Volkssturm, Hitler Youth, and a handful of SS. But under determined leadership, these mixed units, some of them made up of "soldiers" as young as 14 and as old as 60, fought back fiercely against the might of a 16,000-man-strong US division, in this case the 100th Infantry. Not only did they defend the city, but they also counterattacked and almost threw the "Centurymen" back across the Neckar River from whence they had come. With the help of part of the 10th Armored Division, the Americans managed to hang on. But the subsequent assault into the city itself took another three days of bitter house-to-house fighting.

The Hitler Youth, some of them still in the black short pants of the organization, were the worst. They fought to the very end or until they could fight no more. One company commander, Lt. Slade of the 100th Division's 397th Infantry, remembers how, after a terrific mortar barrage on their positions, the group of Hitler Youth holding up his attack finally broke. Crying "kamerad" they flung up their arms and ran to his line, as their officers fired shots into their backs, killing six of the youths. Thirty-six of them, however, made it, "weeping, bleeding, screaming hysterically." "They wasn't nuthin' but kids," Slade commented afterwards. "Before the mortars had hit them, they had fought like demons, but now they were only a disorganized mass of 14 to 17-year-olds . . ." And sometimes, with the "1000 Year Reich" visibly falling apart and with only six more weeks of life to go, the Germans actually beat the Seventh Army and forced them to retreat.

General Morris' 10th Armored Division had taken the German town of Crailsheim without much difficulty in that second week of April. Then the town, located 40 miles southwest of Nuremburg, which was the next objective of the Seventh Army, was counterattacked by two groups of SS troopers. The first force was 500 men strong, the second 700 men strong, and both belonged to the best division still fighting on this section of the German front: the 17th Panzer Grenadier Division.

Supported by 25 jets, the SS succeeded by the second day in surrounding the town and cutting off all supply routes save one; and this was under constant attack. As Richard Johnston, the *New York Times* correspondent, was told by General Morris when the former said he was going to visit the trapped 10th Armored men at Crailsheim, "Start like a bat out of hell and keep going faster."

But Johnston failed to make it, as did all Morris' attempts to send up supplies that particular day. So a force of 50 C-47 cargo planes were assembled to bring in supplies and take out the wounded. Just before they were due to land at Crailsheim, three Me-109s zoomed in at tree-top height, machine guns and cannon blazing. But by now the "Tigers," as the men of the 10th called themselves, had anti-aircraft guns in position. They and the deck machine guns of the 10th's tanks opened up on all sides. One of the Messerschmitts seemed momentarily to falter in its strafing run. Abruptly the pilot lost control and it slammed to the ground in a great burst of flame and exploding metal. "Get that pilot's name and address!" one of the gunners exclaimed in great glee, as the two surviving planes broke off their attack and fled.

Later that same day the transport fleet landed safely, without losing a single plane, while C-47s circled above them warily; for the landing strip the 10th had selected was only 1,000 yards from the German line. They brought up gasoline and ammunition just in time, for shortly before dawn the next day, 600 soldiers of the German Second Mountain Division attacked to the southwest and managed to penetrate into the town for a few hours. That attack was followed as soon as darkness had fallen over the burning town by a night assault from the north. This time 600 more Germans were involved and they were supported by lumbering heavy self-propelled guns, their long hanging tubes spitting fire.

Red-headed, fiery Major T. Hankins, who commanded the force holding Crailsheim, told the correspondents who had now managed to get through, "We fought them off twice and we can fight 'em off again!" Privately, however, the stubby commander prayed that 63rd Infantry Division, which was some 15 miles away from the town, would hurry up and relieve them. The "Tigers," despite all their bold talk, couldn't hold out much longer, in what the newspapers were now calling "Bastogne No. 2."

All that day Crailsheim was attacked from the air, with the German jets streaking in at tremendous speed, leaving the Tigers' gunners helpless. On the ground, meanwhile, the SS pelted the American positions with a deadly, relentless mortar barrage.

That day a Lt. Max Schoenberg, who had been bombed out of two command posts in the last three days, told correspondent A. Goldberg of the Associated Press, "We are sweating this out now." His commander, Hankins, butted in to say, "If they don't throw any more at us than they have over the last two nights, I think we have enough to hold them. They have been attacking in at least six company strength and they are tough SS babies of all ages, but mostly 20 to 25." But that wasn't to be. Hankins wouldn't beat the SS.

For in the end the Seventh Army decided that Crailsheim was not worth the effort. The one supply road that still remained open was constantly being mined and ambushed, taking a heavy toll of truck and jeep drivers. So it was decided that Crailsheim should be abandoned. On the night of April 11th, while the German soldiers watched in relieved incredulity, the last Shermans of Hankins' task force began pulling out of the shattered city. The "Tigers" had been beaten for a while.

On April 15, five days after the "Tigers" evacuated Crailsheim, Eisenhower announced his final strategy for what was left of the Third Reich. According to the dictates laid down by the new plan, Devers' Sixth Army Group would drive south and southeast into western Austria, making its main efforts at first on the right wing of the Seventh Army. Here the objective would be to trap the German Nineteenth Army in the Black Forest. After fighting the Nineteenth ever since the previous August, Patch's men were now going to deliver the death blow.

In order to ensure that Devers could execute this task (and after the battles for Aschaffenberg, Heibronn and Crailsheim, Eisenhower felt the Sixth Army Group still had some tough fighting ahead of it), the Supreme Commander offered him all SHAEF's reserve divisions, plus the First Allied Air Army and the newly arrived 13th Airborne Division. This could be used in an airborne assault to speed the main effort south of Stuttgart, if necessary. For the first time since its creation, the US Seventh Army was being granted maximum resources; and Patch knew why. His army would be advancing into the rugged mountains of Bavaria and Austria.

There, Intelligence had believed since January 1945 that the Nazis had been constructing their "National Redoubt." American spies, working from Switzerland, had furnished information that the Germans had been moving men and material into those remote mountains in large numbers and quantities. There, underground factories and extensive fortifications had been built, that would be self-sufficient and defended by thousands of fanatical SS men. There was even talk that it was up there in the snow-tipped peaks that the Nazis were constructing yet more war-winning secret weapons, ever more deadly than the V-2s which had still been battering London up until March 29, 1945. Later it was found out that "National Redoubt" was a figment of Dr. Goebbels, the Nazi Minister of Propaganda's, lively imagination and the work of smart Swiss journalists, out to earn a quick buck.

But that was later. Now it seemed imperative to General Patch that he must take the key city of Nuremberg before he entered the mountains. For Nuremberg was not just any German city. It was, in Nazi eyes, a shrine to National Socialism, "the City of the Movement," as it had called itself ever since the first annual Nazi Party rally had been held there. Why, every year the Führer had attended the gigantic Party rally, stage-managed by no less a person than Dr. Goebbels himself, and spoken to the hysterical, enthusiastic throng of his supporters in the "Adolf Hitler Platz."

Capture Nuremberg, American Intelligence reasoned, and the capture might just take the heart out of those young fanatics preparing to fight to the last in the mountains. Intelligence knew something else too. On April 20, it would be Hitler's 56th birthday. What a blow it would be for him and his followers, if that city, which symbolized his whole rotten creed, fell into American hands on that very same day.

After two to three years of intensive bombing, Nuremberg had been surrounded by a formidable ring of 88 mm flak cannon, which would now be used in a ground role. With their artillery in place, the Germans now prepared to defend the "City of the Movement" with elements of two crack divisions, the Second Mountain and the 17th SS Panzer Grenadier, plus Gruppe Grafenwoehr. This was two battalions strong and armed with 35 tanks taken from the Grafenwoehr Proving Grounds, where, ironically enough, thousands of young Seventh Army soldiers would receive their combat training in years to come.

It was a sizeable force, even for the two veteran divisions, the 45th and 3rd, which Patch committed to the attack. It was made more formidable, however, by the man who was at the heart of the city's defense. He was Gauleiter Karl Holz, a sulky-faced, opinionated veteran of the Old War, who would remain to the very end a fanatical Nazi.

But General Frederick and General "Iron Mike" O'-Daniel, commanding the 45th and 3rd Divisions, were undaunted by the opposition. Both were well aware of the significance of the city for the Nazis and naturally the two generals knew the kudos of capturing Nuremberg would be rated high in the headlines back home. So they set their divisions racing for the city.

For the 45th, the toughest opposition on the road march towards the city came mostly from the air, with increasing numbers of German jets striking their column time and again, whenever the Allied "umbrella" of fighters returned to base for refuelling. But casualties were few and the Division pressed on, its only encounter of note being that with Mrs. Fritz Kuhn and her daughter Waldtraut. The wife of the former leader of the *Bund*, the American Nazi Party, which had been banned in 1941, was found living comfortably with her daughter in a villa paid for out of Nazi Party funds. Hurriedly the wife of "America's Führer" was placed behind bars.

The 3rd did not have it so easy as it raced for Nuremberg. Although most of the tanks controlled by *Gruppe Grafenwoehr* were dealt with on the flank by the 14th Armored Division northeast of Nuremberg, some of the self-propelled guns managed to get through and began to make life hell for the 3rd. Indeed, on the same day that the Germans counterattacked in an attempt to stop the Americans throwing a circle of steel around Nuremberg, Private Joseph Merrell started a one-man war with the enemy, which would earn him his country's highest honor, the Medal of Honor—and death in battle.

As his company went to ground, pinned down by heavy fire from an SS unit, Merrell charged forward on his own initiative. Running through a hail of fire, he shot four Germans at point-blank range. That done, he continued forward, only to have his rifle smashed by a sniper's bullet. He tossed it away in disgust and went on, armed solely with three grenades. Zig-zagging over 200 hundred yards of rough ground, with enemy bullets snatching up the dirt at his flying feet, he closed with the first German machine gun which was holding his company at bay. He flung two grenades and dived into the gunpit, prepared, as the official citation had it, "to fight with his bare hands, if necessary."

But that wasn't necessary. Somewhere he found a German pistol and shot dead the Germans who had survived the grenades. Re-armed, he now tackled the second machine gun. A burst ripped his stomach apart. But he stumbled on, dying as he went forward, bullets tearing holes in his clothing and his body. Almost out on his feet, he flung his last grenade and wiped out the second machine gun just as he took another burst from a burp gun that killed him instantly.

Young Merrell, a boy in his 20s, would be the first of three 3rd Division men to receive the Medal of Honor in the attack on Nuremberg. Those awards were ample testimony to the severity of the fighting in the "City of the Movement."

Once Nuremberg had been the center of medieval culture, the home of Hans Sachs, the little cobbler, and his *Meistersanger*, the artist Dürer, and celebrated for its fine work in gold. Now, like the rest of Nazi Germany, it and the "land of poets and thinkers" had become that of "the judges and hangmen."

Gauleiter Karl Holz typified that brutal new Germany. As the "Amis" got ever closer to the center of the city, he was here, there and everywhere, encouraging, threatening, cajoling. When the local commander of the *Volkssturm* disbanded his 60-year-olds, sending them home to "*Mutter*," then shot himself, he ordered them reformed at once—or else! It was the same when the head of the local police, General Dr. Martin, told him to his face that "Gauleiter, the defense of Nuremberg is crazy. It can't be held." Holz flushed crimson and bellowed in that typical Nazi style of his, "General, I shall have you indicted before a flying court [a court consisting of three officers who passed judgements and sentences there and then without any legal advice] for not carrying out the Führer's orders. I'm reporting this to Himmler immediately." In the end, as we shall see, he would personally shoot Oberburgermeister Dr. Leibel when the latter refused to carry on the senseless defense of the city.

Three days after the start of the American attack, he gave out the code-word "Puma" which was intended to turn Nuremberg into a desert, part of Hitler's scorched earth policy. It was envisaged that city workers would systematically destroy all electricity and gas works, the water supply, the factories, the various inner city bridges. Fortunately for Nuremberg's surviving civilians, huddled fearfully in the cellars of their ruined houses, most of the city workers had fled and the order couldn't be carried out.

Still the fanatical Holz kept up his resistance, personally threatening anyone he fancied was a defeatist or a coward with the dire warning, "You'll be shot! Shot out of hand like a rabid dog!"

Two days before the city finally fell, he cabled Hitler that "The soldiers are fighting bravely and the population is proud and steadfast. I will stay in this most German of cities to fight and die . . . The National Socialist creed will triumph . . . We greet you, the National Socialists of Gau Franconia in German loyalty. Karl Holz."

Then, after that piece of high-flown bombast, Holz personally led a raiding party in the area of the main station, returning to tell his cronies proudly, "Everyone stays in Nuremberg and will die if necessary."

* * *

"Iron Mike" O'Daniel, the scar-faced commander of the 3rd Division was only too willing to oblige Holz and ensure that anyone still wanting to fight would die. He pushed his men hard, as they breached the medieval wall that enclosed the old city and commenced bitter house-to-house fighting. Indeed, in one instance the 3rd engaged in room-to-room combat in an apartment house which finally yielded 50 prisoners. O'Daniel sent in tanks, but it proved costly because lone snipers armed with the German panzerfaust missile launcher easily knocked them out from rooftop hiding places. In the end, it became standard operating procedure for the tankers to blast apart any building which even looked as if it might conceal snipers; now they were taking no risks.

But the infantry didn't have the protection of armor and they had to take chilling risks if they were ever going to clear the ruined streets of their fanatical defenders.

By noon on April 19, the 3rd Division had reached the famed Adolf Hitler Platz in the center of Nuremberg, where Hitler had spoken to his faithful each year. Hurriedly it was renamed "Michael O'Daniel Platz" in honor of the 3rd's commander. But still the fighting went on. Later that same day a company was surprised by a vicious counterattack on both flanks by Luftwaffe trainees. Hastily another company was whistled up to get them out of the ambush.

Holz threw in his last reserve—a company of middle-aged Nuremberg policemen. But when the 3rd turned its massive tank destroyers on the cops, who were armed only with rifles, some 140 of them surrendered in double-quick time. But the division was running out of men, too. O'-Daniel was forced to throw into combat his anti-tank company, which fought now as infantry for two days and nights without sleep, gaining the brand-new footsloggers the coveted Presidential Unit Citation.

In the early hours of the morning while the fighting still raged in the center of Nuremberg, Holz went to the office of the city's *Oberburgermeister*, which was located in a large aid-raid shelter. For some reason, Holz and Willy Liebel, the *Oberburgermeister*, started to argue—probably Liebel wanted to surrender what was left of the city to the Amis. Holz wouldn't hear of it. Outside, the *Oberburgermeister*'s staff could hear Holz ranting and shouting at the Senior Mayor. Suddenly there was a shot. Moments later a red-faced Holz stormed out of the office, leaving Liebel dead in his chair, a hole blown in the side of his head.

Had Liebel attempted to draw on Holz and been shot for his daring, or had Holz murdered him in cold blood? Probably the latter is true. No one knew and no one would ever know. For now Gauleiter Holz had only hours to live.

That afternoon as Hitler received his birthday visitors in Berlin and then went out into the garden to have the last ever photograph taken of himself, patting the cheeks of 12-year-old Hitler Youth boys who had been awarded the Iron Cross for bravery, Nuremberg, "the most German of all cities," was officially declared captured. At precisely 1830 hours, a rifle platoon from each of the 3rd Division's three infantry regiments, plus tanks and tank destroyers, were drawn up in the debris-littered former Adolf Hitler Platz to be addressed by the American whose name it now bore.

Standing under an improvised flagpole flying "Old Glory," proud "Iron Mike" O'Daniel told his tired soldiers, "Again the 3rd Division has taken its objective. We are standing at the site of the stronghold of Nazi resistance in our zone. Through your feats of arms, you have captured 4,000 prisoners and driven the Hun from every house and every castle and bunker in our part of Nuremberg. I congratulate you upon your superior performance." Then the divisional band broke into "Dogface Soldier," the march of the 3rd Division, and the honor party stamped off over the rubble, watched by a few bemused German civilians.

Now, while a proud "Iron Mike" praised his soldiers, Holz fought his last battle. At the local police headquarters which was still holding out, Holz had personally manned a machine gun in an attempt to stop the policemen defending the place from surrendering. But the cops' morale had broken down completely and Holz decided he would make a break for it before they surrendered, together with an SS officer. They had spotted a shell hole in the outer wall, which led to the courtyard, and felt they could escape through it without being seen by the Amis, who surrounded the place.

That wasn't to be. The SS officer went first. Just as he was about to clamber through the hole, a burst of American machine-gun fire caught him and he fell to the ground dead. That didn't stop Holz. He ran forward and struggled through the hole before the enemy gunner could reload. Running very fast for a man of his age and condition, he started across the courtyard. But now his luck had run out too. Someone spotted him as he doubled back through the smoke of fog and war. A rifle cracked and Holz slammed to the concrete, his jugular vein severed.

There, as the surviving 55 policemen surrendered, being patted on the back by a big US officer and told in German they had "fought bravely, boys" (a little later they would be stripped of all their valuables by some not-so-sympathetic GIs), Holz bled to death, unknown and untended. The man who had been the heart and soul of the defense of the "City of the Movement" had died at last.

The news of the fall of Nuremberg must have pleased Eisenhower, who was in London that day. He realized that his fears about a National Redoubt were perhaps unfounded. There would be no long last-ditch stand by the Nazis in the high mountains. Even in Nuremberg, most German civilians and ordinary soldiers were only too glad to surrender; the Germans were sick of war. In addition, his Intelligence had heard that there was a German resistance group in Munich, the place where Hitler had founded his Nazi Party, prepared to revolt and take the city over in order that it would not suffer the same fate as Nuremberg.

But with one problem apparently solved, another was looming up in the Seventh Army area. In that same week that Nuremberg fell, General Patch had his 63rd, 100th and 44th Infantry Divisions, plus the 10th Armored attacking towards Stuttgart. The drive was supposed to be coordinated with de Lattre's First French Army coming up through the Black

Forest. Once Stuttgart was taken, it would be administered by the US Military Government, as the Swabian city would be part of the post-war American Zone of Occupation.

But urged on by de Gaulle, de Lattre was driving all out for Stuttgart, for French prestige demanded that the major city of the area should be taken by a French Army.

But that was not Eisenhower's only problem. Unknowingly, the French were endangering a highly secret American project. It was the so-called Alsos Group, whose job it was to capture German scientists and material relating to German nuclear fission. By now the team, which had assessed information and documents captured by the T-Force at Strasbourg University the previous November, knew that the remaining German center for research into the production of an atomic bomb was located at the small town of Hechingen, 50 miles southwest of Stuttgart. It had been the plan for the Alsos team to accompany General Brooks' VI Corps in its drive to cut the roads south of the city. Then it would make a dash for Hechingen, for Eisenhower had ordered that on no account should the German scientists and their research data fall into French hands. Just like his political masters, he wanted the atom bomb being prepared for the war against Japan to remain a monopoly of the Anglo-Americans.

On April 19, Eisenhower heard from his Intelligence sources that de Gaulle had ordered de Lattre to take and hold Stuttgart "until such time as the French Occupation Zone had been fixed in agreement with the interested governments." Now, on the same day Eisenhower heard the good news from Nuremberg, it was followed a little later by the bad news that against orders de Lattre had captured Stuttgart. What was the Alsos team going to do?

The thought of the French obtaining the key nuclear fission information and capturing the chief German scientists must have sent a shiver down Eisenhower's spine. He knew General Groves, who was in charge of the gigantic US atomic research project that had been working on the bomb since 1942, distrusted the French nuclear scientists intensely. He felt leading French researchers, such as Madame

Joliot-Curie, whom he thought was a Communist, would simply hand over the captured German material to the Russians on a silver platter.

So while Devers blustered and threatened to cut off supplies to de Lattre if he did not relinquish Stuttgart, Eisenhower tried to cool the situation. He wrote to de Gaulle, deploring de Lattres' on-going defiance of Devers' orders, but said he, personally, did not want to see supplies being cut off from the French Army.

But behind the scenes there seems to have been near panic at Supreme Headquarters. Secretary of War Stimson personally agreed to a plan of campaign with General Marshall. Called "Operation Harborage," it envisaged a reinforced US army corps, consisting of the 13th Airborne Division and the 10th Armored, cutting right through the French zone of operations to take and hold Hechingen, whether the French liked it or not.

However wise heads prevailed. Under the command of Colonel Boris Pash, the Alsos team, reinforced by combat engineers from the Seventh Army, and several British specialists, set off to cross French territory without French permission and reach the German scientists at Hechingen. Pash, a bold and imaginative civilian-soldier, bluffed his way across the first bridge in his path, which was guarded by de Lattre's soldiers. He made a long speech to the officer in charge, about how proud General Devers was that the French had captured this particular bridge and how Devers was sure they would hold it against all odds. Then while his interpreter translated the speech into French, he quietly led the rest of the column across. Before the French tumbled to the fact that they had been tricked somehow or other, the Alsos team had vanished down the road.

A little later, Pash was caught up by a French officer in a vehicle. He thought the Americans were heading for Sigmaringen, where General Petain and the rest of the Vichy Government which had fled France the previous year had their residence. Pash assured the Frenchman eloquently that he was not about to butt into their affairs. The capture of

Petain and his traitors was strictly a matter for the French. Pash was allowed to continue. The miles passed as the column rallied down the white dusty spring roads through half-timbered villages which had yet to see an Allied soldier. Within sight of Hechingen, Pash stopped for a while and signaled to the nearest French Headquarters that the French should stay out of the area for a few hours, "because it is soon to be subjected to a heavy bombardment by American artillery."

On the morning of April 24, while the French hesitated, Colonel Pash and his men moved into Hechingen. There was a short small arms fight which lasted about an hour and then the town was American. Hastily the Alsos team started to search for the precious research documents and, more importantly, the German research scientists. They didn't have to search for long. Under the leadership of Professor von Weizsäcker, a relative of a recent German President, they were only too eager to change sides. Just like Wernher von Braun, the scientist whose rockets had killed some 16,000 Londoners that winter, they were attracted by the land of Uncle Sam and all the goodies it could offer. They were spirited out from underneath French noses and were on their way to America within the month.

Now Germany's remaining cities began to fall rapidly to the Seventh Army just like the "61-minute" street barricades, which attempted to stop the victorious Americans' progress. "Sixty minutes to build them," the GIs sneered, "and one minute to knock 'em down!" If the picturesque Bavarian villages and townships with the murals painted on the houses' whitewashed walls and the great steaming manure heaps just underneath the kitchen windows, displayed white flags and there was no firing, the speeding US columns simply rolled right through the place. If anything to the contrary happened, a little "memorial" to the passing of the US Seventh Army was left behind—in the form of a shattered town center.

Landsberg fell to the 10th Armored and 103d Infantry Division. The latter division claimed the bronze plaque adorning the prison where Hitler had spent a year and a half after the abortive Munich Putsch of 1923 and where he had dictated most of *Mein Kampf* to his self-appointed secretary, Rudolf Hess.

Augsburg seemed as if it might fight. But "Iron Mike" O'Daniel wanted no more casualties; the end of the war was too close. He gave the city time to surrender or suffer the consequences of putting up a fight. The civilians decided for the former course and medieval Augsburg did not suffer the fate of Nuremberg.

Dachau was taken. As the "45 Division News," the Thunderbirds' divisional newsheet, headlined the news of the capture, "Dachau Gives Answer to Why We Fought." It certainly did.

The concentration camp was like a nightmare. Outside it was a kind of moat, where lay 4,000 bodies of inmates who had been slaughtered by machine guns hours before the 45th had taken over. There were also 50 railroad cars standing there, which as one reporter wrote, "At first glance . . . seemed loaded with dirty clothing. Then you saw feet, heads and bony fingers. More than half of the cars were full of bodies, hundreds of bodies.

"The best information we could get was that this was a trainload of prisoners, mostly Poles, which had stood on the tracks several days and most prisoners had simply starved to death."

But this didn't seem to worry the locals, as the reporter noted. "They passed the place daily, but they appeared not to wonder in the least what lay behind the barbed wire. The civilians were looting an SS warehouse nearby. Children pedaled past the bodies on their bicycles and never interrupted their excited chatter for a moment."

But even the battle-hardened veterans of the 45th, which had fought through four countries by now, could not forget—or forgive—what they had just seen at Dachau. They had not that German gift of closing their eyes to anything that might upset them. They went on to their next objective, Munich, with murder in their hearts.

Inside Munich that day, the German opposition's attempt to take over the city and surrender it to the advancing Americans without a fight was about over. Three days before, a group calling itself "Freedom Action Bavaria," under the leadership of a Captain Gerngross, had commenced its bid for power.

Gerngross, a tall, heavy-set young solider, who studied under Professor Harold Laski, the Jewish sage of the British Labor Party at the London School of Economics, and who had twice been wounded in Russia, had spent the last year massing a sizeable number of Munich people who were opposed to Hitler. Now, as the Third Reich was falling apart rapidly, Captain Gerngross decided it was time to take over from the Nazis. His plan was to seize the local radio station, the Munich daily and evening papers and arrest the three most important people in the Bavarian capital—the Gauleiter, the head of the military, and General Franz Ritter von Epp, the well-known right-wing politician and the representative of the Third Reich in Munich.

Gerngross' plan was complex, but the big captain was convinced it would succeed if he could gain the cooperation of the Seventh Army. Two messengers had been sent to General Patch, asking him to stop the air raids on Munich as the city was about to rise against the Nazis. It is not known whether General Patch got the message, but the air raids did cease.

On the morning of April 28, Gerngross assembled his company, most of whom were in on the plot. He told his men, "We're going to do something to liberate ourselves. We are going to end the senseless fighting and devastation of your country. Whoever follows me now must stick it out to the end. I, hereby, release you from your oath to Hitler."

The response was unanimous. Even the few Nazis in the company volunteered to join the Putsch. So the soldiers tied a strip of white cloth around their right arms to indicate to plotters in other companies that they belonged to "Freedom Action Bavaria" and set off to take over power, just as Hitler had done in that same city some 21 years before.

At first things went well just as they had done for Hitler at the head of his Brownshirts. The newspapers and the two local radio stations were seized. The Gauleiter couldn't be found, but at two o'clock on the following morning, Gerngross had located von Epp. Entering his villa, he cut the wires of the General's switchboard and then confronted the old man himself. "You are a prisoner of Freedom Action Bavaria, Herr General," Gerngross said immediately. The haughty von Epp, who had suppressed the Communist revolt in this city back in 1919, looked down his long nose at the captain. Perhaps he felt that the young man's name was indicative of the type he was. "Gerngross" means in German, "would-be-big," literally "upstart."

"Look here," Gerngross said impatiently, "You have a natural responsibility to wipe out your brown [Nazi] past and do something for the Bavarian people. We want you to sign a declaration of surrender for Southern Bavaria." Von Epp turned to his adjutant, "Could I possibly hand myself over to a captain?" he asked. As always in Germany, protocol was of supreme importance. Slightly amused, Gerngross suggested he knew a member in his group, a major, to whom the general could surrender, adding that if von Epp refused, "We'll simply take you prisoner."

By early morning things started to go wrong. When one of his group finally located the Gauleiter Geisler and tried to arrest him, they were met with a hail of hand grenades and fled. At four minutes to 10:00 that morning, while thousands of locals went into the streets crying, "Hitler's dead . . . the war's over!" and waving the blue-white flag of Bavaria, Geisler broadcast to Munich, telling the citizens, "Do not take this Gerngross nonsense seriously. Not a word of it is true, but I call upon you to display your loyalty and love of our Fatherland which you people of Munich in particular have shown to such a marked degree in the trying times of this war . . . These contemptible scoundrels who, during this hardest hour, want to besmirch the name of Germany, will soon be shot and wiped out . . . Long live Germany! Long live the Führer. Heil!"

By mid-afternoon it was all over. Several of the most prominent conspirators had been arrested and Gerngross, with two companions, was fleeing the city in a stolen car bearing SS plates. But the abortive revolt, so typical of the inefficient revolts in that capital which had gone before them in the 20th century, including Hitler's own in 1923, did totally confuse the defenders of Munich.

As the troops of the 45th, 42nd and 3rd Divisions marched into the city they encountered scattered resistance with the only real fight being put up by two battalions of SS troops. Without too much difficulty they took several of the holy "shrines" of the Nazi Party, including its HQ, Das Braune Haus, and Burgerbraukeller, where Hitler had been wont to address the Party faithful each year on November 9, the anniversary of his own abortive Putsch. It was to the advantage of the citizens of Munich that the resistance was so tame, for after the atrocities they had seen in Dachau, the invading troops were in a vile mood. Anyone who stepped out of line was in for trouble, serious trouble.

As Walter Rosenblum, an army photographer, remembers: "There was a firefight between American and SS troops in a square. It looked as though it were a Wild West movie scenario. Only it was real. I was with, somehow, the 42d Division. The Americans were taking a tremendous beating. But they were battle-hardened, had lost a lot of guys and were not to be trifled with. The SS troops surrendered.

"It was in the back of a courtyard. I sat down on a long bench against the wall. It was like a stage-set. They put the Germans against the wall. I was sitting with a single-lens Eimo up near my eye. There were about three or four Americans with tommy-guns. They killed all the Germans. Shot 'em all. I filmed the whole sequence. I still wasn't that battle-hardened and I thought they did the wrong thing. The Germans were quite brave. They sensed what was happening and they just stood there."

Naturally Rosenblum's film of the massacre was never printed by the US Army Signal Corps. As he was told later,

"This film could not be screened, due to laboratory difficulties."

Years later, however, Rosenblum could rationalize the event. "When you're killing and being killed, something happens. You lose your perspective about life and death. These are guys who've been shooting at you and your best friends may have been killed. And those SS troops were so brazen. They acted as though nothing could hurt them."

Eisenhower, who had been physically sick when he had inspected his first German concentration camp in April, neither knew nor cared what happened to enemy soldiers. For him it was now a great relief to know that the cradle of Nazism had been captured without a real fight. The Alpine Redoubt was turning out to be a myth, something dreamed up by Allen Dulles' OSS boys, or "Oh So Social," as the spy organization in Switzerland was mocked at SHAEF HQ.

On May 1, 1945, Eisenhower sent a message to Patch to be read out to all troops under his command. It stated, "To every member of the Allied Expeditionary Force: The whole AEF congratulates the Seventh Army on the seizure of MUNICH, the cradle of the Nazi beast."

At last, it seemed, the unsung Seventh Army was getting some sort of recognition.

Now, as the battered veteran 45th Division finally came to rest in Munich, after two years of combat, the "rat race" commenced once more, as the remaining Seventh Army divisions streamed over the Austrian frontier and into deepest Bavaria.

As always, the 36th Texan Division seemed to be unlucky right to the very end. Elements of its 142d Regiment, together with an attached tank from the 12th Armored, penetrated to the Alpine castle of Itter, where the commandant of the place surrendered himself and his prisoners to the Americans under the command of Captain John Lee.

And what prisoners they were! They included two former French prime ministers; Daladier, who had taken France into World War II, and Reynaud, who had pulled the country out of that same war; the sister of General de Gaulle; a clutch of trade union officials; General Maxime Weygand, the head of the French Army at the time of its surrender in 1940; and Jean Borota, "The Bouncing Basque," as he had been known at the height of his fame as a world class tennis star.

However, just as Captain Lee was congratulating himself on his success, the castle was attacked at dawn by a force of German stragglers equipped with a mobile 88mm cannon. The gun blasted a great hole in the castle's wall and slammed a shell into the 12th Armored tank, wrecking it. Now Lee fought back and surprisingly enough the German major who had surrendered the castle and his prisoners did too, fighting side by side with the Amis as the SS attacked. Even the elderly French politicians joined in, with portly Daladier, the Prime Minister of France who had declared war on Germany on September 3, 1939, hauling ammunition for the defenders.

The German major, ironically enough, was killed by an SS sniper's bullet. The ammunition had begun to run out. Finally it ran out altogether. But help was near. "The Bouncing Basque" had volunteered to go for help disguised as a local peasant. Although his dress and accent were not particularly convincing, he did manage to slip through the SS cordon and now he returned with a full battalion of the Division's 142d Infantry Regiment. They broke through the line of SS tanks and relieved the trapped force. But as always for 36th Division, it had been a near thing.

Now there was only one more prestige objective left in the Seventh Army's zone of operations. It was Hitler's own house, Der Berghof, situated high in the mountains above the resort town of Berchtesgaden. After a tremendous bombing raid in the last week of April, the Berghof, which had started off as a humble mountain chalet but which had been developed into a massive complex, together with its own SS barracks and anti-aircraft battalion, was a smoking shell. As for its one-time master, he was preparing to die in Berlin.

Still, the kudos of capturing Hitler's home were tremendously high and Leclerc, commanding the French 2nd Armored Division, decided they should be his—and France's. Breaking off contact with Haislip's XV Corps, to which the Division belonged, Leclerc set off in an attempt to beat other US units to the "Eagle's Nest," as the Americans insisted on calling the place.

Opposition was minimal—from the Germans at least. As Gaston Eve, the son of an English father and French mother, who served with the 2nd recalled after the war: "We kept rushing on, day after day. A few shots were fired at us here and there, but there was little fight left in the Germans."

Emil Fray, another half-Englishman, remembers, "We pushed on very fast in competition with the Americans. We were operating in groups again and ours had a pretty straight run through, with only odd spots of opposition. . . . Everybody seemed to be waving white flags and nobody knew anything about Hitler."

But if the Germans offered little opposition to these Frenchmen going it alone and without orders, the Americans did. Both the "Screaming Eagles" of the 101st Airborne Division and "Iron Mike" O'Daniel's "Marnemen" wanted the honor of capturing the place. Indeed O'Daniel ordered all bridges across the River Saalach to be guarded by his men. This river formed an effective barrier against anyone trying to reach Hitler's former home. He also ordered that no vehicles but those from the 3rd would be allowed to cross. That done, he commanded his 7th Infantry Regiment to take Hitler's home, although the Berghof was officially out of the divisional zone-of-operations. Not that such things had ever fazed "Iron Mike."

But soon his forward elements were running into the French. As Leclerc's corps commander, General Haislip, recalled after the war, "I soon lost him [Leclerc] . . . Suddenly there was a phone call from divisional commander [O'-Daniel] complaining that the French had appeared and were getting in the way. I said, 'Just you block the roads and that will stop them.'"

In his turn, Leclerc now appealed to Haislip, only to be told by the American, "You aren't supposed to be there at all. You've had Paris and you've had Strasbourg, you can't expect Berchtesgaden as well."

Naturally with *la gloire de la France* at stake, that kind of answer did not satisfy Leclerc. He ordered his men to go all out and damn the Americans. Driving with Leclerc in his jeep, Colonel Chatel recalls, "I was arcing ahead with the General . . . when on two separate occasions American military police on traffic control tried to stop us. . . . He told me to drive right through them and make them jump. I did—and they did!"

After pausing to shoot a platoon of renegade Frenchmen who had served in the French SS Division Charlemagne, Leclerc was stopped by the 3rd's sentries on the River Saalach. The French General demanded to see "Iron Mike." The latter refused to see him. He said Leclerc could cross the river, but not his vehicles. Again Leclerc demanded to see him. "Iron Mike" stalled until he was sure that his Seventh Infantry had captured the Berghof, then he granted the Frenchman permission to cross the river.

But Leclerc was still determined to turn the tables on the Americans and gain for France the honor she deserved. On the morning after the capture of the ruined mountaintop house, "Iron Mike" O'Daniel decided to hold a formal ceremony on the mountain. "Iron Mike" was fond of such ceremonies; he held them all the time.

Unfortunately the French now held the approach roads to Hitler's home and they weren't allowing any Americans to pass. Now the French were holding all the trumps!

O'Daniel fumed. A long and heated discussion followed between the two commanders. Finally they reached a compromise. At the joint ceremony in the ruins of the "Eagle's Nest," both the French and American flags would fly for the benefit of the newsreel cameramen.

So they went ahead with the raising of the flags, the speeches, the saluting, the presenting of arms. Then suddenly the French flag fell down, leaving the Stars and Stripes to wave alone over the Berghof. Perhaps "Iron Mike" had had a hand in it. No one could ever satisfactorily explain that flag falling down. But there it was—"Old Glory" fluttering in the breeze in solitary triumph.

But the Seventh Army was not finished with the French— yet. As the GIs of Patch's army battled their way through the Alpine passes into Austria, intent on linking up with Truscott's Fifth Army advancing up to the Brenner Pass from Italy, de Lattre had plans of his own for his First French Army.

For the most part, Patch's men were hampered more by the weather than the Germans, though here and there the SS were still capable of fierce resistance, slugging it out to the last man in the wet snow and bitterly cold sleet which fell on those first days of May in the mountains. Indeed it was the weather which really delayed General Dean's 44th Division, leading the way.

On the same day that the 103rd Division linked up with men of the 88th Infantry coming up from Italy, General Dean's 44th Division halted. His progress was stopped by weather and a German detachment staunchly defended the serpentine mountain road ahead. The fact encouraged de Lattre to race ahead and try to take the key town of Landeck before the Americans. If the French could succeed, it would at long last bring about the surrender of the Nineteenth German Army, which he and Patch had been fighting since the previous August.

Unaware of what was going on, General Dean, who would one day spend three years in a Korean POW camp and win himself the Medal of Honor, was now approached by five Austrian partisans of the "Free Austria" movement. Austria, which produced Hitler (an Austrian citizen until 1928), Adolf Eichmann, the executor of the "Final Solution," and Ernst Kaltenbrunner, the head of the Gestapo, had suddenly discovered it was anti-Nazi all along. "Free Austrians" had abruptly started to appear from the woodwork everywhere. These particular five volunteered to lead a battalion of Dean's 44th over a secondary road through the mountains and on to Landeck.

Thus it was that emissaries of the German Nineteenth Army, now commanded by General Brandenberger, a veteran of the attack in the Ardennes the previous December, met the men of the 44th to arrange a surrender and not de Lattre. The Frenchman known as "King Jean" was going to be out of luck.

Meanwhile the 3rd Division, which had suffered 35,000 casualties since first going into action in North Africa in 1943, was landing even bigger fish. On May 3, the division's 7th Regiment was attempting to negotiate the surrender of the Austrian city of Salzburg in a small rock-walled room, sunk 100 feet in a shaft below street level, when suddenly the phone rang.

A German noncom in the room picked it up, clicked his heels together and snapped, "Jawohl Herr General." The NCO then summoned the senior German officer present to the phone. He talked rapidly for a few moments with the "Herr General" before saying, "General Zimmerman, chief-of-staff of Field Marshal Kesselring's Army Group wanted to know if Salzburg was in US hands. If so, would the US commanding general receive an armistice delegation from Kesselring's HQ?"

"Iron Mike" O'Daniel certainly would!

It was agreed that the Kesselring armistice delegation would proceed through the US lines under a white flag and meet O'Daniel's representative, General Robert Young, in Room 49 at a Salzburg hotel, the *Osterreich Hof*. Time passed, but no Germans. Had something gone wrong? Had they changed their minds? General Young started to send out search parties for the missing delegation. At 7:00 that night, two of the officers who had been sent out came into Room 49 with the bad news that "They blew the bridge up right under our faces!"

They meant the bridge near Hallein south of Salzburg. Apparently the SS had blown the bridge to stop the Americans crossing. General Young sucked his teeth and said,

"Maybe they've been picked up by some of our men and taken to the PW cage. We'd never find them."

The deal was given up as a bad job and the party started to drift downstairs. One of the correspondents present, Howard Cowan of AP, had hardly reached the bottom when "I was almost knocked down by [General] Foertsch and his party striding up the stairs two steps at a time. The party was covered with white chalk which gave their faces a deathly pallor and grayed their hair. They were loaded with briefcases and parcels of paper." Kesselring's delegation had been found by another search party and guided to the hotel.

Hastily the Germans showed their credentials and General Foertsch said, "I have full authority to ask for an armistice as soon as possible to complete arrangements for unconditional surrender of the German army, navy and air forces. I have full authority to act for the German army and German government. It is imperative that I see your Sixth Army Group Commander immediately. The meeting should be as near this spot as possible because of the state of our communications."

The party was led immediately to "Iron Mike's" CP. "All along the route, which was cleared of heavy tank and truck traffic by scouts speeding ahead," AP Correspondent Cowan reported, "parties of doughboys lined the roads and you could hear the babble of comments as we passed by.

"'Von Kesselring,' one ejaculated.

"'Is it over?' was shouted scores of times."

It nearly was, but there were still difficulties on the way.

On May 4, "Iron Mike" accompanied the German party to Munich where they met General Devers just outside the Bavarian capital at a large house which had been built by Hitler's architect and Minister of Munitions, Albert Speer.

Here while Devers, Patch and "Iron Mike" remained stubbornly seated, General Foertsch introduced his team standing, and the two sides got down to business.

The German explained that Field Marshal Kesselring was prepared to accept the US terms but there were difficulties in communication and there was also the problem of breaking off action with the Russians who were moving into Austria from the East.

Devers nodded his understanding and told the interpreter, "Tell them there can be no offer of an armistice. It has to be unconditional surrender!" He waited until the interpreter was finished and said, "Do you understand that?"

Foertsch stiffened. After a long minute's silence he said, "I can assure you, sir, that no power is left at my disposal."

At approximately 2:30 p.m. on the afternoon of that May 5, the two sides signed the terms of the unconditional surrender. All German troops still remaining in the Austrian-Czechoslovakian region right up to the Swiss border, three armies in all, including Seventh Army's old enemy, the German Nineteenth Army, would cease fighting on the morrow.

The war was virtually over. Unfortunately for the Seventh, at 6:00 on that same day in a British tent set up in the rainy heath landscape just outside the little northern German town of Luneberg, another German surrender delegation sent by Nazi Germany's last Führer, Grand Admiral Doenitz, surrendered the whole of Germany unconditionally. The surrender deal would be repeated for Eisenhower's benefit at his HQ and then for the Russians in Berlin. But on that gloomy wet afternoon, Patton's "little fart," Field Marshal Bernard Montgomery, had upstaged them all. Once again the great achievement of the US Seventh Army became merely a minor sideshow, forgotten in the worldwide euphoria created by the German surrender to Montgomery.

One ally, however, decided it would continue the war in Austria a little longer. It was of course "King Jean" de Tassigny's First French Army. On May 4, General Schmidt, commanding the German Twenty-fourth Army, which came under Field Marshal Kesselring's command, had approached de Lattre about surrendering. By the time Schmidt's emissaries returned to their HQ with details of the French demands, they learned that a mass surrender of the whole army group to Devers' Sixth Army Group was going to take place near Munich.

General Schmidt decided that this was an excellent way of not having to suffer the personal indignity of surrendering to the French. Accordingly, he sent the First French Army commander a note, mentioning the general surrender and suggesting that de Lattre should get in touch about the matter with Devers' Sixth Army Group.

Predictably, "King Jean" was shocked by the "insolence" of the German's note. He signalled Devers his demand that any plenipotentiaries from the German Twenty-fourth Army that might approach the American forces should be sent forthwith to him. Indeed, he signalled, he was going to continue hostilities against the Twenty-fourth until the Germans presented themselves at his HQ.

So de Lattre put up a show of continuing the war on his own. Frustrated as always by the French, Devers sent an emissary to "King Jean" to explain the situation. De Lattre was not placated. He said that he should at least have had a representative at the surrender talks.

When at this juncture, Devers' liaison officer asked "King Jean" to sign his name to the surrender document, he flatly refused. Again he demanded that General Schmidt should present himself at French headquarters. General Devers refused and there the matter rested. Hostilities on the First French Army front continued, finally fizzling out ignominiously a day or so later because de Lattre simply couldn't find enough Germans still willing to fight.

Still, here and there fanatics resisted. Returning to Field Marshal Kesselring's HQ, a party from the 3rd Division was held up by SS troopers blowing up the bridges to their front, and Captain Clem, who led the party, was treated to the spectacle of an "SS second lieutenant arguing with a German lieutenant general [Foertsch] and actually being abusive."

On May 6, three airborne troopers of the 101st Airborne Division were kidnapped by other SS soldiers and for a while feared for their lives. Next morning, however, wiser heads prevailed and they were released and told to send officer representatives from Division to accept the SS unit's sur-

render. But some, like the notorious SS Colonel Oto Sko-
rzeny, "Public Enemy Number One," as Eisenhower had
called him; the man who rescued Mussolini from his mountain prison in 1943 and supposedly had undertaken to kill
Ike himself in 1944, hid out in the mountains for days until
he finally decided to surrender.

By now the Seventh Army was engaged in what
amounted to a mopping-up operation, tidying up their zone
of operations prior to the peace soon to come. While most of
the Army went into reserve or were engaged in guarding the
huge number of prisoners—nearly a million in the end—
who were flooding into the divisional cages by the thousand,
others searched for Nazi gold, looted European art treasures,
and kidnapped European *prominenten*, as the Germans
called them.

On May 7, the 106th Cavalry Group liberated Leopold,
King of the Belgians, who had surrendered his country to
the Germans five years before. On that same day a Lieutenant Burke of the 45th Division captured Field Marshal
von Rundstedt, the brain behind that 1940 campaign and
the 1944 offensive in the Ardennes. The incredibly wrinkled old soldier, who had a fondness these days for good
French cognac, maintained, however, that the only soldiers
he could give his orders to were the sentries outside his
door.

Field Marshal Albert Kesselring, "Smiling Albert," as he
was known to his soldiers, surrendered himself to 101st Airborne Division and was passed on to the 3rd Division, which
was highly gratified, for the 3rd had fought against Kesselring for too long in Italy in 1943 and 1944. Asked by Sey-
mour Korman, war correspondent for the *Chicago Tribune*,
"What was the best division faced by troops under your
command on either the Italian or Western Fronts?" the Field
Marshall named, without hesitation, the 3rd Infantry as the
best. Now Kesselring would be heading for the war crimes
courts in due course of time.

So would the 36th Division's most prominent prisoner in
all its long combat career. On the morning of May 7,

Colonel von Brauchitsch, son of the German War Minister at the start of the war, presented himself to the 36th Division's CP at Kufstein in Austria. He told the Americans he was Field Marshal Goering's senior adjutant and he had brought with him the number two Nazi's offer of surrender. He also brought Goering's plea for an interview with the Allied Supreme Commander so that he could talk to Eisenhower "as one soldier to another."

The order was given to apprehend Goering in his secret hideout. Led by the 36th's assistant divisional commander, General Stack, the party contacted the man who once had been regarded as Hitler's successor and took him prisoner. During the process, one of the SS officers guarding him proved, as the Divisional History records, "unmanageable," adding laconically "and had to be shot."

For his part, Hermann Goering (known behind his back to the German populace as "Fat Hermann" on account of his enormous girth) was "very affable." The politico, who rouged his fat cheeks, sniffed cocaine through a bejewelled tube, rolled precious stones through his chubby fingers like Greek worry-beads, and was reputed to change his self-designed uniforms at least a dozen times a day, was interrogated at length. Then he was flown away. Naturally he never had that talk "as one soldier to another" with Eisenhower. Now Ike was refusing even to shake hands with top-ranking Germans after what he had seen in that Nazi concentration camp.

As Goering was flown, instead, to "Camp Ashcan" in little Luxembourg where he would be joined by the rest of the Nazi big shots until the time came to try them at Nuremberg, one wonders whether he realized that the grand illusion had collapsed. He was no longer one of the chief actors in the German nation's greatest drama; he was simply a prisoner of war who would soon answer for the crimes that Hitler's Germany had committed in those last six years. That mad National Socialist dream with its loud-mouthed effrontery, gold-braided vulgarity, strutting jack-booted cruelly, was over.

He—all of them—had become mere trash to be consigned to the ashcan.

On the following day, May 8, 1945, the day of victory in Europe, General Patch issued an order of the day expressing his pride and appreciation for what his soldiers had done.

It stated, "I have just received the following cable from the Secretary of War: 'I join a grateful nation in applauding the heroic part you and your men have taken in our triumph. Each soldier of the Seventh Army shares in congratulations for success gained through magnificent courage at the front. You can be proud of a distinguished accomplishment.'"

Now Patch added his own comments: "Observe you glorious men of the Seventh Army, our efforts and exploits are not unrecognized in our country. To you, who have done the fighting, I send my deepest and most patriotic thanks. Alexander M. Patch"

The prose was a little purple, somewhat florid for retiring, unassuming "Sandy" Patch, but it was spoken from the heart. Whether their "efforts and exploits" had been really recognized in their home country did not matter. Patch knew, in part, just what his fighting men had undergone in that long trail through France, Germany and Austria, and before that in Sicily. Between August 1944 and June 1945, the Seventh Army had suffered 83,507 casualties in men killed, wounded, captured and missing in action: the population of a medium-sized town back home vanished in ten short months.

They included Colonel "Paddy" Flint, half-naked and wearing his black scarf in Sicily and swearing the "Krauts" could never hit an "old buck" like him. Audie Murphy's friend, Sergeant Tipton, on that beach at Pampelonne on the Riviera, now a favorite place for wealthy French nude bathers, crying, before he died: "They can kill us, but they can't eat us, Murph. It's agin the law." Well, there had been very little law in the frontline these last ten months.

Day after day, week in, week out, one month after another, they had slugged it out with the enemy, plodding down those blinding white, so-straight French roads in the blazing sun with the guns rumbling menacingly to the rear. They had toiled up into those snow-capped Vosges Mountains with the machine guns hissing hysterically and the enemy mortars tearing the air apart. They had lain on their snow-bound foxholes in the Saar and watched, sweating with fear and apprehension, as the SS had come surging forward in their hundreds.

Some of them had broken down and run. Some of them had collapsed and lost their nerve. But the great majority of these citizen soldiers had stuck it out, living in constant, permanent apprehension that they would be injured, captured or killed at any moment.

"The nice young kid" holding off the advancing Germans with his .45 while his comrades escaped. "Little Boy Blue" dying at that window as he tried to warn the unsuspecting soldiers below. Private Joseph Merrell starting his personal little war with the Germans at Nuremberg and sacrificing his life when the war was almost won. Young men all—dead before they had begun to live . . .

Now it was over at last.

Some got drunk on that first day of the peace in Europe.

Some wandered around in a daze, puzzled by that strange loud silence, now that the guns no longer rumbled.

Some couldn't quite believe it. They had longed for peace for months, perhaps years in some cases. "Then suddenly, it was upon them all and the impact of the fact was a thing that failed to register— "like the sudden death of a loved one," so the historian of the 3rd Division wrote. "Like some involved bit of philosophical reasoning [it] had to be taken in again and again, in small doses. The sure knowledge of the fact was there, but the full implication of it needed much time and serious consideration."

Most would absorb the fact that the war was over in time, but there would be those who would never rid themselves of the conflict. In the years to come there would be odd moments when they would become pensive, sulky, cut off, knowing that the civilians all around had never understood what they had been through "over there." As Paul Fussell, who had been wounded as a platoon leader with the 103rd Division, wrote many years later: "[They were possessed] of the conviction that optimistic publicity and euphemism had rendered their experience so falsely that it would never be readily communicable . . . what had happened to them had been systematically sanitized and Norman Rockwellized, not to mention Disneyfied."

Some, a few, would bear the great conflict with them every hour of their remaining lives until the day they died. Audie Murphy on leave in Cannes already sensed he was cut off, as he went into the streets crowded with merrymakers. "I feel only a vague irritation. I want company and I want to be alone. I want to talk and I want to be silent. I want to sit and I want to walk. There is V-E day without, but no peace within."

And there never would be any "peace within" for Audie Murphy for the rest of his life. He would sleep with a loaded .45 under his pillow and with the lights on. "America's Most Decorated Soldier" would be plagued by a recurrent dream in which "I am on a hill and all these faceless people are charging up at me. I am holding an M1 Garand rifle, the kind of rifle I used to take apart blindfolded. And, in my dream, every time I shoot one of these people, a piece of the rifle flies off until all I have left is the trigger guard. The trigger guard!"

But one day later, May 9, 1945, it was all back to normal. Close order drill, company formations, parades. The US Army was getting back to "real soldiering" once more. As the "head shirts" would wise-crack in the long years to come in Germany, "War is hell, but peace-time will kill ya . . ."

7

1990

"Remember me when I am dead and simplify me when I am dead."

—CAPTAIN KEITH DOUGLAS, killed in action,
Summer 1944

ON the morning of Thursday, March 1, 1990, something very unusual happened in barracks and camps all along the old demarcation line between West and East Germany. That Thursday, cool and a little foggy, there was none of the usual bustle and haste among the Seventh Army's troops in the area. In the mess halls the soldiers, who normally would be hurrying into their combat gear by now, took a leisurely breakfast and sipped another cup of coffee. In the motor-pools there were no harassed, worried mechanics fussing over armored cars and jeeps which wouldn't start. There wouldn't be much need for "wheels" this day. And in the company and battalion HQs, officers sat around, openly reading the Stars and Stripes, idly wondering how they were going to pass the rest of the day.

Year in, year out, three generations of Seventh Army GIs—some two million in all—had been accustomed to the morning haste, irate noncoms barking orders, the cough and splutter of jeep engines reluctant to start, the frowning battalion commanders staring at their watches and wondering just how much more time it would take before they could shout, "Okay, let's go!" But on this particular March morning there was none of the usual urgency. Of course, the GIs had known that it was an exercise, a kind of showing the flag. But there had always been the off-chance that one fine morning when they breasted the next rise, they might just encounter the real thing—the Soviet Eighth Guards Army barreling straight toward the Fulda Gap.

So it was that for the first time since the Americans and the Russians had once met at Torgau on the Elbe at 12:05 p.m. on April 26, 1945, there were going to be no US patrols along the "frontier of Freedom," as the Seventh Army had long called the border between East and West. Then, when recent West Point graduate Lieutenant Kotzebue of the US 69th Infantry Division had first shaken hands with Lieutenant Colonel Gardiev of the Russian 58th Guards Infantry Division, the picture of that historic meeting between the representatives of the two victorious allies had been flashed around the world. The press corps and newsreel cameramen had swarmed to the site in their hundreds. Now no one in the media took the slightest bit of notice. The Cold War had died this morning, but as always with America's Forgotten Army, the event passed without the least attention.

It was left to the troops themselves to wonder at the strange ending to their 40-year-old mission. Master Sergeant Robert McCord of the 11th Armored Cavalry confessed jut how perplexed he was when he first encountered the "enemy" in person. "It was unnerving to see an East German officer whom I clearly recognized from the cameras walking through Fulda." It was equally strange for the 11th Cavalry's top kick to cross the border himself for the first time. As he stated, "We always had strict exercises on not crossing the line. We practiced this. We showed this to our people, here's the line, don't cross it. So when I did the first time, I felt I was doing something immoral. It was a very strange feeling." Now the noncom felt the 11th Armored's mission was accomplished and it would be the regiment's final job "to turn out the lights if the United States leaves Germany."

On the same day the Seventh Army ceased patrolling the frontier with the East, the traditional "Soviet Threat" briefing regularly given to newspapermen and visiting firemen at Army HQ in Patrick Henry Village, Heidelberg, ceased, too. As Captain Tony Neal, the briefing officer, told the press,

"Threat is a four letter word these days," and another intelligence noncom remarked to the correspondent of the *Boston Sunday Globe*, who was present, "the threat just went away."

Year after year the men of the Seventh Army had guarded and patrolled that lonely frontier with its ominous watchtowers, minefields and automatic killing devices. Even the dullest of the Seventh's GIs had understood that if World War III was going to start, it would probably begin here. Regulars had come back to this place for tour after tour. Officers like George Blanchard had first come here as a humble captain to return at the end of his military career as a four-star general commanding the whole of the Seventh Army. Children had been born in those gray military "housings" who would come back years later as officers and noncoms to serve in that same army. In due course they would produce another crop of "army brats" to repeat the process. Many of the Seventh Army's "homesteaders," especially the civilians attached to the force, had spent their whole working lives in Germany with the Seventh. They had, in many cases, German wives, children who spoke German as easily as they did English. They wore German clothes, ate German food, mixed socially with the Germans off-duty. For some of them America was almost a foreign country.

Now many agonized about their futures. What was the Forgotten Army going to do now? What role would Washington assign to the Seventh, now that the threat had gone away? Washington, of course, realized it no longer possessed the kind of economic and political muscle it had possessed back in the '50s and '60s. Then it had been able to dictate policy to the Europeans. Now that was no longer possible. In due course, the Europeans might well ask why there was any need for a large foreign army to be stationed in the middle of Central Europe? Then the pressure would be on to remove the Seventh.

It would be little different back home in the USA. The American public would be eager for the "peace dividend." How could John Doe be convinced that there was a need for a large and expensive standing army in Europe when the visible threat to US interests had vanished? President Woodrow Wilson had tried it back in 1918 and failed lamentably.

While the thinking members of the Seventh Army pondered seriously what their future role in Europe might be, the reunited Germans were making it quite clear to the Russians in East Germany that the Red Army's role was played out. The rank-and-file of the Red Army stationed in East Germany seemed totally demoralized. Every day Russian soldiers deserted and asked the contemptuous Germans for "political asylum." The sale of Russian uniforms, even weapons, was widespread.

Informants from across the one-time border reported to the 11th Armored Cavalry that Russian officers' wives were leaving their husbands and looking for Germans to marry so that they could stay in the country. Others related that they had bought a Kalashnikov assault rifle for $460 and a pair of Russian pistols for $160. One informant told the 11th Armored's Intelligence that "they [the Russians] are starving. If you come here [the city of Gotha] in the morning, you'll see that they've ripped up their roof timbers and have burned their furniture because they have no more fuel."

In one celebrated case the German magazine *Tempo* set up a trap for a senior Russian officer. The latter sold the cheap publication a surface-to-air missile for the equivalent of $3,000—and then threw in a free lesson on how to use it for good measure!

Once the huge Russian headquarters at Wuensdorf had been known to the German locals as "little Moscow." It had been a feared place. You didn't hang around the headquarters' mile-long perimeter fence for long. You risked ending up in some Soviet gulag if the sentries didn't like the look on your face. Now the newly reunited East Germans, with all the power of the hard D-Mark behind them, openly insulted the Soviet troops stationed in the great sprawling HQ. Contemptuously they called the place "little Mexico." After all, the Germans, who were now paying the Russian soldiers' wages, reasoned the conditions inside the HQ were no

better than in some corrupt, third-rate South American ba-
nana republic.

In exchange for Moscow's agreement not to oppose re-
unification of the two Germanies, Chancellor Kohl of West
Germany had promised to pay the wages of the whole Red
Army stationed in East Germany until the last Russians left
in 1994. Now, with the anti-Russian attitude among the local
German populace hardening rapidly, it was hoped in Bonn
that the Red Army would leave earlier, perhaps in 1992. In
Washington, it was realized that when that happened and the
Russians had safely disappeared behind the Urals, the Germans would commence asking when the Americans would
do the same—and depart.

Suddenly the whole structure on which the Cold War had
been based, militarily and politically, had changed virtually
overnight. Everything was in a state of flux. All was confusion, perhaps even chaos. The reunification of Germany, the
breakdown of the Warsaw Pact, the arms control treaties being worked out in Paris and Vienna meant there had to be a
drastic re-thinking of the future of the US Seventh Army.

For the Seventh Army that summer there appeared to be
two basic choices. Either the Army would go home in its en-
tirety, or the majority would go, leaving behind a small US
token force. The days of the Seventh Army in Germany, at
least, seemed to be numbered.

But then, just as suddenly and startlingly as when the
Berlin Wall had been torn down the previous year, the situation changed again on August 2, 1990. While the world still
rejoiced at the new era of universal peace and good will to
all men, Saddam Hussein, the dictator of Iraq, took the
plunge. His army crossed the border into the neighboring
oil-rich state of Kuwait. Within hours, his 100,000 troops,
some driving to war in civilian buses, had crushed all
Kuwaiti opposition. After the Emir's younger brother was
killed in the fighting at the royal palace, all remaining resistance collapsed. In the words of one US official, it was "just
like a cakewalk."

For once the UN in New York, which has often been compared to a "talking shop," acted with dispatch. Backed by a UN resolution condemning Saddam Hussein, President George Bush decided to send in US troops. That old faithful, the 82d Airborne, which had spearheaded the old Seventh's attack on Sicily 47 years before, was flown into Saudi Arabia. It was followed by the 24th Mechanized Infantry Division, another outfit which had served with the Seventh in Germany after the war. Another stalwart of the old Seventh, the US 1st Infantry Division—"the Big Red One"—followed it. The pressure started to mount. Saddam Hussein had to withdraw from Kuwait. Or else.

Instead he blustered and started taking European and American civilian hostages. President Bush reacted with more force. He called up several thousand reserves. Then he dropped a bombshell. Half the Seventh Army in Germany would be going to the Gulf! One hundred thousand soldiers, plus 2,000 tanks would have to be in position in Saudi Arabia by the first week of January, 1991.

On Friday, November 16, 1990, several hundred soldiers of the 1st Armored Division were ordered to report to a converted Army gym at the Bavarian town of Katterbach for their "Gulf Briefing." Here doctors peered down their throats while orderlies gave them vaccinations against a variety of desert diseases. New dogtags were handed out and the chaplain gave Bibles to those who wanted them. Several soldiers lined up to revise their wills or sign forms giving relatives power-of-attorney. "Should I make this good for one whole year, or two?" a clerk was heard to ask of one noncom. The latter replied, "Better make it for two."

Some of the 1st Armored men were shocked by the dramatic change in their circumstances, "I never expected it to happen," a helicopter mechanic told the correspondent of the *New York Times*. "We've been at peace for so long that this is something you don't really think about." Some looked forward to the excitement, the thrill of possible combat. A sergeant said, "We've got a few people who thought they were joining the Army to get an education. We have to shake them once in a while to show them what the Army is really about. Right now we're shaking them pretty good." And some were downright belligerent. One specialist told the correspondent, "Every generation has its war. This is going to be a big one. It's not going to be some little Panama-type operation. I've been waiting for this for 18 years!" The belligerent specialist was all of 23 years old!

The scene was similar all over Germany. The 3rd Armored was departing from its base in Frankfurt. The 2nd Armored (Forward) was on its way from Nuremberg. VII Corps at Stuttgart was on its way, as was II Corps HQ. Everywhere the troops were on the move.

Now hospitals all over Europe were alerted to take casualties. From the island of Crete to that other island, Britain, military and civilian hospitals began clearing wards and preparing surgical teams for what might soon come. At US air bases in Southern Germany—Ramstein, Wiesbaden, Rhine-Main and others—gigantic transports packed with troops were taking off every minute on the minute.

Rhine-Main's commander told the press that his was the biggest airlift since the Berlin Blockade. "Over 40 years ago," he said, "a multi-national force took a stand. . . . Today, history repeats itself." Everywhere there was movement, convoys, packing, arming, with thousands of soldiers and civilians, many of them Germans incidentally, who would soon lose their jobs, working around the clock to get nearly 200,000 men on their way. It looked as if, after winning the Cold War, "America's Forgotten Army" was on its way to a shooting war 45 years after it had fired its last shot in anger.

Late on the night of Wednesday, January 16, 1991 that shooting war commenced, as the first squadron of US F-15 fighter-bombers roared into the night and President Bush told the nation, "The liberation of Kuwait has begun. The United States has moved, under the code name 'Operation Desert Storm,' to enforce the mandate of the United Nations' Security Council."

Colonel Keith Kellogg of the US Air Force put it more

succinctly when he returned from his air strike against Saddam Hussein. He told the press, "This is how the big boys play. If you're gonna piss on a tree, you'd better be a pretty big dog!"

The rest is history. In a mere 100 hours, the men—and women—of those regiments and divisions which had beaten the tyrant Hitler in World War II—the 1st, 2nd and 3rd Armored Divisions; the 82nd and 101st Airborne Divisions; the 1st, 3rd and 24th Infantry Divisions; and all the rest of those proud traditional formations—had done it again. After nearly half a century, they had settled with yet another tyrant, Saddam Hussein.

All the strains, the sufferings, the stresses of those long years in Germany fighting—and winning—the Cold War, its existence virtually unknown to the greater American public, had been vindicated. And America was suddenly aware that she possessed the Forgotten Army and that she should be grateful to the sons and grandsons of those "good ole boys," who had themselves once helped to overthrow a dictator. The Forgotten Army won another decisive victory in the Gulf. After half a century of obscurity, it was time for the US Seventh Army to come in from the cold.

BIBLIOGRAPHY

Arnold, E. *The Trailblazers: The Story of the 70th Infantry Division*. Richmond: 70th Division Association, 1989.

Bar-Zohar. *Die Jagd auf die deutschen Wissenschaftler*. Berlin: Propylaen, 1965.

Bradley, O. *A Soldier's Story*. New York: Henry Holt, 1951.

Breuer, W. *Operation Dragoon*. Novato, CA: Presidio Press, 1987.

Brooks, T. *The War North of Rome, 1944–45*. New York: Sarpedon, 1996.

Buckenridge, J. *History of the 550th Airborne Battalion*. Nancy: privately printed, 1945.

Cheves, W. *Snow Ridges and Pillboxes: A True History of the 274th Infantry Regiment in World War II*. Privately printed, 1946.

Churchill, W. S. *Great War Speeches*. London: Corgi, 1953.

Clark, M. *Calculated Risk*. New York: Harper, 1951.

Clarke, B. *Training a Combat Ready Field Army. Army Information Digest*, March, 1958.

Clostermann, P. *The Big Show*. London: Corgi, 1960.

Codman, C. *Drive*. Boston: Little Brown, 1957.

Combat History of the 44th Infantry Division, 1944–45. Atlanta: Albert Love Enterprises, 1946.

Cunningham, A. B. *A Sailor's Odyssey*. London: Hutchinson, 1950.

Daly, H. *The 42nd "Rainbow" Infantry Division: A Combat History of World War II*. Baton Rouge: Army Navy Publishing, 1946.

Darby, W. and Baumer, W. *We Led the Way*. Novato, CA: Presidio, 1980.

Dawson, W. *Saga of the All Americans*. Atlanta: Albert Love Enterprises, 1946.

D'Este, C. *Bitter Victory.* London: Collins, 1988.

De Gaulle, C. *War Memoirs, Salvation.* New York: Simon and Schuster, 1960.

Die Letzen Tage von Nurnberg. Nuremberg: Edited 8 Uhr Blatt, 1952.

Docken, D. *Combat History Company C, 1st Battalion, 275th Regiment, 70th Division.* Privately printed, 1990.

Eisenhower, D. *Crusade in Europe.* New York: Doubleday, 1948.

Ellis, W. and Cunningham, T. *Clarke of St. Vith.* Cleveland: Dillon, 1974.

Farago, L. *Patton.* London: Barker, 1966.

The Fighting Forty-Fifth: The Combat Report of an Infantry Division. Baton Rouge: Army Navy Publishing, 1946.

Froberg, L. *63rd Infantry Division Chronicles.* The 63rd Infantry Division Association, 1991.

Fussell, P. The Real War. *The Atlantic Monthly,* August 1989.

Garland, A. Sicily: *The Making of an Army.* Armor, 1970.

Gavin, J. *On to Berlin.* New York: Bantam, 1978.

Goddard, W. *Report of Operations, the Seventh United States Army in France and Germany 1944-1945.* Nashville: Battery Press, 1988.

Hamilton, N. *Monty,* Vol. III. London: Hamish Hamilton, 1986.

Houston, D. *Hell on Wheels.* Novato, CA: Presidio Press, 1977.

Huff, R. A *Pictorial History of the 36th "Texas" Infantry Division.* Nashville: Battery Press, 1979.

Huie, W. *The Execution of Private Slovik.* London: Pan, 1952.

The Invisible Soldier. Detroit: Wayne State Press, 1975.

Irving, D. *The War Between the Generals.* London: Lane, 1980.

Jackson, R. *Coroner: A Biography of William Bently Purchase.* London: Odhams, 1956.

Klein, P. and Ropp, R. *Seventh Army's Other Mission. Army Information Digest,* April, 1963.

Knickerbocker, H. *Danger Forward: The Story of the First Division in World War II.* Atlanta: Albert Love Enterprises, 1948.

MacDonald, C. *The Last Offensive.* Washington, DC: Office of the Chief of Military History, 1973.

Martin, R. *The GI War.* Boston: Little Brown, 1967.

Maule, E. *Out of the Sand.* London: Corgi, 1970.

Middleton, D. *The Seventh Army. Combat Forces Journal,* August, 1952.

Mittelman, J. *Eight Stars to Victory: A History of the Veteran Ninth US Infantry Division.* Columbus, OH: F.J. Heer, 1948.

Montagu, E. *The Man Who Never Was.* London: Evans Brothers, 1953.

Morrison, S. *The Invasion of France and Germany.* Boston: Little Brown, 1964.

Mueller, R. and J. Turk. *Report After Action: The Story of the 103rd Infantry Division.* Nashville: Battery Press, 1945.

Murphy, A. *To Hell and Back.* London: Corgi, 1950.

Nichols, L. *The Battle Story of the Tenth Armored Division.* New York: Bradbury, Sayles, O'Neill Co., 1954.

Patch, A. *The Seventh Army: From the Vosges to the Alps.* Army and Navy Journal, December, 1945.

Patton, G. *War As I Knew It.* Boston: Houghton Mifflin, 1947.

Pence, D. Recollections of Philippsbourg. *Trailblazer Magazine,* Nov. 1976.

Polk, J. *Our Men in Germany, Tough, Young, Ready. Army,* November, 1968.

Rapport, L. and A. Northwood. *Rendezvous with Destiny: A History of the 101st Airborne Division.* Washington, DC: Infantry Journal Press, 1948.

Robichon, J. *Le Debarqument en Provence.* Paris: Laffont, 1962.

Salute to the Numbered U.S. Armies. Army Information Digest, October, 1962.

Seventh Army Tells the Troops. Army Information Digest, March, 1965.

Spore, J. *U.S. Seventh Army: The Search for Excellence. Army,* September, 1963.

The Story of the Century: The 100th Infantry Division in World War II. Nashville: Battery Press, 1979.

Strong, K. *Intelligence at the Top.* London: Cassell, 1968.

Taggart, D. *History of the Third Infantry Division.* Nashville: Battery Press, 1987.

Terkel, S. *The Good War.* London: Hamish Hamilton, 1985.

Toland, J. *The Last 100 Days.* New York: Random House, 1966.

Truscott, L. *Command Decisions: A Personal Story.* Dutton: New York, 1954.

Welcome to the Headquarters. Seventh Army, 1968.

Webster, P. *Petain's Crime.* London: Macmillan, 1990.

Werth, A. *France 1940–55.* London: Hamish Hamilton, 1957.

Ziemke, E. *The U.S. Army in the Occupation of Germany.* Washington, DC: Office of the Chief of Military History, 1975.

INDEX